The Politics of Jurisprudence

For Ann, David and Linda, again

The Politics of Jurisprudence

A Critical Introduction to Legal Philosophy

Roger Cotterrell

University of Pennsylvania Press
Philadelphia

Copyright © 1989 by Roger B. M. Cotterrell
First published 1989 by Butterworth & Co Publishers
First published in the United States 1992 by the University of Pennsylvania Press
All rights reserved
Printed in the United States of America
Library of Congress Cataloging-in-Publication Data
Cotterrell, Roger (Roger B. M.)
   The politics of jurisprudence : a critical introduction to legal
philosophy / Roger Cotterrell.
      p.   cm.
   Originally published: London : Butterworths, 1989.
   Includes bibliographical references (p.   ) and index.
   ISBN 0-8122-3175-9 (cloth). — ISBN 0-8122-1393-9 (pbk.)
   1. Jurisprudence.   2. Law—Philosophy.   3. Law—Great Britain—
History.   4. Law—United States—History.   I. Title.
KD640.C67   1992
340′.1—dc20   91-40233
                                                          CIP

Second paperback printing 1994

Contents

Preface   ix

1. **Legal Philosophy in Context**   1
    Jurisprudence, Legal Philosophy and Legal Theory   1
    Legal Philosophy and Legal Practice   4
    Justifying Normative Legal Theory   6
    Unity and System in Law   9
    Professionalisation and Politics   12
    Legal Philosophy in Social and Political Context   14
    How Should Legal Philosophy be Interpreted
        Contextually?   17

2. **The Theory of Common Law**   21
    The Character of Common Law Thought   22
    The Common Law Judge   25
    Can Common Law Thought Explain Legal
        Development?   26
    Common Law and Legislation   30
    The Political and Social Environment   33
    Savigny: A Theory for Common Law?   37
    Maine's Historical Jurisprudence   41
    Maine on Politics and Society   44
    Historical Jurisprudence and the Legal Profession   47
    The Fate of Maine's New Science   49

3. **Sovereign and Subject: Bentham and Austin**   52
    The Empire of Darkness and the Region of Light   54
    Positive Law and Positive Morality   57
    The Coercive Structure of a Law   59
    Sanctions and Power Conferring Rules   63
    Sovereignty   67
    Some Characteristics of Austin's Sovereign   69
    Must the Sovereign be Legally Illimitable?   72
    The Judge as Delegate of the Sovereign   75
    Austin's Theory of the Centralised State   77
    Austin and the Legal Profession   79

4. Analytical Jurisprudence and Liberal Democracy: Hart and Kelsen 83

Empiricism and Conceptualism 85
Hart's Linguistic Empiricism 87
The Character of Rules 92
Sociological Drift 94
The Structure of a Legal System 96
The Existence of a Legal System 100
Hart's Hermeneutics 101
Judicial Decisions and the 'Open Texture' of Rules 103
Kelsen's Conceptualism 106
'The Machine Now Runs By Itself' 109
Democracy and the Rule of Law 112
Conclusion 116

5. The Appeal of Natural Law 118

Legal Positivism and Natural Law 118
Is Natural Law Dead? 122
Natural Law and Legal Authority 125
The 'Rebirth' of Natural Law 127
Anglo-American Lessons from the Nazi Era 129
The Ideal of Legality and the Existence of Law 132
A Purposive View of Law 136
Fuller and the Common Law Tradition 138
Politics and Professional Responsibility 142
Natural Law Tamed? 145

6. The Problem of the Creative Judge: Pound and Dworkin 150

Pound's Rejection of the Model of Rules 152
The Outlook of Sociological Jurisprudence 156
A Theory of Interests 159
The Search for a Measure of Values 162
The Wider Context of Pound's Jurisprudence 164
Dworkin and Pound 166
Principles and Policies 168
The Closed World of Legal Interpretation 172
Politics, Professionalism and Interpretive
    Communities 177

7. Varieties of Scepticism 182

Pragmatism and Realism 185
Realism and Normative Legal Theory 188
Llewellyn's Constructive Doctrinal Realism 194
The Political Context of American Legal Realism 202

Post-Realist Policy-Science   206
Post-Realist Radical Scepticism   210
Legal Professionalism and the Legacy of Realism   213

8.   The Uses of Theory   216
Some Political and Professional Uses of Theory   216
Who Is Listening?   220
Normative Legal Theory and Modern Legal Practice   223
Normative Legal Theory as a Partial Perspective   228
The Destiny of Legal Theory   231

Notes and Further Reading   236

References   258

Index   271

Preface

This book aims to survey key theoretical contributions to the field of modern Anglo-American legal philosophy in order to outline debates about the nature of law which these contributions have provoked. In this sense it is intended as a general introduction to central areas of modern legal theory. However, it attempts something more than most such introductions. It seeks to put the debates in the literature into a broader context than that in which they are usually presented in introductory texts. It is intended not just as a survey of theories but also, more specifically, as a discussion of what Anglo-American legal philosophy, in some of its dominant forms, is and has been *for*.

This task involves examining approaches to legal philosophy in the United States and Britain in the light of conditions in which those approaches have emerged since the beginnings of modern legal professionalisation in both countries. I argue in these pages that the succession of dominant approaches in Anglo-American legal philosophy since the nineteenth century – the approaches which today make up much of modern jurisprudence – can usefully be understood, to a large extent, as responses to particular political conditions and also, especially, conditions of legal professional practice. Thus, the book suggests that this legal philosophical literature has helped to reinforce views about the nature of law which have seemed important for the legal professions' status and objectives at particular times. And this legal philosophy has also had political significance insofar as it has promoted, reinforced or reflected wider currents of political thought. The professional and political roles of what is often seen as an esoteric region of legal thought and literature ought not to be exaggerated. But it is important to bring those roles to light. This perspective may provide a way of showing that debates in jurisprudence which tend to be portrayed as timeless, and which often seem interminable and incapable of resolution, are better understood as reflecting specific responses in legal philosophy to pressures, developments and conditions arising in particular times and places. Viewed in this perspective, such matters as the controversies around modern theories of sovereignty, the enduring (but problematic) appeal of legal positivism in its various forms, the ebb and flow of natural law theory and the character of certain varieties of sceptical theory in legal philosophy appear quite differently from the way they usually appear in standard textbook treatments. This book claims that the patchwork of philosophical views of the nature of law contained in modern Anglo-American jurisprudence can be understood as a response to social and political change – but a response shaped substantially by perceived problems arising in the professionalisation of legal practice.

Such an interpretation is used here as an organising framework for an introduction to major orientations in legal philosophy. Is it justifiable, then, to offer, as such a framework, what can be no more than a tentative sketch of a way of interpreting this material? I think it is. First, this approach can suggest a structure or unity in much of the vast, unwieldy mass of modern theoretical literature on law which is not necessarily otherwise readily apparent. Second, the approach may reveal this literature as more vital and engaged in the practical affairs of law in society than it has sometimes seemed to be and, indeed, than it has often presented itself as being. The development of modern legal philosophy – at least in part – has been a kind of running commentary on the changing conditions of law in Western societies. If an attempt is made to put legal philosophy "in context" – particularly by bringing to light assumptions contained within it about the social, political and professional environment of law – it may be possible to appreciate that some of legal philosophy's central issues and debates have a broader significance (for both lawyers and ordinary citizens) than is often assumed. Finally, the question of what is and what has been "central" in this field might be clarified and even reshaped by the kind of approach adopted here. Indeed, in the case of most major writers considered in these pages the contextual approach encourages a different assessment from that which represents the current orthodoxy.

No attempt at comprehensiveness is made, even within the particular areas of theory highlighted. The book examines contributions to legal philosophy which have been influential in the Anglo-American common law world in the period of modern professionalisation of law. It seeks to identify the general orientations of each of these contributions, especially in the light of their professional and political relevance. It includes detailed exegesis only where this throws light on the central issues with which the book is concerned. Most of the theory discussed is indigenous to the United States or Britain, but influential imports from elsewhere are included where a knowledge of them seems essential in understanding Anglo-American developments. Each contribution is discussed insofar as it offers a *theory of law*, that is, insofar as it tries to clarify theoretically the nature of law, laws, or legal institutions in general. This emphasis makes it possible to focus consistently on what I take to be a unifying thread running through much of the diverse literature of modern jurisprudence (while in no way denying the wide variety of intellectual aims attributable to the theorists whose work is discussed in these pages). I hope that the book as thus conceived will provide a useful introduction to the areas of theory it surveys while conveying a distinctive view of them. I hope also that its discussions show why this theory needs to be studied in the light of its professional and political ramifications, and how such a contextual approach – far from undermining or explaining away in reductionist fashion what it examines – can actually demonstrate the enduring value of this material more clearly than can most traditional approaches to the subject. Legal philosophy, like law itself, reveals its full significance only when considered in social and political context.

These aims dictate the relatively straightforward organisation of chapters. Chapter 1 elaborates the approach underlying the work as a whole. Each of Chapters 2 to 7 then deals with a particular cluster of contributions to legal theory, setting the discussion in the context of wider problems to which that theory can be seen as, in part, a response. Thus, these chapters focus on material which has had great historical prominence in legal scholarship and also retains major significance in present-day jurisprudence. The final chapter offers, in the light of the discussion contained in the previous chapters, an assessment of the present position and likely destiny of the approaches to legal theory with which this book is concerned.

I am especially grateful to my friend and colleague Dr David Nelken for reading and commenting on several sections of the manuscript, and for the stimulus of many productive conversations on questions of legal theory. Parts of this book were written while I was visiting professor and Jay H. Brown Centennial Faculty Fellow in Law at the University of Texas during the spring semester of 1989. I benefited greatly from the research facilities and the experience of teaching jurisprudence in that environment, both of which have contributed significantly to this book. I am also grateful to my college for a term's sabbatical leave during the early stages of research on the project; and to Dr. M. W. Bryan, now of Melbourne University, and Professor W. C. Powers of the University of Texas Law School, who also read and commented on sections of the manuscript in draft. Parts of Chapter 6 are adapted from an article which I previously published in the 1987 volume of the *American*

Bar Foundation Research Journal (pp. 509–24). The A. B. F.'s permission for reproduction of some passages from that essay is gratefully acknowledged. Finally, I owe thanks to my children for putting up stoically with the disruption to their lives which is caused by other members of their family writing books; and to my wife, Ann, for her constant support and encouragement through the period of researching and writing this volume.

The Politics of Jurisprudence was first published in Britain in 1989. I am delighted that it now appears, with revisions, in a United States edition. In writing it I was conscious always that its material bridges two closely comparable and interrelated, yet also instructively contrasting, common law cultures. The theoretical debates discussed in these pages are, in part, a record of a highly productive interaction between different traditions of legal philosophy developed in the United States and Britain. In fact, the book's outlook is closer in some respects to modern American traditions than to British ones. I find congenial the example of openness to context and sharp professional self-consciousness provided by some of the best work of American legal realism – a breath of fresh air in legal thought which, regrettably, largely bypassed the traditional mainstream of British legal studies. This book's approach is, however, best understood as related to recent critical movements in legal thought which have developed independently – with different orientations but increasingly productive cross-influences – on the two sides of the Atlantic. Legal theory is a terrain on which the intersection of legal experience in different jurisdictions holds out the prospect of overcoming the limitations of narrow professional perspectives on law, a development never more necessary than at the present time.

Roger Cotterrell
Faculty of Laws
Queen Mary and Westfield College
University of London
August 1991

1   Legal Philosophy in Context

Most lawyers have little difficulty in recognising 'law' as a clearly identifiable field. No deep reflection on the matter seems necessary. Treated as the lawyer's practical art or as the special expertise possessed by a legal profession, law seems an area of knowledge and practice with well understood unifying features and distinctive character. In normal conditions of legal professional practice, there may seem no need to think systematically about the character of law-in-general, or to pose broad questions about the nature of legal institutions. It may well seem enough for legal practice that the lawyer has the expertise to deal with particular legal problems in hand, knows or can find and interpret the specific areas of legal doctrine – rules, principles and concepts of law – needed to give clear legal answers to those problems, and has the appropriate 'know-how' to be able to recognise and make good use of appropriate channels of influence and procedures by which the legal resources of the state can be harnessed to clients' interests. Given the complexities of law and regulation, this kind of understanding of law may seem as much as anyone could reasonably ask of a legal specialist. In practice, the particular, the specific and the appropriate are what count.

Jurisprudence, Legal Philosophy and Legal Theory

However, the legal realm can be looked at in ways that go beyond the immediate experiences and needs of professional practice. Law is assumed to be socially significant, although the nature of this significance, and what kinds of study are appropriate to reveal it, are always controversial matters. Law has long been thought worth studying for its intrinsic philosophical or social interest and importance, which relates to but extends beyond its immediate instrumental value or professional relevance. In this sense, law is 'a great anthropological document' (Holmes 1899: 444). In the Anglo-American world the term most often used to refer to the whole range of actual and possible inquiries concerned, in one way or another, with this broader significance of law, is *jurisprudence*. Jurisprudence is not united by particular methods or perspectives. It includes work grounded in the diverse perspectives of the various social and human sciences and of many kinds of philosophy (lay and professional), as well as other intellectual disciplines.

Jurisprudence is, therefore, probably best defined negatively as encompassing all kinds of general intellectual inquiries about law which are not confined solely to doctrinal exegesis or technical prescription. The qualification 'general' is important. If jurisprudence is unified at all it is by a concern with theoretical generalisation, in contrast to the emphasis on the particular and the immediate which characterise most professional legal practice. Thus, it has been described as the theoretical part of law as a discipline (Twining 1984). But such a view is controversial insofar as it ties jurisprudence firmly within a conception of some overall disciplinary unity of law. Given the diversity of law and legal activity and the sheer range of material and types of inquiry which can be included within the scope of jurisprudence, this disciplinary unity is perhaps a hypothesis to be examined rather than a postulate to be assumed (Cotterrell 1986a).

The unwieldy category of jurisprudence can be further broken down or even replaced with designations of more specific fields or modes of inquiry. For example, *legal philosophy* can be taken to encompass all philosophical speculation (rather than empirically-based social scientific theory) on matters of law or related to law. Thus, it excludes empirical social theories of law (such as those associated with sociology of law) which would also be encompassed by jurisprudence as defined above. Insofar as philosophy is concerned with examining the conceptual apparatuses by which human experience is interpreted, legal philosophy's major focus is on clarifying or analysing the ideas or structures of reasoning implicated in, presupposed by or developed through legal doctrine, or which constitute the environment of thought and belief in terms of which legal processes are justified and explained. It is not concerned with empirical inquiries about law's social effects and about legal behaviour such as are pursued in sociological studies of law. Legal philosophical inquiry in this sense cannot be clearly demarcated from the kind of conceptual inquiries with which sociology of law is concerned. The difference is perhaps primarily one of emphasis. In legal philosophy generally, conceptual clarification tends to be treated as much more important than – and sometimes independent of – systematic empirical analysis of legal institutions[1] in their historical context and social environment. By contrast, in sociology of law, analysis of law's conceptual structures is to be undertaken only in relation to this empirical analysis.

This book is concerned with legal philosophy, but not the whole of this huge field. The following chapters deal only with the part of legal philosophy which contributes to what can be called *legal theory*. Like the terms jurisprudence and legal philosophy, this term is not used uniformly by different writers. Here, however, legal theory is taken to refer to systematic theoretical analysis of the nature of law, laws or legal institutions in general. It excludes, on this definition, those parts of legal philosophy concerned primarily with the moral justification of particular aims or policies related to or expressed in legal doctrine. Legal theory does not directly address, for example, such matters as the nature of justice as a general concept, the philosophical justification of particular legal or governmental policies in relation to morally controversial matters (such as abortion), or the general question of how far the enforcement of moral principles as such is an appropriate task of contemporary criminal law. Legal theory seeks specifically to develop theoretical understanding of the nature of law as a social phenomenon. While philosophical justifications of particular aims or tasks of law are not irrelevant to this concern (and may follow directly from certain types of legal theory, such as natural law theory), they are not central to it.

It follows from this definition of legal theory that both legal philosophy and sociology of law can and do contribute to it, the latter in ways which are beyond the scope of this book (cf. Cotterrell 1984). For convenience, I term legal philosophy's contributions to legal theory *normative legal theory* and sociology of law's contributions to it *empirical legal theory*. Just as it was necessary to note above that the distinction between legal philosophy's conceptual inquiries and those of sociology of law is often more a matter of emphasis than of rigid demarcation, so the same is true of these two kinds of legal theory. Discussion in subsequent chapters will be directly concerned, however, only with those parts of the literature of legal philosophy which in the past century or

---

[1] By legal institutions I mean here patterns of official action and expectations of action organised around the creation, application and enforcement of legal precepts or the maintenance of a legal order. More generally, throughout this book the word 'institution', in the sense of social institution, refers to a system of patterned expectations with regard to the behaviour of individuals fulfilling certain socially recognised roles. Cf. Cotterrell 1984: 3.

so have sought to contribute to legal theory and, in doing so, have exercised a dominant influence on the shape and outlook of modern Anglo-American jurisprudence. Hence, this book's focus is on the development of normative legal theory in this context.

Legal Philosophy and Legal Practice

Since the 1960s, Anglo-American legal philosophy has become more closely linked to academic philosophy in various ways. First, it has been developed to a greater extent than previously by scholars who see themselves as owing disciplinary allegiance to academic philosophy, or dual allegiance to law and philosophy, rather than to law. Secondly, issues and modes of inquiry in legal philosophy have been increasingly influenced by the wider disciplinary concerns of philosophy, rather than by issues close to the concerns of legal practice. This drift towards academic philosophy threatens to make legal philosophy esoteric in a way which – as this book seeks to show – is at odds with its modern history. Indeed, it should be kept firmly in mind that, apart from this very recent philosophical professionalisation, legal philosophy, in the sense defined above, has been an enterprise pursued, in modern times in the Anglo-American environment, primarily by lawyers with little that today would pass for professional philosophical training. Indeed, it may be more appropriate to refer to them generally as jurists rather than legal philosophers; as legal scholars with a speculative concern, rather than members of any branch of a philosophical establishment.

There is something puzzling about this state of affairs. What have these speculating jurists, whose work today makes up a considerable part of modern jurisprudence, seen as their role? What has been the function of legal philosophy? What is its status as an intellectual field in relation to other such fields and in relation to the lawyer's professional knowledge of law? Clear answers to these questions would help considerably in understanding the nature and significance of issues and disputes which have arisen in the literature of jurisprudence or legal philosophy. Yet, very rarely are convincing answers given in general texts surveying the legal philosophical components of jurisprudence. In this book, in considering some areas of legal philosophy which dominate the literature of modern jurisprudence, it will be necessary to try to make some assessment of legal philosophy's contribution to the wider world of political and legal activities – including especially the professional practice of law as it has developed since the mid-nineteenth century during the period in which most of the theoretical contributions discussed in this book were made.

Where could we begin to look for answers? Some relationships between conceptual inquiries in legal philosophy and the concerns of professional legal practice seem obvious. The everyday notions which lawyers use include such concepts as justice, responsibility, obligation, rights and duties, causation, validity, ownership, possession, personality – all of them pregnant with philosophical complexities and wide social significance. Insofar as legal philosophy focusses attention on these kinds of concepts as they relate specifically to legal settings in which lawyers have to play a role, it seems merely a more general version of what lawyers do in everyday practice in interpreting the complexities and contradictions of legal doctrine. Further, a concern to identify conceptual inquiries in jurisprudence specifically with issues relevant to professional legal practice, may underlie the attempts of some writers clearly to distance jurisprudence from (academic) philosophy. Thus, Julius Stone writes that most of jurisprudence's problems are in substance different from those of philosophy, and that jurisprudence's classifications are acceptable to the extent that they allow its concerns to be introduced to law students and discussed by lawyers generally, in an orderly way (Stone 1964: 8, 16, 17). On this view, jurisprudence's major constituency is clearly a legal professional one.

On the other hand, this legal professional constituency has long tended to be distrustful of many aspects of the jurisprudential enterprise, if not necessarily of all of them (cf. Cohen 1933: 327). Even conceptual clarification in legal philosophy may not be valued highly by those concerned with the practice of law, and sound reasons can be constructed in defence of this attitude. First, much legal practice does not involve issues of doctrinal interpretation of sufficient depth to lead the lawyer into philosophical thickets. The conceptual puzzles of legal philosophy, insofar as they deal with issues of immediate practical significance, are usually puzzles for appellate courts, not for most office lawyers or trial judges. Issues of everyday practice are more often strategic or tactical than conceptual; routine rather than innovative; issues of fact rather than of law; and matters of care and competence rather than of doctrinal creativity. But this is not always so, and some forms of legal practice undoubtedly require high levels of conceptual ingenuity and theoretical imagination.

Secondly, a more fundamental point can be made. Surely modern Western law, by its nature, does not lend itself to broad conceptual generalisation? It seems to be a mass of technicalities in no way unified by broad principle or philosophically coherent concepts. Certainly, lawyers seek rationality and system in legal doctrine. Indeed, their ability to interpret that doctrine and predict the outcome of litigation or the effects of legal documents and transactions depends on this. But the rationality of modern law is a piecemeal rationality. Legal doctrine is to be organised, systematised and generalised just sufficiently to meet the needs of the moment. Concepts are used pragmatically and not necessarily with any concern for broad consistency of meaning (cf. Harris 1961). Short-term strategy rather than broad-view conceptual rigour may be what is significant. In complex modern legal systems, in which doctrine undergoes rapid change and develops ever more technical refinements of regulation, system and order in doctrine are features to be created and recreated continually, as far as possible, to meet the needs of professional practice. System and order – conceptual clarity – are, however, produced (if at all) with the knowledge that they cannot be more than provisional; they are valid only until the next input of new doctrine from legislation, judicial decisions, or administrative rule-making.

These conditions of legal practice are not new, although the complexity and scale of modern regulation have greatly increased. They certainly raise doubts, however, as to why legal philosophy should be thought significant for the professional world of law. It seems necessary to look elsewhere for the functions legal philosophy has fulfilled, at least in its contributions to legal theory, unless we are to conclude that this legal philosophy has served no functions in relation to the wider world of legal activities. If the latter were true, however, it would still be necessary to explain why an immense modern literature of the kind under consideration in this book exists, and why some of that literature has had a considerable impact on discussion and opinion among legal and political elites. Finally, it would be necessary to explain why legal philosophy's contributions to modern legal theory have been, predominantly and continuously, contributions by lawyers addressed primarily to lawyers. Despite jurisprudence's ostensibly broad, open perspectives, the part of it under consideration here has been very much a lawyer's enterprise. Its whole intellectual organisation has presupposed a single community within which practising legal professionals and legal theorists are members.

Justifying Normative Legal Theory

The justifications which Anglo-American jurists have given for their work in normative legal theory often emphasise its practical role in improvement of law. For Jeremy Bentham, the English legal reformer, this kind of theory was central to a science of law which would provide a secure foundation for rational reform. Bentham's less radical follower John Austin, like many later writers, put more emphasis on legal theory's rationalising, systematising task – making sense of the chaotic jumble of legal materials – and its educational value in providing a 'map of the law' – a framework upon which the detail of legal technicality could be arranged (Austin 1863: 379–80; Clark 1885). For influential American theorists such as Roscoe Pound and Oliver Wendell Holmes, legal theory could be justified in even more explicitly instrumental terms. Pound refers to its modern task as facilitating social engineering through law, with the jurist cast in the role of expert in fair and efficient governmental and judicial decision-making (see Chapter 6). For Holmes, the engineering analogy gives way to an architectural one. 'Theory is the most important part of the dogma of the law, as the architect is the most important man who takes part in the building of a house' (Holmes 1897: 477). Theory is the ally of the scientifically-minded lawyer engaged in 'the eternal pursuit of the more exact', the establishment of law's principles 'upon accurately measured social desires' (Holmes 1899: 452, 455).

Ronald Dworkin, one of the most influential of contemporary legal philosophers, sees legal theory as justifying law and so guiding and supporting the judge in the task of legal interpretation: 'If a theory of law is to provide a basis for judicial duty, then the principles it sets out must try to *justify* the settled rules by identifying the political or moral concerns and traditions of the community which, in the opinion of the lawyer whose theory it is, do in fact support the rules' (Dworkin 1977: 67, emphasis in original).

Other theorists are more ambiguous in asserting practical relevance, subsuming this in wider intellectual justifications. For both the English jurist H.L.A. Hart and the Austrian Hans Kelsen – who worked for many years in the United States and has significantly influenced modern Anglo-American jurisprudence – legal theory could be justified as clarifying through conceptual inquiries the nature of law as a social phenomenon. Thus Hart (1961: vii) suggests that clarification of the nature of legal ideas can cast light on the social contexts in which they are used. Kelsen describes law as a 'specific social technique' (Kelsen 1941a) and sees his task as, in part, to show clearly through an examination of the nature of legal knowledge and reasoning where its specificity lies. In both cases the reference to the 'social' should not mislead the reader into thinking that the theory proposed is sociological in orientation. It remains, like all normative legal theory, grounded in abstract philosophical speculation, rather than in empirical examination of actual patterns of legal behaviour or actual social and historical contexts in which law exists. Nevertheless, where serious attempts to understand the wider cultural resonance of law's conceptual frameworks are undertaken in legal philosophy, it may become sensitive to sociological dimensions of law to an unusual extent.

Finally, some other writers treat the appropriate role of legal theory as a 'debunking' or demystifying one – not to rationalise, justify, clarify or improve the conceptual structure of law, but to expose it or explain it away. Certain tendencies in legal philosophy which can be labelled 'sceptical' in one sense or other, seem in their most radical manifestations to be concerned not to praise law's abstract conceptual structures but to bury them. The explicit justification for these kinds of approach is usually that they offer 'realism'; they explain realities about law which are obscured in orthodox legal thought and other legal theory; they look behind legal doctrine to the political positions, individual and social interests, or personal value judgments (for example, of judges or other legal decision-makers) which doctrine may hide. How deep the radicalism of these approaches runs and whether they are to be seen as providing a substantial rejection of (rather than a supplement to) the more general characteristics of normative legal theory outlined in this chapter, are matters to be explored later in this book. Examples of these sceptical legal theories are discussed in Chapter 7.

Given such a diversity of implicit or explicit aims underlying modern Anglo-American legal philosophy's contributions to legal theory, generalisation becomes dangerous. As subsequent chapters will suggest, the relationship between particular kinds of theory and the political and legal professional environment of the time in which they developed varies. Jurisprudence and legal philosophy are made up of bodies of literature which have been intended to serve different purposes at different times. Further, whatever the motivations of particular theorists, any influence which their work has actually had on professional or political life may be equally varied. And the collecting together of this material in legal education – as part of taught jurisprudence courses – often reflects yet other considerations, expressed in such aspirations as to relate 'the law to the spirit of the time' (Laski 1967: 577) or to provide in legal education 'an orderly view of the law's "external relations"' with other fields of knowledge (Stone 1966: 30). All these matters are important in considering the nature of legal philosophy in general and normative legal theory in particular. The latter is typically treated as a cumulating corpus of knowledge focussed on a single concern to 'theorise law'. Indeed, by definition, this is what normative legal theory is. But it would be unwise to assume more consistency of aim and effect than is implied by this purely definitional unity.

Unity and System in Law

So the puzzle still remains. What if anything can be said, in general terms, about the significance in the practical world of affairs of legal philosophy's contributions to legal theory? What all of them seem to have in common is that, in some way, they attempt to offer a general perspective on the nature of law. This frequently involves trying to demonstrate some kind of *unity* of law. The search for unity can be pursued in many different ways, however. It may involve trying to identify a consistent moral or cultural foundation of legal regulation which validates and gives moral meaning and social authority to laws. It may entail trying to show how the entirety of legal rules and regulations can be seen as part of a single rational structure, or how legal reasoning entails consistent methods or epistemological assumptions, or how the diverse elements of legal doctrine applicable in a particular jurisdiction (for example, England and Wales, or the United States) link to form something which can actually be understood as a system of elements organised in a unified whole. It may involve a search for a purposive unity of law, so that all its elements are to be interpreted and evaluated in terms of some fundamental objectives (for example, social, moral, economic or political) which they are thought to serve. Unity is sometimes sought in a common source of authority of laws, or in consistent patterns of legal reasoning which appear as law's unifying characteristics.

Unity may be sought in a universal sense, so that the law of all times and places is seen as necessarily having common foundations. In modern Anglo-American legal philosophy this approach is rare but is exemplified in the claims of the American jurist Lon Fuller that the very nature of rules as a legal mechanism of government presupposes certain universal moral criteria of their development and application in *any* social context (see Chapter 5). More typically, however, modern legal theory tries to explain how the law of a *particular* nation, state or jurisdiction can be thought of as a legal system, with all its diverse rules and regulations somehow rationally or purposively interconnected and yet clearly distinguished from the components of other such systems.

These kinds of inquiries may seem highly abstract, but they are very relevant to practical legal reasoning and problem solving. This is because they involve examining the background assumptions in relation to which those practical activities take place. Thus, when lawyers recognise uniform general tests which determine in a legal system which rules are *valid* as (for example, English or American) law or which decisions have legal force, they seem to presuppose the distinct identity of the system as a whole; that there are conclusive means of distinguishing the legal from the non-legal and marking the boundaries of legal doctrine. Equally, some similar presuppositions about the distinctiveness of 'the legal' are entailed when it is necessary to develop a general conception of what can count as legal arguments, or justiciable issues, in contrast with non-legal or non-justiciable ones (see e.g. Craig 1983: 485–6). Finally, legal reasoning links rules together and presupposes that the legal relationship between them can be conclusively determined. For example, it deals with such questions as: What is the position if the rules conflict? What is their relative authoritativeness? In what circumstances can one rule determine the validity of another? In doing so, this reasoning presupposes an internal structure of the legal system, and a theory of the relationship between its elements. Thus, unity as a practical matter entails two things. It entails predictably consistent *internal* relationships of elements (rules, principles, concepts, decisions, etc.) within a legal system. Equally, it entails predictably consistent *external* relationships between the system and what lies outside it, so that the determination of the legal from the non-legal (for example, legal rules from moral rules; judicial decisions from political decisions) can be a reliable one.

This need to mark out what is 'internal' to law and what 'external' shows itself in many different ways besides those just mentioned. The internal-external dichotomy is complex and many-sided but closely connected with the problem of demonstrating some kind of unity of law or some kind of distinctiveness of legal thought or reasoning. One writer notes: 'the very unity of a field of knowledge [such as law] is comprised in its delimitation from other fields of knowledge' (Tur 1978: 158). Given what has been said earlier about normative legal theory's typical concern with system and unity in law it is unsurprising that the problem of the internal-external relationship pervades it. This is explicit, for example, in the influential work of H. L. A. Hart (1961), who distinguishes what he calls internal and external views of legal (and other) rules.

The internal view is that of legal 'insiders' who orient their thinking in terms of legal rules treated as guides for conduct – whether or not the rules are approved by such insiders. For Hart, however, the internal view is certainly not restricted to lawyers. He defines it in such broad terms that it encompasses many different kinds of perspectives of citizens on law. The external view seems to be restricted to those who cannot really reason with rules at all or, for their own purposes, see no point in doing so (see Chapter 4).

Another way of looking at the internal-external dichotomy is illustrated in the recent writings of Ronald Dworkin. Dworkin sees legal questions as, essentially, questions of interpretation. One can understand what the law is, in a particular community, only by becoming involved as a participant in the 'game' of interpretation. Judges and lawyers, of course, are so involved, and – according to Dworkin – so also are legal philosophers. By contrast, on the 'outside' is anyone who rejects or avoids involvement in these interpretive debates which determine the content and meaning of law. Thus, Dworkin puts matters very differently from Hart. In particular, because for Dworkin insiders – participants in the interpretive exercise – actually determine the law, knowledge of law is essentially restricted to these participants. They can and do include ordinary citizens, as Dworkin (1977: 214–5) makes clear, but it is hard to see that the citizen will usually be able to compete effectively in interpretive debate with the professional community of lawyers and judges on the meaning of laws. Consequently, Dworkin's image of the internal-external dichotomy seems to move us closer to a parallel distinction between legal professional insiders and other outsiders (see Chapter 6).

These brief remarks on areas of theory which will be considered in later chapters at least suggest that the internal-external dichotomy can refer to several different kinds of demarcation. It may focus on the distinction of 'legal' phenomena or characteristics from 'non-legal' in many contexts – for example, with regard to rules, systems of doctrine, types of reasoning, institutions or decisions. It may focus on the idea of a distinctive field of legal knowledge or understanding, separable from other knowledge-fields; or on the idea of a community of legal 'insiders', distinguishable from outsiders in some consistent way; or on the idea of a distinct professional practice of law, marking lawyers off from other occupational groups or from lay citizens.

Professionalisation and Politics

The concern of normative legal theory with such matters as unity, system and the internal-external dichotomy can, therefore, be linked not only with practical problems in interpreting law within a legal system but also with characteristics or conditions of legal *professional* organisation. A sociologist viewing a legal profession and its members' practices might emphasise the profession's collective claim to possess special professional skills or knowledge as central to its continuing assertion of distinct professional status (e.g. Larson 1977: 231). The clear marking out of what count as legal knowledge, legal reasoning and legal issues might be thought of as the identification of an autonomous professional field, a field of special legal expertise, belief in which helps to ground and maintain the lawyer's professional status. Undoubtedly, this conscious identification of a distinctive legal realm in explicit terms is not something lawyers normally need to worry themselves with. It has often been taken for granted as has the idea of a secure, distinctive and autonomous professional knowledge and expertise centred on an identifiable field of law. Equally, the idea of this autonomous legal field might not necessarily be important to all forms of legal practice, or to professional practice in all times and places. There might be more important conditions for securing and maintaining status than the acceptance of the claim to possess special, distinctive expertise and knowledge. But this claim has been, and may still be important in certain contexts. In subsequent chapters an attempt will be made to show that legal philosophy's varied images of law as unified or systematic have sometimes been powerful, in particular conditions and at particular times in the development of modern Anglo-American law, in helping to reinforce the idea of a special professional knowledge and expertise underpinning lawyers' claims of professional status.

Equally, attempts in legal philosophy to explain a unity, distinctiveness or systematic character of law may have a wider *political* significance. They may suggest, for example, how far law can be considered separate from politics. Obviously, some provisional conception of 'the political' is necessary if this issue is to be raised. Accordingly, for this limited purpose, we can take politics to refer to the struggle to acquire and make use of power (cf. Weber 1948: 78), especially through established institutions and formal processes, and without resort to direct violence. On such a view, the most widely visible and extensively organised politics naturally centres on what is thought of as 'government' and the state. Law is clearly related to the political. But what is the relationship? How far can legal reasoning and judicial decisions be seen as different and distinct from policy argument and political decisions? Are legal institutions to be thought of as special or specialised, as regards their functions, forms, character or controlling values, in comparison with (other) political institutions associated with government, administration and the varied activities of the state. If legal reasoning, decisions and institutions do have particular unifying, distinguishing features, should law be considered a distinct *aspect* of politics or government, or should the 'legal' be *counterposed* to the 'political'? How far should legal institutions be treated as 'independent' of political institutions? These issues are not unimportant when questions about the legitimacy or authority of a legal system, its laws and its institutions, are raised. They help to define law's place in society and the degree of autonomy which law can be considered to have in relation to other aspects of society or political life. Hence, the kind of demarcation of the sphere of law, which normative legal theory tends to offer in terms of unity, system, distinctiveness and the internal-external dichotomy, might be far from insignificant in influencing views on the scope and limits of – and relationships between – legal and political actions and issues.

A postulated relationship between normative legal theory's demonstrations of unity or system in law, on the one hand, and legal professionalism and the political context, on the other, provides a merely provisional framework within which to consider, in the following chapters, some influential currents of Anglo-American legal philosophy. Such a framework does, however, make it possible to look at this material in a less abstract manner than is usual, and to keep consistently in mind some relatively concrete questions: what practical relevance in wider professional and political arenas of law do legal philosophy's contributions to legal theory have? What insights do particular types of normative legal theory provide for issues of legal and political practice? How can we best understand the significance of ideas and debates in this literature? How do they relate, if at all, to particular historical conditions, to changes in Anglo-American law itself during the period in which the literature has developed, and to changes in the situations of professional practice? What assumptions about the nature of societies are being made in these writings which purport to clarify the nature of law? In this way a literature that often seems highly abstract and whose concerns seem frequently ahistorical can be confronted with the specific context and conditions which have shaped it but which are rarely admitted explicitly and directly in the theory itself.

Legal Philosophy in Social and Political Context

Objections might be raised to this kind of emphasis in interpreting normative legal theory. Does this theory have no intellectual significance in its own right? Why emphasise its professional or political ramifications when its explicit concerns are not normally these but are frequently expressed in terms of general philosophical curiosity, a desire to understand law better, or to interpret it in broader terms than those of everyday legal practice?

An answer might begin by noting some well recognised difficulties in interpreting normative legal theory without a serious attempt to locate its abstractions in specific historical contexts. The first of these difficulties tends to be acutely felt by undergraduate students of jurisprudence, whether or not generally admitted by legal philosophers. There is often a sense that in the battle of abstract arguments no-one ever wins, and, further, that there are no reliable criteria by which one could recognise victory anyway. The disputes seem timeless; the issues never resolved. Philosophy in this state of affairs appears to lead nowhere. The jurist Tony Honoré wrote of one such fundamental theoretical dispute: 'Decade after decade Positivists and Natural lawyers face one another in the final of the World Cup. . .. Victory goes now to one side, now to the other, but the enthusiasm of players and spectators alike ensures that the losing side will take its revenge' (Honoré 1973: 1–2; cf. Honoré 1987: 32–3). Perhaps this interminable dispute (which will surface in subsequent chapters) reflects issues of such supreme difficulty and significance that agreement can never be obtained. But if so, should the debate continue? Or should it be restructured with its elements related to particular contexts, times and places, and the *causes* and *conditions* of disagreement made the centre of attention, rather than the abstract battles themselves? Otherwise, at legal philosophy's cup finals, perhaps 'the legal theorist can only cheer or jeer, label his opponent a moral leper or a disingenuous romantic' (Honoré 1987: 33).

Secondly, there seems good reason to suggest that the timelessness of many debates in normative legal theory is not just due to the intractability of abstract issues. Clearly legal philosophy must relate at many points to what it treats as legal experience – that is to lawyers' and judges' (and, to a lesser extent, citizens') knowledge, understanding and use of particular elements of legal doctrine and particular legal processes. Inevitably, its claims are tested for plausibility against this experience. Yet, still it seems that little progress is made. Perhaps there is something suspect about the 'testing' process itself, or about the way legal experience is being interpreted. One writer has recently suggested that although Hart's fundamental contribution to normative legal theory has been shown, even by some of his staunchest defenders, to be replete with uncertainties and difficulties, these defects have seemed irrelevant to its immense reputation and influence (Campbell 1988). If this is true it is, at least, puzzling.

Perhaps changing intellectual fashions related to the changing social context of legal development have been relevant to the assessment of some theories, as the legal scholar William Buckland claimed in discussing John Austin's mid-nineteenth century English jurisprudence. At the age of 85, Buckland noted how attitudes in the legal world to Austin had altered since Buckland's late nineteenth century youth: 'He was a religion; today he seems to be regarded rather as a disease' (Buckland 1949: 2). The general point seems strengthened when it is realised that, in Austin's case as in some others, a particular part of the writer's theoretical enterprise – and not necessarily that which he considered most fundamental – is consistently treated in most later commentary as if it were his entire theoretical contribution[2]. Such matters require explanation, as do consistent misrepresentations of a jurist's ideas, where such misrepresentations are sufficiently widespread to assume the proportions of myth. Again, Austin has been claimed as a victim of this kind of misrepresentation (Morison 1982: 170–7).

These kinds of problems are clearly not unique to normative legal theory. They suggest, however, that, if we are to try to understand how legal philosophy has developed and how its debates and disputes have been formed and conducted, the answers cannot be found entirely in the logic of philosophical argument. They are, in part at least, located in the wider context of ideas and activities in which theories are developed and evaluated. Reasons have already been suggested in this chapter for considering that context to be, in part, professional and political. The approach to understanding legal philosophy adopted in this book, therefore, in no way denies the significance of the substantive content of legal philosophy's debates about the nature of law. It argues, however, that that content is to be understood not as timeless but as a response to conditions and problems existing at particular historical moments in Western legal development.

By its nature, normative legal theory tends to exclude systematic consideration of the social context of law. It does so in two ways. First, unlike the empirical legal theory which is a major concern of sociological studies of law, normative legal theory, as it has

---

[2]   See on this e.g. Moles 1987; Sugarman 1986: 43.

been defined in this chapter, attempts to explain the nature of law almost exclusively through philosophical analysis and clarification of the values, concepts, principles, rules and modes of reasoning entailed in or presupposed by legal doctrine. Empirical legal theory, by contrast, relies heavily on systematic empirical analysis of legal institutions in their social environment and historical context. These behavioural and contextual inquiries relating to law are largely absent from normative legal theory.

Secondly, as argued earlier in this chapter, normative legal theory's concern to offer a general account of the nature of law tends to entail the creation of some sharp internal-external dichotomy, marking the legal from the non-legal. Since what is being attempted is often a rigorous clarification of the concept of law (or laws), it follows that this clarification seems to be attained best if the concept is analysed to distinguish conclusively the legal from the non-legal and so to show how the components of the legal can be explained and interpreted without reference to non-legal criteria. It should be said immediately that in most normative legal theory no claim is made that this can be *totally* achieved. If it could be the result would be a total 'closure' of the legal as a self-contained realm of knowledge.

The view taken in this book is that legal theory, as the attempt to understand law as a social phenomenon, *should* require that the limited, partial perspectives of particular kinds of participants in legal processes – for example, lawyers, judges, legislators, administrators, various categories of citizens – be confronted with wider theoretical perspectives on law which can incorporate and transcend these more limited viewpoints in order to broaden understanding of the nature of law. While there are many difficulties in the way of pursuing this objective of transcending partial perspectives, it may be the one which has guided most serious attempts to advance knowledge. Normative legal theory has, however, usually been produced from the perspectives of very specific kinds of legal participants – especially lawyers. Thus, it has often served systematically to express (rather than to challenge) their outlook; to confirm and refine their view of the nature of law while being influenced by their special practical needs with regard to the ordering and interpretation of legal knowledge.

Normative legal theory is often said to be concerned to answer the question 'What is law?'. But if this were really so it would surely explicitly seek to look at law from many perspectives: not just in terms of unity and system and the internal-external dichotomy, but also in terms of law's social origins and effects; not just philosophically but also sociologically; not just as concepts but also as behaviour (cf. Chapter 7); not just in terms of logical structures and rational foundations of doctrine but also through rigorous historical study of legal institutions. Thus, it might be said that normative legal theory in general has not seriously addressed the question 'What is law?'. It has more typically asked how it is possible to organise, in an intellectually satisfactory way, the diversity of doctrinal materials associated with legal regulation. But, in trying to answer this question it has often *implied* a great deal about the nature of law in society.

This book, therefore, is a discussion of normative legal theory which tries to adopt a broader view of what is required for an adequate legal theory than that which normative legal theory itself often presupposes. To remain true to that broader view the discussion seeks consistently to read normative legal theory 'in context'; to suggest the wider implications of some of this literature and what has promoted or inspired it, as well as to discuss its major claims and arguments about law.

How Should Legal Philosophy Be Interpreted Contextually?

The method advocated here is related to those now widely adopted in several other intellectual fields. A recent writer on social theory asserts the value of emphasising 'the non-theoretical "conditions of existence" of theory' and the need to examine what he calls theory's 'external and internal history'; that is, not only the pattern of its intellectual development but also the pattern of events and conditions which have provided the environment and stimulus of that development (Elliott 1987: 8, 9). Equally, if the word 'legal' is substituted for 'political', Quentin Skinner's influential interpretive outlook on political theory has much relevance for an understanding of normative legal theory: '[legal] life sets the main problems for the [legal] theorist, causing a certain range of issues to appear problematic, and a corresponding range of questions to become the leading subjects of debate'. This view does not entail that theoretical ideas are to be treated as 'a straightforward outcome of their social base', but they are certainly to be read in terms of their wider intellectual context (Skinner 1978: xi).

However, more is involved than just a reading of ideas in social and intellectual context (cf. Stone 1964: 5). They are also to be considered as far as possible in terms of their origins and effects. This can be a highly complex matter but one which may be integral to an understanding of the development of theories and their interrelations. For example, it cannot be assumed that there is a direct line of intellectual development which threads its way as a kind of triumphal progress of increasing enlightenment as one major theory or theoretical approach is refined and eventually gives way to a later one. As suggested earlier, ideas and theoretical orientations seem to be adopted and discarded in ways which cannot simply be explained in terms of intellectual superiority or inferiority. The great figures of Anglo-American normative legal theory do not necessarily appear as a succession of writers diligently building on their successors' work in a continuous intellectual endeavour[3]. It seems that the wheel is sometimes re-invented. Equally, central concerns of earlier writers are sometimes simply discarded or ignored by later ones. The impression is not one of continuity. To try to link in a historical development the contributions of a few major theorists is often like trying to see a route from one mountain top to the next without casting one's gaze down to the valleys between the mountains where the travellers' tracks actually wind. This is not to deny that leading theorists explicitly relate their ideas to what they take to be the ideas of their predecessors. It is merely to assert that these relationships are much more complex than they are often made to appear.

The sociologist Karl Mannheim well expressed some aspects of this problem in writing of what he termed the 'illusion of the immanent flow of ideas'. 'The works of the past appear to the scholar as pictures in a gallery – an array of discrete entities. The temptation to construe this array as an organic and continuous growth is well-nigh irresistible to those who confine their interest to the historical records of creative expression. What is ignored in this imagery are the intervening areas in which men act and react as social beings' (Mannheim 1956: 30). Thus, while ideas have intellectual origins and may exert intellectual influence, these relationships and lines of development may be mediated by *social* factors – the acts of people as 'social beings'. In relation to legal ideas, these factors may relate – as has been suggested earlier – to professional and political considerations.

This is not, however, a book about intellectual history, but about theories which are major components of contemporary Anglo-American jurisprudence, or have provided essential foundations of it. Thus, a concern with context is solely for its contribution to a more satisfactory understanding of the nature of these theories. How then, finally, is it possible to reconcile a concern for ideas

---

[3]   Cf. Collini, Winch and Burrow 1983: 4, noting parallel problems in interpreting the development of what is now seen as political science.

on their own terms, with a concern to interpret them in terms of their consequences and origins?

Earlier it was suggested that normative legal theory generally propounds a sharp dichotomy between the legal and what is external to law. The clear marking out of a realm of the distinctively legal is characteristic of much of this literature. And certainly, from particular points of view – especially those of the lawyer anxious to know clearly what rules and regulations are valid as *law* – it makes good sense to treat law *as if* it can be identified as a wholly distinct realm. But it will be suggested in the following chapters that normative legal theory has had only partial success in this demonstration of legal distinctiveness (and related claims about law's unity or systematic character). To the extent that it has tried to portray a distinct field of specifically legal knowledge it has often failed to show the autonomy of that knowledge from sociological, political or moral conditions or ideas. Indeed, partly because 'the legal' can never be totally separated from such matters which normative legal theory often treats as external to law, the theory itself often implies interesting ideas about the very social context which it apparently seeks to exclude from its concerns. It will be important to highlight these ideas in subsequent chapters since they often reveal very important presuppositions on which normative legal theory is based.

Any study of law must make some provisional identification of its subject-matter. Such a marking out does not, however, require the kind of exclusory definitions of law which some normative legal theory has defended. If a rigid internal-external dichotomy is hard to accept in considering law, a productive replacement for it is an approach which tries to understand *both* the insistent attempts to defend an autonomous realm of legal knowledge *and* the conditions which equally inspire and seem to defeat those attempts. Hence, normative legal theory itself needs to be looked at from the 'inside' and the 'outside' since each kind of viewpoint is inadequate without the other. The theory should be viewed on its own terms *and* in context. Each contribution to normative legal theory should be assessed for the persuasiveness of its particular explanation of the legal reality it chooses to emphasise. Equally, it should be viewed as a reflection and expression of a climate of thought, a particular perspective on law which is sociologically interesting insofar as that perspective has been influential or an important intellectual response to developments in law as a field of practice or experience. Thus, a view of normative legal theory in context is an attempt to relocate its perspectives on legal reality within a broader perspective of a 'larger' social reality, of which both the activity of philosophising about law and the particular legal experience philosophised about form only a part.

The following chapters discuss particular contributions to theory which have powerfully influenced Anglo-American ideas about the nature of law in general. Their order of treatment seems to me to correspond roughly to a progressive unfolding of the difficulties normative legal theory has faced in attempting to portray, in changing conditions, the unity, structure or autonomy of modern law, especially in the Anglo-American world.

2 The Theory of Common Law

Any serious attempt to understand the dominant ideas which have surrounded Anglo-American law must begin by confronting the great tradition of thought and practice summed up in the words 'common law'. The mere sound of them 'thrills the hearts of all good English lawyers', according to an eminent French legal scholar (Levy-Ullmann 1935: 3). However that may be, the common law tradition is rooted in centuries of English history. It emphasises the centrality of the judge in the gradual development of law and the idea that this law is found in the distillation and continual restatement of legal doctrine through the decisions of courts. Of course, modern law is predominantly *legislative* in origin. The production or refinement of legal doctrine by judges according to time-honoured common law approaches is increasingly subordinated to other ways of making or stating law: for example in statutory provisions, numerous forms of delegated legislation, administrative regulations, directives, guidelines and codes of practice. Nevertheless, common law thought as a way of conceptualising law and reasoning with it still exerts a fundamental influence in those jurisdictions which have inherited its historical legacy. Comparative lawyers still refer to a common law 'family' of legal systems. And in English legal education and scholarship, the 'common law frame of mind continues to overshadow the way we teach, write and think about law. Its categories and assumptions are still the standard diet of most first-year law students; and they continue to organise law textbooks and case-books' (Sugarman 1986: 26).

This purpose of this chapter is to establish the general theoretical ideas about the nature of law and its place in society which underpin the common law tradition. By doing so it is possible to identify some of the earliest and, in a sense, most fundamental normative legal theory from which modern Anglo-American legal philosophy has built its images of law. The theoretical problems which common law thought poses have had to be confronted in this modern legal philosophy, and, as later chapters of this book will argue, they remain to haunt it. The place of the judge in the legal and political order; the relative significance of community values and political power as foundations of law; the relationship between interpretation of law and legislative activity – these are some of the fundamental problems which the theory of common law poses and attempts to answer.

Although this book is concerned with the relevance of legal theory for the situation of law in society today, common law thought cannot be understood without taking a long historical view. Its character has been shaped by centuries of English legal practice. Consequently the picture of common law's theoretical outlook presented in this chapter has to be pieced together from ideas and events widely scattered in time and place. Classical common law thought certainly does not present a kind of legal theory comparable with the explicit, systematic theories developed in modern legal philosophy. But, as will appear, it has provided conceptual building blocks for much later legal theory.

The Character of Common Law Thought

What is common law? A limited, but direct, historical answer might be that it consists of the rules and other doctrine developed gradually by the judges of the English royal courts as the foundation of their decisions, and added to over time by judges of those various jurisdictions recognising the authority of this accumulating doctrine. Henri Levy-Ullmann notes that the expression *la Commune ley*, is used, from the end of the thirteenth century onwards in the ancient reports of legal arguments known as the year-books, 'in contra-distinction to terms denoting legal rules derived from sources other than those upon which the King's judges normally based their decisions' (Levy-Ullmann 1935: 4; cf. Blackstone 1809 I: 68). So common law, as the law of common jurisdiction applied by these courts, was distinguished from various kinds of special or local law. Much later, the term came to refer frequently to judge-made or judge-declared law in contrast to legislation.

But how far is this common law an affair of *rules*? Here, as in many other inquiries about classical common law thought it is important to avoid imposing on the common law tradition modern interpretations reflecting views about law derived from wholly different theoretical premises (especially those to be discussed in Chapters 3 and 4). To write of common law as a system of rules (cf. Neumann 1986: 244–5) is to impose just such an alien conception on it. A commentator remarks on the surface 'chaos' of judicial decisions, underlying which is, however, 'an internally coherent and unified body of rules'. But he goes on to note that 'principles' of law stand behind these rules and, in common law thought, are more important than them (Sugarman 1986: 26). In fact, however, it is probably more true to common law tradition to see its essence not in rules at all. 'To represent it as a systematic structure of rules is to distort it; it is to represent as static what is essentially dynamic and constantly shifting' (Postema 1986: 10). The idea of common law as *principles* of law seems more appropriate for capturing this shifting, dynamic character, if only because principles suggest flexible guidelines for legal decision-making rather than rules which control.

Much more lies behind all this than a terminological quibble. As Brian Simpson has noted, if common law's existence is thought of in terms of a set of rules 'it is in general the case that one cannot say what the common law is' (Simpson 1973: 16). This is because it is impossible to mark out conclusively such a rule-set corresponding to common law. While some continental writers have interpreted the common law as a 'complete, closed and logically consistent' system (Neumann 1986: 245), Simpson seems on much firmer ground in saying: 'As a system of legal thought the common law. . . is inherently incomplete, vague and fluid' (1973: 17). Thus, for Jeremy Bentham, the great English legal reformer, who insisted that law should be a matter of clear rules, common law was no more than 'mock law', 'sham law', 'quasi-law'. Judicial development of law exemplified 'power everywhere arbitrary' (quoted in Simpson 1973: 16).

Issues of the clarity and completeness of law therefore arise. Common law resides in judicial decisions rather than rules. But something stands behind the decisions, justifying them, guiding them and giving them authority as law. For the American jurist Roscoe Pound, common law is 'a mode of treating legal problems' rather than rules. But principles of common law shape rules (Pound 1921: 1). Pound also identifies the spirit of common law in distinctive institutions: 'supremacy of law, case law and hearing of causes as a whole in open court' (1921: 2). Associated with these are the institution of trial by jury and 'judicial empiricism' (Pound 1921: ch 7) – pragmatic case-by-case decision-making guided by past judicial precedents; a method of working that, for Pound, 'combines certainty and power of growth [of law] as no other doctrine has been able to do' (1921: 182). But still it can be asked what, if anything, unifies these institutions and what gives them legal authority or legitimacy.

Common law's unity has been attributed to 'the fact that law is grounded in, and logically derived from, a handful of general principles; and that whole subject-areas such as contract or torts are distinguished by some common principles or elements which fix the boundaries of the subject. The exposition and systematisation of these general principles, and the techniques required to find and to apply them and the rules that they underpin, are largely what legal education and scholarship [in the common law environment] are all about' (Sugarman 1986: 26). Indeed, a long tradition of thought sees the classical essence of common law in broad legal guidelines, as much concerned with how to reach proper judicial decisions (Simpson 1973: 21), as with the specific content of them. On this view it is best seen as 'a method of legal thinking' (Cohen 1933: 333) or of deciding disputes. A.V.Dicey, using terms similar to those of the eminent eighteenth century jurist Sir William Blackstone (cf. Blackstone 1809 I: 67), wrote at the end of the nineteenth century of common law as a 'mass of custom, tradition or judge-made maxims' (Dicey 1959: 23–4).

Maxims of common law symbolised the broad guidelines which could be considered to underlie and direct loosely individual decisions. One writer examining a crucial period of common law development in the first half of the seventeenth century remarks that maxims 'were the essential core of the common law, woven so closely into the fabric of English life that they could never be ignored with impunity'; as 'high level general principles or fundamental points of the law' they were used in interpreting the past decisions of the courts – evaluating their significance as precedents to be applied to new cases (Sommerville 1986: 94). Maxims, indeed, were far more important than precedents themselves. In modern times, as legal doctrine became more detailed and complex, these maxims lost their force and have ceased to be of much practical significance. But they point to the enduring idea that the heart of common law is not in specific decisions or in rules distilled from them but in broad notions which are difficult to unify or systematise, but which may, indeed, in some way, be 'woven into the fabric of life'.

Because many of these notions are extremely hard to pin down, the unifying element of common law often seems mystical. Sometimes in classical common law thought it is portrayed as a vague historical destiny, a working out in history of an obscure but immanent logic of the law, or a kind of superhuman wisdom reflected in the collective work of the common law judges throughout the centuries but impossible for any single person to possess. Thus, for Blackstone, law is 'frought with the accumulated wisdom of ages' (quoted in Postema 1986: 63). And Coke CJ, early in the seventeenth century, wrote: 'we are but of yesterday. . . our

days upon the earth are but as a shadow in respect of the old
ancient days and times past, wherein the laws have been by the
wisdom of the most excellent men, in many successions of ages,
by long and continual experience. . . refined, which no one man
(being of so short a time) albeit he had in his head the wisdom
of all the men in the world, in any one age could ever have effected
or attained unto. And therefore. . . no man ought to take upon
him to be wiser than the laws'[1].

The Common Law Judge

Though such statements date from long ago they express honestly
and directly a set of assumptions which underpin the classical
conception of common law judging. According to the declaratory
doctrine of common law, judges do not make law[2]. They are, in
Blackstone's words, 'the depositories of the laws, the living oracles,
who must decide in all cases of doubt' (Blackstone 1809 I: 69).
The authority of law is seen as a traditional authority. The judge
expresses a part of the total, immanent wisdom of law which is
assumed to be already existent before his decision. The judge works
from within the law which is 'the repository of the experience of
the community over the ages' (Postema 1986: 32). Thus, even though
he may reach a decision on a legal problem never before addressed
by a common law court, he does so not as an original author
of new legal ideas but as a representative of a collective wisdom
greater than his own. He interprets and applies the law but does
not create it, for the law has no individual authors. It is the product
of the community grounded in its history. Judicial decisions,
according to Matthew Hale writing in the seventeenth century, do
not make law 'for that only the king and parliament can do' but
are *evidence* of law, and 'though such decisions are less than a
law, yet they are a greater evidence thereof than the opinion of
any private persons, as such, whosoever' (quoted in Levy-Ullmann
1935: 56). Thus the judge is spokesman for the community about
its law, but a particularly authoritative spokesman.

Such a viewpoint could lead to apparently radical conclusions.
A judge could mistake the law (Postema 1986: 9–11; 194–5).
Blackstone (1809 I: 70) writes: 'The doctrine of the law then is
this: that precedents and rules must be followed, unless flatly absurd

---

[1]   *Calvin's Case* (1608) 7 Co Rep 1, 3.
[2]   See e.g. per Lord Esher MR in *Willis v Baddeley* [1892] 2 QB 324,
      326.

or unjust'. But law (wiser than any individual) is the perfection of reason, so an unjust or absurd decision cannot be declaratory of the law. It is not bad law but, in Blackstone's view, no law at all. It follows that the doctrine of precedent – the doctrine that judges are bound to treat as binding on them the essential legal grounds of decision adopted in similar cases previously determined in courts of higher or perhaps equal status – is a complex one in classical common law thought. It is also perhaps much more flexible than it is typically portrayed as being. The judge must attach great weight to previous decisions, not only for practical and political reasons (maintaining sufficient certainty in legal doctrine, avoiding usurpation of the legislative function) but also for theoretical reasons. Those decisions provide, in general, the best available evidence of the collective wisdom of the common law. An individual judge or court must subordinate individual reasoning and values to those enshrined in the law. On the other hand, the reasoning and values of the law are greater than those not only of the presently deciding judges, but also of any of the precedent-creating judges of the past. Hence the theory of common law does not dictate a slavish adherence to precedent. Even where prior judicial decisions can be considered to state accurately the common law, a later judge is bound not by those decisions but by the principles implicit or explicit in them (cf. Postema 194– 5). Further, while classical common law thought denies that the judge is creative as a maker of law, he is not merely passive as a finder or revealer (Levy-Ullmann 1935: 54) of it. The judge is the privileged representative of the community, entrusted with its collective legal wisdom, which he is authorised to draw upon constructively in order to produce solutions to novel issues raised before the court.

Can Common Law Thought Explain Legal Development?

A paradox seems to lie at the heart of classical common law thought. Common law as the embodiment of ancient wisdom is revealed by judges, not created by them. It is, therefore, always already existent. Yet obviously it develops with the accumulation, reinterpretation and restatement of precedents and the adjustment of legal doctrine to new circumstances reflected in the never-ending succession of cases brought before courts (cf. Pocock 1957: 36– 7). How is the evolution of law explained in this conception? And why is it not possible to assert openly that judges *make* law, even if only within strict limits which would fix them as clearly subordinate to recognised legislators, such as (in the context of English history) a parliament or the monarch?

The formal answer to this last question is that law embodies an ancient wisdom which may, according to some conceptions of common law, be considered timeless or, according to others, be seen as continually evolving through collective experience. On either view judges can only reflect this wisdom and not change it. In some classical common law thought the claim of timelessness is taken to fantastic lengths. Influential seventeenth century lawyers, such as Sir Edward Coke, 'argued on the flimsiest evidence that the common laws, including their most detailed procedural provisions, dated from the earliest times' (Sommerville 1986: 90). Even Magna Carta was treated as declaring ancient law, confirming and making enforceable rights which had long existed (Sommerville 1986: 98). Coke claimed that in all its major parts the law and constitution had remained unchanged since the Saxon era and even before (Postema 1986: 19). These strange views were always controversial but the reason for asserting them at times when the authority of common law was seriously challenged (as in the early seventeenth century) is not hard to see. This authority was traditional in nature. Rooting it in a distant or even mythical past emphasised that it was certainly not derived from the present power of any monarch or other political authority.

The authority or legitimacy of common law as a legal order entitled to the highest respect was seen as residing not in the political system but in the community. If a judge *made* law this could only be as an exercise of political power. The deliberate making of law would be a political act. But according to common law theory, the authority of the judge is not as a political decision-maker (certainly not as delegate of the king or parliament) but as representative of the community. Hence he has authority only to *state* the community's law, not to impose law upon the community as if he were a political ruler or the servant of one. And the community is to be thought of here as something uniting past and present, extending back through innumerable past generations as well as encompassing the present one. Clearly, if the term 'community' were to be defined rigorously in this context it would be necessary to ask who exactly is within this community and what is its nature. It would also be necessary to consider the compatibility of this communitarian conception of law with the fact that the judges referred to here are judges of the *royal* courts, the instruments of a centralised justice promoted by kings. But such issues are typically absent from classical common law thought. Thus, common law is, for Coke, simply 'the most ancient and best inheritance that the subjects of this realm have' (quoted Sommerville 1986: 103).

The usual way of conceptualising this apparently unchanging inheritance in classical common law thought is as *custom*. As Brian Simpson remarks, it is odd nowadays to think of law in this way because lawyers are used to treating this law as posited by the judges. But this is another example of the tendency to impose alien modern theoretical conceptions on common law (Simpson 1973: 18). Just as common law is not strictly to be thought of, in the classical conception, as rules, neither is it to be thought of as decisions. To term it 'a residue of immutable custom' (Sugarman 1986: 40) is more accurate, but does not confront the fact that common law thought embraces complex notions explaining and justifying past practices (not just stating them as custom) and providing guidance for future conduct. Equally common law thought allows the development of new doctrines and ideas, so has a dynamism which custom may lack. Because of these characteristics Simpson (1973: 20) prefers to term common law customary law, rather than custom. But this hardly seems to solve the theoretical problem of its development. Customary law still has the character of custom, looking back to the past rather than guiding the future. It is concerned with stating established practice rather than with means of developing legal doctrine to meet changing times.

The problem here is not that custom is changeless. There is no reason why it cannot be considered to change over time. Law as an expression of custom can, therefore, also change. The problem is that common law thought itself cannot really address this change or explain it as a *legal* process. The mechanisms of change are in society (or the community). Law changes solely through the mysterious processes by which custom changes. To explain or even recognise explicitly processes of legal change, classical common law thought would require some kind of sociological or anthropological insight. But the common lawyers were hardly sociologists. Common law thought predated any modern social science and, in any event, its practical case-by-case view of legal development would have found little room for any explicit general theory of social or cultural change. So classical common law thought emphasised continuity (which it could interpret legally in terms of precedents and fundamental principles), rather than change (for which it could find no specifically legal criteria of evaluation).

Historically, the conundrum of law as changeless yet always changing was avoided by devices made possible by cultural conditions. Common law was considered to be unwritten.

Blackstone (1809 I: 67), following Hale, distinguished 'the common law, or *lex non scripta* of this kingdom' from the written law of Acts of Parliament. Even though this unwritten law was eventually reported in written form, the fact that the law itself was still considered unwritten presumably allowed individual innovation to be forgotten, subsumed in the image of a changeless collective legal knowledge. As the anthropologist Jack Goody has noted about societies lacking writing, it is not that the creative element is absent in them or that 'a mysterious collective authorship, closely in touch with the collective consciousness, does what individuals do in literate cultures. It is rather that the individual signature is always getting rubbed out in the process of generative transmission' (Goody 1977: 27). Certainly common law's unwritten character was seen as one of its strengths, making possible 'a flexible system which had developed along with the English people itself' (Sommerville 1986: 91).

In the early ages of common law the lack of writing allowed a convenient amnesia. Blackstone wrote in the eighteenth century that 'in our law the goodness of a custom depends upon its having been used time out of mind; or, in the solemnity of our legal phrase, time whereof the memory of man runneth not to the contrary. This it is that gives its weight and authority' (Blackstone 1809 I: 67). The traditional authority of common law required that its customs be shrouded in antiquity. But in the Middle Ages two or three lifetimes would be enough to make a principle of common law immemorial (Pocock 1957: 37); 'in ten or twenty years a custom was of long standing; in forty years it was "age-old" ' (Gough 1955: 14). Later the flexibility of memory was less satisfactory. When, in the seventeenth century, lawyers such as Coke found it necessary to assert with the greatest possible force the traditional authority of common law against the king, the 'idea of the immemorial . . .took on an absolute colouring. . . It ceased to be a convenient fiction and was heatedly asserted as literal historical truth' (Pocock 1957: 37). It can easily be seen, therefore, that common law thought eventually backed itself into a corner. First, the idea that the law was unwritten eventually became a mere fiction as the common law was recorded – preserved, explained and digested in written form in public records, law reports and 'the authoritative writings of the venerable sages of the law' (Maine 1861: 8; cf. Blackstone 1809 I: 73). Secondly, the purely traditional authority of the law eventually demanded an utterly unrealistic claim of unbroken continuity from ancient times. And, finally, the declaratory theory of common law judging had to be maintained in the face of abundant evidence of conscious judicial innovation in legal doctrine (cf Levy-Ullmann 1935: 53).

Three responses to this situation were possible. One was to declare that common law possessed no authority by which it could develop further. Legal innovation could only come through Acts of Parliament, or other legislative acts. Thus, as one judge put the matter, 'It is in my opinion impossible for us now to create any new doctrine of common law'[3]. A second response was to embrace openly the idea that judges sometimes make law, discard all fictions and go on to ask serious questions as to *how* and under what conditions they should make it. But this pragmatic approach also involved discarding all the standard assumptions underpinning the authority and legitimacy of common law. Traditional authority would need to be replaced with something else – perhaps the charismatic authority of individual wise judges, a conception of delegated political power (see Chapter 3) or, as in the United States, the authority of a specific constitutional document providing the ultimate foundation of legal and judicial systems (Cotterrell 1984: 241–3). In any event such a new foundation of judicial authority, if it could be found, would be something different from that presupposed in classical common law thought.

A third solution was to discard the notion of common law as custom and the formal idea of an unchanging ancient law, and to emphasise instead the complex conception of the judge as spokesman of the community – neither individual creator of law nor mere restator of ancient truths, but representative of an evolving collective legal consciousness[4]. As will appear later, this view of common law thought, which maintains what might be considered fundamental elements in it but avoids the *cul-de-sac* of an appeal to custom, has been reflected in various forms of modern legal philosophy. It is restated in the historical jurisprudence to be discussed later in this chapter, and reworked in various ways in the writings of certain modern authors, such as Roscoe Pound and Ronald Dworkin, considered in Chapter 6.

Common Law and Legislation

So far legislation – the deliberate creation of new law by a formal

---

[3]   Per Farwell LJ in *Baylis v Bishop of London* [1913] 1 Ch 127, 137. Cf. *Mirehouse v Rennell* (1833) 1 Cl & F 527, 546 (per Parke J).

[4]   Cf. Hale's interpretation of the evolution of common law discussed in Postema 1986: 19–27.

law-making body such as Parliament – has received hardly any mention in this discussion. But in classical common law thought the relationship between legislation and the law-finding of the courts had to be settled not just as a practical and political matter, but as a theoretical one. How should legislation be viewed from the standpoint of common law theory? Nowadays, English lawyers generally have no doubt that in a conflict between statute law and judge-determined law, the former prevails over the latter. It is of superior legal authority. Equally most lawyers (and probably most non-lawyers) have no doubt that judges in the higher courts frequently make law through their decisions, whatever classical common law theory may suggest. But there is much doubt as to how far judges are justified in doing so. We have considered the explanation of judicial authority which classical common law thought gives. How does it explain the relationship between legislation and common law?

In English history, statutes only gradually emerged as something clearly distinct from common law. In medieval times, legal opinion treated them as performing 'in a more explicit and general way, the same task which occupied the judiciary' (Postema 1986: 15) – stating customary common law. Early statute law could be regarded as part of common law (Postema 1986: 24). In an influential study, Charles McIlwain described the English parliament of the Middle Ages as a court, with its statutes considered as no more than affirmations of common law (McIlwain 1910: ch 3; Levy-Ullmann 1935: 232–3). Some of McIlwain's claims may be exaggerated (Gough 1955: ch 1) but the general picture of a slow historical separation of statute and common law and a gradual emergence of the idea of deliberate law creation by a formal body seems clear.

Concern here is not with historical events but with strands of theory related to them. As such, it is possible to see a common law theory of legislation emerging. In the seventeenth century, in the great struggle between royal and parliamentary power which culminated in the English Civil War and Revolution and its consequences, common lawyers 'elevated Parliament to a position of near-sovereignty, while at the same time insisting that unwritten custom was superior to statute law' (Sommerville 1986: 95). As Parliament's supremacy in law creation was affirmed, common law thought treated the authority to enact statutes as, itself, grounded in common law. It followed that Parliament could not abolish the whole of the common law without abolishing itself (Sommerville 1986: 95), although it could obviously overrule – with legal if not necessarily moral force – particular principles of common law or decisions founded on them. Thus, although an Act of Parliament was 'the exercise of the highest authority that this kingdom acknowledges upon earth' (Blackstone quoted in Manchester 1980: 33), common law authority, in a sense, 'trumped' that of Parliament. Parliamentary supremacy over common law was claimed as *given by* common law. Legislation could be thought of as an island or archipelago in a broad sea of common law (Postema 1986: 18). This suggests why it remained possible in common law thought up to modern times to treat legislation as somehow peripheral to common law despite the ever-increasing bulk of enactments. Similarly, such a view justified a restrictive approach to legislation, which should be interpreted so that it could be integrated into the common law (Postema 1986: 17), at least where ambiguity or uncertainty of legislative meaning allowed this.

This view of legislation could hardly be satisfactory in modern times and always entailed inconsistencies. It certainly did not mean that judges were superior to Parliament (Blackstone 1809 I: 91; Levy-Ullmann 1935: 236–7). In Coke's time, for example, the threat of royal pressure on the judges would have made any such doctrine dangerous to the image of law as the defence of the subject's liberties (Sommerville 1986: 96). Coke wrote of Parliament's power as 'transcendent and absolute', although according to one view he may have been thinking of Parliament in its old sense as the highest court of the land and thus still the instrument of common law (cf. Grey 1978: 856). But, in any case, common law thought had to recognise that from early times 'novel law' in Acts of Parliament, ordinances, provisions and proclamations 'defeated' common law (Gough 1955: 14–5). It seems that the common law outlook could not come to terms with modern legislation in a realistic way. It offered a powerful defence of the jurisdiction of common law judges as autonomous, while fully recognising the supremacy of Parliament; and it explained the role of the judge in interpreting legislation as one derived from his position as declarer of the community's law, not as the servant of a political legislator. But it failed to provide an adequate theory of the political authority underlying legislation. It remained firmly rooted in a social world predating the modern legislative state. Conversely, as will appear in the following chapters, the theories which challenged common law thought and provided powerful justification for state law-making often remained ambiguous or unsatisfactory in their explanation of the sources of judicial authority. The idea of judicial authority rooted in community remains perhaps the strongest, most vibrant, contribution of common law thought. Its explanations of political law-making through legislation remain perhaps its weakest, flimsiest elements.

The Political and Social Environment

So far, in this chapter, common law thought has been presented merely as a set of abstract conceptions of law's attributes. But how does common law thought view the social and political environment of law? How might it help to define the lawyer's place in society and the relationship between law and politics? Since no attempt is being made here to present any part of the history of common law thought as such, a few illustrations of very general contextual considerations may be sufficient to suggest further dimensions of what has been sketched here as the classical theory of common law.

Legal Knowledge and Community

Common law thought has no rigorously developed conception of the nature of law's social environment. The term 'community' seems to capture best the vague assumptions about the nature of this social setting which are presupposed in common law thought. Yet, although law is assumed to be deeply rooted in this environment and to derive essential meaning from it, the nature of the environment remains largely unelaborated. Gerald Postema sees the common law image of community as entailing a 'broad consensus and an already constituted social unity', which is confirmed and maintained by common law decisions but not created by them (Postema 1986: 19). But almost the only thing which can be said with certainty about social life in common law terms is that law is an *aspect* of it, inseparable from the rest. The American jurist James Carter probably best expressed this in asserting that 'Law, Custom, Conduct, Life – different names for almost the same thing – true names for different aspects of the same thing – are so inseparably blended together that one cannot even be thought of without the other. No improvement can be effected in one without improving the other, and no retrogression can take place in one without a corresponding decline in the other' (Carter 1907: 320; cf Hale quoted in Postema 1986: 73). The common lawyers saw society through the lens of law. In a sense, society *was* the structure of relations, customs, claims and obligations expressed in legal knowledge.

But what kind of knowledge is law? In the classical conception common law is, above all, rational, excelling all other human laws in rationality (Sommerville 1986: 89, 92–5). But there are probably at least two conceptions of rationality at work here. Common law entailed a kind of particularistic analogical reasoning making it possible to link cases and compare precedents (Postema 1986: 31). It could thus tolerate broad illogicalities arising out of particular analogical linkages of ideas or cases. Equally, however, common law is, for Blackstone, 'a rational science' of 'general and extensive principles' (Blackstone 1809 I: 2, II: 425). Therefore, such a view might permit illogicalities of detail within an overall framework of broad principle[5]. Reason could, consequently, serve opposite roles in linking detailed particularities or broad tendencies in legal thought. There is, thus, no simple key to unlock the assumed rationality of common law.

In particular, there is no key which an untrained person could use. If the law is that of the community it is, nevertheless, inaccessible to most members of the community, at least in detail. According to common law thought, law is not natural reason but refined or *artificial* reason which, as Coke asserted, 'requires long study and experience, before that a man can attain to the cognisance of it'[6]. Although the law is reason, reason alone will not give mastery of it. Experience of the practice of law (such as the common law judge possesses) is also essential (Postema 1986: 33, interpreting Hale), and apprenticeship is the most appropriate means of acquiring it. Thus, obviously, actual knowledge of law is denied to the community. This knowledge is necessarily – by its nature – the monopoly of lawyers, who appear as the absolutely indispensible representatives of the community in stating, interpreting and applying the community's law.

The point is strengthened by aspects of the linguistic history of common law. 'Legal ideas were transmitted largely orally, and even the available literary sources were, as late as the seventeenth century, written in a special and partly private language' (Simpson 1973: 21). After the Norman conquest the language of the English common law courts became Norman French and then a unique 'Franco-English jargon', long maintained as such by the lawyers for documents, despite efforts to change the language to English by statute (Levy-Ullmann 1935: 123–4). Only in 1731 was there finally a conclusive enactment making English, rather than Latin

---

[5]   Cf. Lord Devlin's remarks in *Hedley Byrne & Co Ltd v Heller & Partners Ltd* [1964] AC 465, 516.

[6]   *Prohibitions del Roy* (1608) 12 Co Rep 63, 65. Cf. Pound 1921: 61; Sommerville 1986: 89, 93–4.

or French, the exclusive language of court proceedings, requiring records to be made in legible writing rather than obscure 'court hand', and forbidding abbreviation of words[7].

There is, therefore, an apparently profound inconsistency between, on the one hand, the thoroughly esoteric form in which legal knowledge existed and, on the other, the way classical common law thought understood law as having 'developed along with the English people itself' (Sommerville 1986: 91); or as 'a part of the lives of men' (Holmes 1897: 473). The assumed link between law and community has a primarily *symbolic* significance in common law thought, wholly different from any modern notions of participation or popular justice. It would be wrong to characterise common law knowledge as 'professional knowledge' since the 'artificial reason' of the law predates the emergence of an organised legal profession in any modern sense. Nevertheless, the classical common law conception of law was undoubtedly admirably suited for the promotion of the collective status of lawyers as a group. On the one hand, the implied deep community roots of law suggested that legal knowledge was a central part of the collective wisdom of society. It was therefore of the greatest social significance and the possessor of it spoke with obvious authority. On the other hand, what the historian Maitland called the 'occult science' of law (Maitland 1893: 483) was defined in such a way that no-one but legal practitioners could have access to it. Although all these claims about the community roots of common law and about the inevitable 'artificiality' of its reason could be (and were) challenged at various times, their forceful advocacy served very well the interests of common lawyers as a group.

Common Law Thought and Political Authority

The relationship between law and politics in classical common law thought derives directly from the ambiguous relationship between law and community discussed above. Again, it will be sufficient to illustrate some aspects of the political significance of common law thought by taking a few themes from a very complex history.

How does common law thought view the political realm? Essentially, it finds great difficulty in recognising such a realm in any modern sense. English common law still has no definite and elaborated concept of the state (Maitland 1901; cf. Buckland 1949: ch 7) and refers instead to the Crown. Originating in a social order in which political authority could be conceptualised as a set of

[7]   Statute 4 Geo. II, c. 26.

private property rights held by monarchs or their subordinates (Cohen 1933: 41ff.), common law thought recognised royal authority, and later parliamentary authority, as given by common law or by some fundamental principles of reason underlying it. Maitland made great play of the fact that, when the king died, 'we see all the wheels of the State stopping or even running backwards' (for example, litigation stopped and had to be restarted; military commissions had to be renewed) since there was no coherent general conception of a continuing abstract political authority (Maitland 1901: 253; cf. Stoljar 1958: 27–30). Today such problems are of merely historical interest. The inadequacies of common law conceptions were marginalised long ago by legal solutions reflecting other theoretical views of law and politics, or by purely pragmatic legal developments. But they illustrate again the fact that common law thought cannot easily come to terms with the concept of the modern legislative and administrative state with its complex network of intersecting and self-renewing authorities.

Classical common law thought did not really produce a theory of the relationship of law and politics either. In the great political struggles of the seventeenth century in which common lawyers, such as Coke, sought to protect the authority of common law against the claims of monarch and parliament, the main theoretical effort was, it seems, to elaborate and extend common law's authority claims. Thus, if the roots of its authority are in an intertwining of reason and tradition, both of these elements were elevated or exaggerated in ways which emphasise their centrality for any theory of common law, and the fact that they are entirely independent of political authority.

Common law's reason was often claimed to be derived from God's reason (Sommerville 1986: 92). Certainly, as has been noted earlier, it was considered to transcend the reason of individuals, however wise. Thus a fundamental *natural law of reason* was held to inform common law, allowing highly controversial claims to be made in a few famous seventeenth century cases that 'when an Act of Parliament is against common right and reason, or repugnant, or impossible to be performed, the common law will control it, and adjudge such act to be void'[8]. On the other hand, in the same period, the appeal to traditional authority became, in the doctrine of the Ancient Constitution, the mythical idea that

---

[8]   *Dr. Bonham's Case* (1610) 8 Co Rep 114, 118 (per Coke CJ). See also *Calvin's Case* (1608) 7 Co Rep 1; *Day v Savadge* (1615) Hob. 85; *City of London v Wood* (1701) 12 Mod 669. And see further Chapter 5, below, pp 121–2.

English common law remained essentially unchanged since a time that predated all relevant *political* authorities, and so had a transcendent authority unaffected by political change. Some common lawyers even denied that there had been a military conquest in 1066 which entailed any legal discontinuity. 'To admit a conquest was to admit an indelible stain of sovereignty upon the English constitution' (Pocock 1957: 53). Thus, with what now seem bizarre claims about the authority of transcendent natural reason and the significance of myths about the sources of common law in history, common lawyers fought to maintain the independent force of common law at a time when already it was preparing to give way to types of authority rooted in political sources which it could not theoretically comprehend.

Savigny: A Theory For Common Law?

The discussion in previous sections should suggest that the legacy of classical common law thought in itself is seriously inadequate to provide a convincing legal theory. In particular, although the nature of law is seen as rooted in the nature of society, no explicit conception of society or social development is offered in common law thought. One consequence of this is that, insofar as law is considered to be customary, it becomes extremely difficult to explain or even clearly identify the processes of legal development in common law. Secondly, the relationship between judge-declared law and legislation – the dominant source of law in modern Western societies – remains unclear. Thirdly, the sources of law's authority frequently appear mystical; grounded in myths about history or in claims, unsupported by rigorous argument, about the character of natural reason.

In the nineteenth century, various types of legal philosophy developed which tried to take serious account, in an explicitly elaborated legal theory, of the conditions of law in the modern state. Some of these theories reflected ideas which had been in currency long before, but all of them, in one way or another, had to take account of obvious changes in the character of law and legal institutions – and especially the increasing dominance of legislation as a source of new law. The rest of this chapter will be concerned with certain theories from this period which can be interpreted as defences and elaborations of conceptions of law very similar in important respects to the conception suggested in classical common law thought. In an age of legislation – of extensive, deliberate law-making by political authorities aimed at reshaping society or its legal traditions – common law thought implied only an ambiguous, undeveloped legal theory disdainful of rigorous concepts and incoherent in fundamental respects. The nineteenth century legal philosophy which came to be known as historical jurisprudence can be seen as partly filling the need for a theoretical defence of common law methods. Indeed, the following discussion will argue that, today, in the Anglo-American context, the most fruitful way of interpreting historical jurisprudence in relation to normative legal theory is in these terms. But, as will appear, the rich and complex literature of historical jurisprudence is in no way confined in its concerns to Anglo-American common law.

The dominant original influence in historical jurisprudence is usually traced to the Prussian jurist and statesman Friedrich Carl von Savigny. Writing at the beginning of the nineteenth century, Savigny opposed the political movement of the time pressing for the codification of the law of the German states. Many of those favouring codification saw it as an instrument for promoting German political unity. However, the modern idea of codification as an attempt to produce a complete statement of fundamental principles of law in some systematic arrangement suggests a culmination of legal development, the result of which can be captured in perfected, rationally elaborated legal forms and structures.

For Savigny, this idea denies the character of law as spontaneously and continually evolving with the culture – the whole way of life – of a people (*Volk*). The optimum time for codification of law would be at the peak of cultural development, but then such a fixing of law in final form would be unnecessary when law and culture are vibrant and dynamic. Codification would be merely for the benefit of 'a succeeding and less fortunate age, as we lay up provisions for winter', and such foresight is rare (Savigny 1831: 43). Thus, in Savigny's view, codes are usually made at the wrong historical moments – in the early phases of cultural development when legal development is lively but technical skill in distilling fundamental concepts and principles from this changing law is likely to be lacking; or in a time of cultural decline, as with the Emperor Justinian's remarkable codification of Roman law in the sixth century A.D.. Savigny notes, of the efforts of this period, that when 'all intellectual life was dead the wrecks of better times were collected to supply the demand of the moment' (1831: 51).

Immediately, in these comments, a view of law is suggested which emphasises the pervasiveness of change and which ties law firmly to cultural evolution. Behind all this are ideas close to those which underpin classical common law thought, although Savigny writes in a different legal context. Thus, law is seen as an aspect of social life, not something set apart from other social phenomena as distinctive. For Savigny, law 'has no self-dependent existence. . . its essence is the life of man itself' viewed from a certain standpoint (1831: 46). In place of the ancient wisdom, rooted in a perhaps mythical past, which grounds and guides common law, Savigny puts 'the common consciousness of the people' (*Volksgeist*) as the 'seat of law' (1831: 28). In his descriptions of it there seems an almost exact parallel with the elusive ideas of profound communal sources of reason and authority, spanning the centuries, which are presupposed in classical common law thought. 'That which binds them into one whole is the common conviction of the people, the kindred consciousness of an inward necessity, excluding all notion of an accidental and arbitrary origin' (Savigny 1831: 24).

Because Savigny has no hesitation about describing culture explicitly in evolutionary terms, his picture of law also is one of continuous evolution. As language develops spontaneously by essentially uncontrolled communal processes, so law develops 'by internal silently operating powers, not by the arbitrary will of a lawgiver' (Savigny 1831: 30). As in classical common law thought legal ideas are assumed to have no individual authors. They are a wholly collective product. Legislation, as deliberate lawmaking, is definitely treated as subordinate to the demands of the common consciousness.

Although much of the common lawyer's mystical conception of law's origins remains in this theory, a much more explicit statement of the stages of cultural change is offered and, with it, a more definite view of the role of legislation and the state in aiding the spontaneous processes of legal development. Savigny was writing at the beginning of a new age in which legislation would have a specific vocation (Savigny 1831). Although, like the common lawyers, he sees law's primary form as custom, he also recognises that modern law cannot be thought of in such terms. He notices at least some simple sociological considerations regarding social development. With the development of societies to a certain level of complexity, social classes emerge and society fragments into different interest groups (cf. Savigny 1831: 28; Savigny 1867: 14, 36). One might imagine that this recognition would lead Savigny to doubt whether any common consciousness could continue to co-exist with such social divisions. However, it leads him only to note the special role which lawyers now assume, and some special tasks of legislation. The common consciousness still exists but it is harder to focus it to produce new law directly. As the common lawyers distinguished natural reason from the artificial reason of law, so Savigny notes that law 'perfects its language, takes a scientific direction' and 'devolves upon the jurists, who thus, in this department, represent the community'. Thus it becomes 'artificial and complex' and leads a twofold existence as part of community life and also as the specialised knowledge of lawyers (Savigny 1831: 28; 1867: 36–40). This idea closely parallels the uneasily ambiguous common law view of law's relationship with community. For Savigny, as for the common lawyers, it is vital to affirm that the link with community is not broken, however complex law becomes, for where else is the source of law's utility and authority to be found?

As regards legislation, its task is explained by Savigny, in terms reminiscent of Blackstone, as that of putting settled law into systematic form and clarifying law in transitional phases where new legal principles reflecting the developing common consciousness are emerging but not yet crystallised (Savigny 1831: 33, 152–3; cf. Blackstone 1809 I: 86–7). There seems to be an important difference from classical common law ideas, however, in Savigny's recognition that legislation eventually becomes central to the task of developing the law, not peripheral and supplementary as it often appears to be in common law thought. The appropriate scope of legislative activity seems to depend on the stage of development of culture which has been reached. Cultures rise, flourish and then decline. In certain late phases of cultural development conditions 'are no longer propitious to the creation of law by the general consciousness of a people. In this case this activity, in all cases indispensable, will in great measure of itself devolve upon legislation' (Savigny 1867: 34). It seems to be implied, therefore, that the eventual dominance of legislation as a legal form is inevitable – though hardly to be taken as a sign of cultural vitality.

A consequence of this more definite view of the eventual pervasiveness of legislation is that Savigny is forced to make explicit the strange consequences of treating the authority of legislation as deriving from the same communal and traditional sources as other legal authority – such as, particularly, that of the law-declaring judge. The legislator must, as Savigny puts it, stand in the centre of the people or nation 'so that he concentrates in himself their spirit, feelings, needs, so that we have to regard him as the true representative of the spirit of the people' (1867: 32). This awkward and unreal formulation probably points not so much to a democratic assembly with a popular mandate as to an enlightened monarch with the common touch. But Savigny's need to address the legislative role in direct terms at the dawn of the age of modern legal codes does seem to lead him finally to a different emphasis from that of classical common law thought. In the latter, law originated in community life and became the esoteric knowledge of lawyers as an independent occupational group, in which it found its ultimate expression. For Savigny, writing in a German context in which lawyers lacked the political independence and occupational autonomy of the common lawyers, the development could not realistically be seen to stop there. The most influential legal scholars were the university jurists. With the threat of what Savigny undoubtedly considered the legislative megalomania of codification hanging over the Germanic 'common law' (*Gemeines Recht*) of his time (a mixture of customary law and adopted principles of Roman law), he seems to have felt the need to recognise the legislator as central to future legal development in partnership with the jurists. But, like the English common lawyers, he defines the scope of legislative authority not in political terms but in cultural terms. In this way the power of the state to impose law is restricted by a clear obligation on the lawmaker to act as representative of the community – in Savigny's term, the *Volk*.

Savigny's writings had considerable influence on legal scholarship in Britain and America in the nineteenth century, especially since the spectre of codification – the symbol of rational legislative law-making dominating over judicial law-finding – arose to challenge common law thought in both countries. Because he offers a more explicit theory of cultural development than did the common lawyers, he supplies a conception of legal development largely lacking in common law thought. Equally the role of legislation is directly addressed in terms which clearly (if reluctantly) recognise its modern importance. But there is no hint that culture itself might be a complex, fragmented phenomenon; that cultural development might vary immensely in different societies and that cultural change itself has causes requiring explanation. Savigny's legal theory makes reference to culture, but only as a symbol which, merely by being invoked, guarantees the integrity and legitimacy of legal doctrine in evolution.

Maine's Historical Jurisprudence

The immense influence in England and America of the work of the English jurist Sir Henry Maine in the second half of the nineteenth century may be partly because of its relevance in meeting this need for a sound underpinning of common law methods in an age of legislation. But Maine wrote relatively little on common law thought as such in his most important books. His historical jurisprudence was primarily concerned with examining legal ideas and institutions in terms of their evolution in cultural history. It might appear, therefore, that Maine's work has little relevance to normative legal theory as it was defined in Chapter 1. But its importance here is to show one route which might be taken by efforts to develop a general theory of the nature of legal doctrine which is compatible with fundamental assumptions of classical common law thought.

Maine's major writings show vast geographical and chronological range. Roman law, ancient Irish (Brehon) law, Hindu law and Biblical law, as well as English law, provide many of his major sources. Legal concepts such as contract, property, crime and delict are traced through centuries of development or decay and across several continents. One outcome of this broad comparative concern is a general thesis about legal evolution expressed in his most influential book *Ancient Law*, first published in 1861.

According to Maine, law originates not as custom but from judgments handed down by human authorities (such as kings) or attributed to superhuman ones (such as gods). These judgments he terms 'themistes' (Maine 1861: 2–5; and cf. Maine 1883: ch 6). The idea of a judgment thus arises in the legal history of the world before the idea of a rule. The judge predates the lawmaker. But the 'epoch of kingly rule' is succeeded by 'an era of oligarchies' (Maine 1861: 6) in which the purely charismatic authority of particular rulers gives way to the rule of military, political, religious or other elites. At this stage the authority to make 'inspired' judgments requiring no special justification has ceased to exist. 'What the juristic oligarchy now claims is to monopolise the *knowledge* of the laws, to have the exclusive possession of the principles by which quarrels are decided. We have in fact arrived at the epoch of Customary Law' (Maine 1861: 7). Judgments are no longer considered divinely inspired but are justified as being based on established custom. Customary law may, however, be viewed as having a divine origin. Law, in this stage of evolution, is unwritten and so its knowledge can easily be monopolised by a juristic elite. But, Maine is anxious to assert, this unwritten law should not be confused with English common law which became written – whatever classical common law thought might suggest – once cases and legal arguments were recorded in the year books and elsewhere.

The third stage of legal development comes with the era of codes. Here Maine is writing particularly of the ancient codes (such as the Twelve Tables of Roman law of the fifth century BC) which Savigny had identified with the early stages of cultural development.

Codes became possible with the discovery and diffusion of the art of writing and, in some contexts, gave rulers or communities a means of breaking the knowledge-monopoly of juristic elites. Maine, like Savigny, notes the generally unsystematic character and lack of technical precision of these codes. They tended to mix 'religious, civil, and merely moral ordinances, without any regard to differences in their essential character' because the separation of law from morality and from religion belongs 'very distinctly to the *later* stages of mental progress' (Maine 1861: 9). But we should note that Maine intends in writing of the era of codes merely to mark the transition from unwritten to written law. Accordingly, English common law, presented in the form of written reports and records, is 'only different from code-law because it is written in a different way' (1861: 8).

The transition to written law in the evolution of civilisations is fundamental. Without it, Maine suggests, there can be no further significant legal development. Unwritten custom, arising perhaps for good reasons, may degenerate into unreasonable and irrational ritual and be distorted by extension through irrational analogies, since the law exists, inseparably from numerous interpretations of its meaning and purpose, only in collective memory. A reduction of law to writing fixes rules in such a way that they must be changed, if at all, deliberately. It marks the end of 'spontaneous development' of law and the beginning of the possibility of law's *purposive* development (Maine 1861: 13). Thus, like Savigny, Maine sees the question of the point at which codification occurs in the evolution of a culture as being of the utmost importance (1861: 9–10). If custom has already degenerated by the time it is codified the result will be very different from a codification of living custom animated by manifest reasons intelligible from experience. But whereas Savigny treats early codes as merely clumsy and primitive and later systematic and comprehensive ones as of value only to preserve legal achievements from future cultural decline, Maine treats codes – in the sense of written compilations of customs – as the keys to all future progress, as long as codification occurs while custom retains its vitality.

Thus, all major civilisations reach the era of written law but, while 'stationary' societies show little further legal development, 'progressive' societies – which for Maine certainly included those of western Europe but not many others (1861: 13–4) – continue to undergo substantial social and legal change. Three devices are available to allow modification of law to follow social change. They are legal fictions (maintenance of legal forms while concealing the fact of their operation in new ways), equity (principles distinct from ordinary law but claimed to be able to supersede it by virtue of their superior authority) and legislation (enactments deriving authority from some 'external body or person' creating them) (Maine 1861: 15–8).

Maine's use of evidence to support this general picture of legal evolution is certainly restricted. The history of Roman law looms large. But at least the need for evidence is clearly recognised and Maine's broad knowledge of legal and cultural conditions in a wide range of periods and civilisations is evidenced throughout *Ancient Law*. Culture, for Maine, has ceased to be the simple backcloth of legal development which it is for Savigny. Maine's historical jurisprudence accepts, for virtually the first time in English legal scholarship, the need for detailed knowledge of the specific cultural settings of law if the development of legal doctrine is to be understood. And, instead of the assertion in classical common law thought that law is merely *found* in its cultural setting, Maine tries to show the numerous devices by which law is *made* – not just through legislation, but through the use of fictions, the development of equity jurisdictions as competing legal authorities (in England the Court of Chancery and the common law courts) jostle with each other for prestige and power, and the use of conceptions of some fundamental or natural law of reason. Common law, like the law of all 'progressive' societies, is not spontaneous – merely found in culture. It is constructed by technical devices validated by long use in progressive societies generally. Thus, Maine tries to show how law is inseparable from cultural development but (after its reduction to writing) has its *own* mechanisms for regulating legal change. It seems that the riddle of common law development is solved.

Nowadays, many of Maine's specific claims can be criticised and the overall thesis of legal evolution is hard to defend in the face of numerous exceptions and historical complexities. But for the first time in English legal scholarship a theory is offered which clearly links law and culture, does so with a wealth of specific empirical reference, shows processes of law-making other than legislation as of great historical significance, and emphasises the gradual pace of legal development and the roots of modern legal ideas in history.

Maine on Politics and Society

There is little reliable evidence that Maine was directly influenced by Savigny (Burrow 1966: 142-3; cf. Stein 89), although he was certainly affected by the ideas of the German historical school generally. Further, although *Ancient Law* was published only two years after Charles Darwin's *Origin of Species* it does not seem that Maine's innovative empirical approach to the study of legal evolution owed anything to Darwin's evolutionary theory (Feaver 1969: 46; Burrow 1966: 139, 152–3; Stein 1980: 88). Darwin's ideas were quickly adapted by many writers in the second half of the nineteenth century to explain social evolution in terms of some kind of natural selection or 'survival of the fittest' thesis. And this 'social Darwinism' thesis was congenial to Maine as an explanation of why some legal ideas and institutions flourished and others withered. In his later writings he 'hastened to borrow new weapons from the armoury of Darwin' (Barker 1928: 161). But the source of Maine's dramatically new approach to legal scholarship first revealed in *Ancient Law* is obscure (Burrow 1966: 142).

It is tempting to see it, in part, as a timely response to a need to put together in some orderly theory the immense traditional and historical baggage attached to legal thought in the common law environment. And Maine's work did seem to provide possible solutions to some of the difficulties which arise in attempting to construct a normative legal theory consistent with common law thought. It was seen earlier that, if common law is treated as judge-*made* law, serious theoretical difficulties arise. The most important difficulty is in explaining where judges get their authority to make new law, and how far that authority extends. Maine's work implies an imaginative answer. The source of authority of judge-made law is (as classical common law thought had suggested) no different in essence from that of legislation. But Maine finds that source in historical necessity demonstrated by the lessons of comparative history. Social change in progressive societies demands that the law change to keep in step. The methods of judicial innovation (fictions, invocation of equity and natural law ideas), like those of legislation, are shown in his work to be more or less common to the entire civilised world. The implication is, thus, that they can be treated as 'natural' elements in civilisation. Fictions, equity and legislation, emerging successively in history, reinforce each other as remedial devices to ensure law follows social progress.

Maine's conception of the process of social change explains, for him, not only the forms of law but also law's changing content. Progress depends on Darwinian competition. Social change is governed by the principle of the survival of the fittest (Barker 1928: 161). Thus, in progressive societies, legal rights and duties gradually cease to be based on rigid statuses of individuals (for example, as member of a clan, head of a family, wife, son or daughter) which, in general, are not freely chosen by them. Instead, law increasingly recognises the dynamic nature of social life by treating transactions, situations and arrangements as the result of deliberate choice or decision. Status relationships cease to dominate law and society and give way to contractual relationships. Hence the dictum for which Maine is most famous: if status is taken to refer to personal situations not the direct or indirect result of agreement 'we may say that the movement of the progressive societies has hitherto been a movement *from Status to Contract*' (Maine 1861: 100). Maine's image of modern society is, thus, clearly very different from that of the close-knit communities which he associates with the past. He welcomes the individualism of the present; the movement from status to contract is progress. The guarantee of the naturalness of *laissez-faire* individualism is in the great evolutionary sweep of history from the ancient village communities to the present.

But this conception of the nature of society also explains why, for Maine, legislation is not a specially privileged type of law-making. A critic of his ideas, in the late nineteenth century as now, could argue that legislation represents *democratic* law-making in modern states in which representative democracy flourishes. Hence it necessarily has a greater legitimacy and acceptability than judicial law-making. In Maine's view, however, this special legitimacy evaporates on examination. Society is largely composed of a mass who do not lead but only follow. Social competition for survival does not seem to offer for most people 'any guiding thread of growing freedom' (Barker 1928: 167). Like other late nineteenth century jurists, Maine was interested in the bases of popular obedience to authority and found them in habit and inertia rather than reason or fear (Maine 1885: 63; Bryce 1901: ch 9). Thus, authoritative prescription rather than coercive command is the essential quality of law (cf. Maine 1875a: ch 12). Equally, society (the mass who follow rather than lead) must be governed by elites of some kind, whether the elites are considered to be judges or legislators. Which are the most appropriate lawmakers should depend simply on which have the best expertise.

One commentator has described Maine's 'administrative' mentality: 'cool, unsentimental, honest and just, but tending always to identify with authority, and lacking in sympathy with the feelings and aspirations of the mass of mankind' (Burrow 1966: 174, 177–8). While other writers, also seeing democracy as problematic, might think that able natural leaders would emerge despite it to form the inevitable governing elites (Bryce 1901: 29–43), Maine feared demagogues as the enemy of efficient modern state administration. His last book *Popular Government* (1885) is a polemical condemnation of democracy. Thus, just as the common law concern with community requires no popular participation in law-finding (even if a jury might find the facts), and Savigny's spirit of the people does not demand democratic institutions to express it, Maine's picture of law's evolution as part of civilisation as a whole is of an evolution to be managed by elites, not by the democratic representatives of the people.

Historical Jurisprudence and the Legal Profession

What can be said of the relevance of Maine's work for the concerns of lawyers as an occupational group within common law systems? In considering the period when Maine wrote and the decades before *Ancient Law* appeared, it is certainly possible to see a modern legal 'profession' self-consciously shaping itself and building its status, whatever may have been the nature of the occupational group of common lawyers in earlier times (Cocks 1983; cf. Duman 1983: ch 7). In the nineteenth century fundamental issues about legal education and training began to be seriously addressed[9] and, with them, difficult and controversial questions about the nature of the lawyer's professional knowledge and expertise, about what the student of law should learn in order to be well equipped as a member of a modern learned profession, about the possibility of a 'science' of law comparable with the other modern sciences then flourishing, and about whether and in what ways legal knowledge could be considered autonomous, unified and systematic.

Maine's writings are of great importance in this context. As has been seen, common law – as portrayed in classical common law thought – can certainly be considered to be knowledge which is both esoteric and of central social importance. But it cannot easily be considered a 'science' in the nineteenth century sense of a rational organisation of ideas. Such a rational science 'could never hope neatly to capture within its four corners the rich, living tradition of Common Law' (Postema 1986: 37). Equally, as noted earlier, classical common law thought lacked grounding in any serious historical inquiry[10]. It existed in substantial isolation from knowledge of other legal systems or methods (Feaver 1969: 45; Pocock 1957: ch 3). Finally, it lacked any rigorous intellectual criteria separating it from other branches of learning. Its relationship

---

[9]   For a summary of developments see e.g. Manchester 1980: 54–63.
[10] For discussion of this see e.g. Maitland 1888; Gordon 1981; cf. Holdsworth 1928: 4–5.

with them was parasitic yet unsystematic (Sommerville 1986: 93). The implication of all Maine's major work is that a sound knowledge of law as an intellectual field, rather than as merely a disordered jumble of precedents and principles, demands comparative, historical and philosophical studies. Other sources of influence – such as the Select Committee appointed in 1846 to investigate the state of legal education in England and Ireland – had reached similar conclusions[11]. and Maine was active in campaigning for legal education to be developed along these lines (Feaver 1969: ch 3). 'The fault of our legal system', he declared in 1855, 'is that it is exclusively practical. . . with us, law is not a science' (quoted Feaver 1969: 24). Maine's science of law was, thus, a 'new sort of empirical history that could nonetheless be fitted into a theoretical framework explaining the general evolution of legal systems' (Feaver 1969: 46).

Maine's books and their methods had immense influence in the latter part of the nineteenth century. By 1871 *Ancient Law* was widely used in the law schools of Europe and America. Maine reported that an eminent American lawyer had told him that 'he thought almost every attorney in the States had a copy' (Feaver 1969: 128, 129). The book went through eleven editions in twenty five years. The impact was not just on lawyers. 'The extent and profundity of Maine's influence among the intellectual class would be hard to exaggerate. . .'; his 'method dominated a whole generation's reflections on politics', reflecting 'the immense prestige and unimpeachable respectability of his achievement' (Collini, Winch and Burrow 1983: 10, 210, 252).

The reasons for Maine's success in reaching the attention of the legal profession are crucial here. He presents attractively something which looks like a genuine science of law based on sound empirical data, and, moreover, one which demonstrates both the impressive weight of legal knowledge and its centrality in social life and the history of civilisation. He offers ideas consistent with the inbuilt conservatism of common law thought and its preference for gradual legal adjustment through case law rather than wholesale legislative reform. Finally, he seems to offer the comforting message that the time-honoured methods of common law and the doctrine and institutions it has produced are validated by the natural scientific laws of social progress. And he connects legal scholarship neatly with what were in his time widely seen as the most advanced ideas in other social studies. Thus, in the late nineteenth century, as an eminent public figure and an eloquent spokesman on legal

[11]   Report from the Select Committee on Legal Education no. 686 (1846).

matters he could appear as a powerful force in promoting the status of the legal profession and its knowledge in the wider world of politics and intellectual life.

The Fate of Maine's New Science

In 1875 Maine set out a programme for 'a new science', foreshadowed by his already published work, which would apply comparative methods, already used in other fields in illuminating the evolution of civilisation, to the investigation of 'laws, institutions, customs, ideas, and social forces' (Maine 1875b: 230). Yet, despite his popularity and renown, the new science did not produce a lasting influence on legal scholarship. Although a few eminent jurists followed Maine's lead to some extent, historical jurisprudence did not reshape legal thinking in the common law world. What went wrong?

In the previous chapter it was suggested that legal theory may serve the professional needs of lawyers by clarifying the nature of professional knowledge, demonstrating a unity or system in it, and distinguishing the legal from the non-legal (the internal-external dichotomy) in definite terms. But Maine's jurisprudence is seriously defective in this respect since it does not portray legal knowledge as a well-defined, manageable field. Instead, it suggests that legal studies consistent with a scientific reworking of common law thought must embrace vast areas of cultural knowledge extending over many nations and many centuries of history. The problem from the standpoint of professional legal education is especially clear. Maine's books were prescribed for examinations of the Inns of Court, universities in Britain and the colonies, and the Indian Civil Competitive Examination. In the late nineteenth century brief 'nutshell' books for students offered simplified versions of major law texts (Sugarman 1986: 52). The preface to one of these, dealing with Maine's works, declares: 'In these works there is a great deal of writing that is absolutely useless to the student for examination purposes, and page after page has to be waded through in the search for a criticism or a theory; and to discover any complete theory or criticism on any one question or theory, it is often necessary to search through not only each one of the books, but also many different chapters or lectures in each of those books. This necessitates a great waste of time and mental energy on the part of the student, there being over two thousand pages in all' (Evans 1896: v-vi). No matter that Maine's writings offered a sincere attempt to turn legal study into a pursuit of real cultural value, and to escape the idea that law was no more than an 'occult science' vastly inferior to the real sciences explaining the nature and progress of civilisation. His work did not offer a conception of a manageable professional knowledge.

Thus, with the eclipse of historical jurisprudence, the problem of finding a normative legal theory compatible with common law thought seems no nearer solution. Maine's writings pointed not towards normative legal theory but instead to the value of what has been called, in the previous chapter, empirical legal theory – theory aimed at explaining the nature of law in terms of its social origins and effects. Maine is, to this day, treated as a significant figure in the history of anthropology and his work exerted major influence on the development of sociology, including sociology of law.

Even here, however, we should keep clearly in mind that he was, first and foremost, a jurist. To some extent, Maine is closer to Savigny, to whom culture appeared merely as the motif which made sense of law's claims to doctrinal integrity, than he is to modern social science. He was not a 'thorough sociologist' (Burrow 1966: 151) and many writers have commented on his unreliable use of empirical evidence. Adherents of historical jurisprudence distanced themselves from the writings and outlook of sociologists (Collini, Winch and Burrow 1983: 213, 220). Equally, historical jurisprudence in England had a different orientation from anthropology. Whereas the latter appeared to take all mankind as its province, the former, as Maine established it, was concerned only with those peoples whose cultural history fed into what was seen as the evolution of civilisation (Collini, Winch and Burrow 1983: 212). Historical jurisprudence traced a line of descent of civilisation, validated essentially in terms of the historical development of comparable legal ideas and institutions and grounded in assumptions about an original Aryan family of peoples. Maine wrote: 'Civilisation is nothing more than a name for the old order of the Aryan world, dissolved but perpetually reconstituting itself under a vast variety of solvent influences' (1875b: 230). It is almost as though the seventeenth century appeal to an ultimate timeless and mystical cultural foundation of common law in the idea of the 'ancient constitution' is resurrected in the idea of the timeless cultural unity of the Aryan world. The unity underpinning Maine's thought, like that of common law thought, is a unity of culture.

If such a unity is hardly satisfactory to ground a normative legal theory, where else might one look for foundations? Having followed assumptions of classical common law thought to what may seem their ultimate consequences without finding adequate solutions perhaps it might be fruitful to start from virtually opposite positions: to treat legislation as central to law and judicial law-making as peripheral and to see the foundations of law in political power rather than in community. The theory to be considered in the next chapter does exactly that. In leaving classical common law thought and historical jurisprudence it is important, however, not to lose sight of their strengths. Despite much ambiguity and some incoherence, the theory of common law, and the nineteenth century legal philosophy which developed ideas consistent with it, emphasise the vital importance of maintaining law's link with community life. By implication they pose a warning against the arrogance of legislators who treat law as no more than an affair of efficient rules organised as an instrument of coercion.

3 Sovereign and Subject: Bentham and Austin

John Austin's wife wrote that he lived 'a life of unbroken disappointment and failure'[1]. Yet Austin, more than any other writer, provided the compact and systematic formulation of a conception of law which allowed an escape from the tradition-bound theory implicit in classical common law thought. Equally, Austin provided what historical jurisprudence could not: a clear designation of the scope of legal knowledge, an orderly theory of law which allowed the legal to be distinguished from the non-legal and the logical connections between legal ideas to be made explicit. Finally, he offered a way of looking at law which made legislation central rather than peripheral. Thus, his legal theory recognised the reality of the modern state as a massive organisation of power. It tried to show law's relationship with this centralised and extensive power structure. It seemed in tune with modern times in which government, not community, was the apparent source of law. Thus, noting Sarah Austin's comment quoted above, one of Austin's most important successors goes on to remark that 'within a few years of his death it was clear that his work had established the study of jurisprudence in England' (Hart 1955: xvi). Austin died in 1859, believing that his neglected writings and unsuccessful lectures had made no mark whatsoever. Four years later all of his most important work had been republished, largely through the efforts of his widow. For reasons to be considered in this chapter, it caught the legal mood of the times. It established or clarified ideas about the nature of law which still provide basic elements in the vocabulary of concepts which lawyers in the Anglo-american world use (cf. Dworkin 1977: 16).

Austin's legal theory is contained primarily in the lectures he prepared as the first professor of jurisprudence in what was to become the University of London. Much of his legal philosophy is heavily indebted to earlier writers. It represents the packaging of a set of ideas distilled from a long tradition of political theory concerned with the concept of sovereignty, together with a selective plundering of the legal theory of Austin's original mentor, the

[1] In a letter quoted in Rumble 1985: 56.

English philosopher and law reformer, Jeremy Bentham. Today, the received wisdom is that Austin's work is much less important than Bentham's and, indeed, there is no doubt that its intellectual range is far more limited. But, partly because of the accidents of publication, Austin exerted an influence on the development of legal theory and on wider concerns in legal scholarship far beyond that of Bentham.

The fact that all of Austin's major work in legal theory was in print from the 1860s, whereas the major writings of Bentham which cover similar ground were not, is, however, only part of the explanation. The form of Austin's legal theory and the ordering of its concerns enable it to offer a normative legal theory which was particularly appropriate to the political and legal professional concerns of its time. Further, it exemplifies a certain general conception of law in an extremely concise and straightforward manner. In fact, Austin's 'failure' in so many worldly things may have been the condition of his success in this. He pursued with apparently total singlemindedness a distinct image of how a 'science' of law might be possible. Lacking Bentham's restless intellectual curiosity – which diverted the greater writer into an immense diversity of projects – Austin meticulously worked on the theory of law which had been merely a part of Bentham's concerns. Where his ideas differ from Bentham's it is often because he prefers a stubborn logic (for example, on the nature of sovereignty) or a hard-headed realism (for example, in discussing judicial law-making), where Bentham equivocates or tries to develop more radical analyses in the cause of legal or political reform.

For the moment it will be necessary to keep an open mind about the relative merits of Bentham and Austin in their development of normative legal theory – the theory which is the exclusive concern of this book. But it will be argued in the following pages that a strong defence can be made on Austin's behalf against many of the most serious criticisms which are routinely made of his legal theory. In this chapter he occupies centre stage simply because it is he rather than Bentham who has exerted by far the greater influence on later jurists and on legal scholarship generally, and he who offers a version of normative legal theory which in its clear (even dogmatic) pronouncements provides an effective contrast to the vague theory underpinning the common law tradition. In considering Austin's ideas and their political and professional consequences, however, comparisons with Bentham's theories will be made. And it will be necessary to trace the roots of Austin's thinking beyond Bentham to make the point that the evolution of common law thought, considered in Chapter 2, is parallelled by a long tradition of quite different thinking about the nature of law.

The Empire of Darkness and the Region of Light

A key to understanding the motivation behind and orientation of the legal theories of Austin and Bentham is to recognise the profound hostility of both writers to the methods and outlook of English common law, and the profound difference between their reactions to it. Towards the end of his life Austin may well have modified his views but his London University lectures on jurisprudence, originally written for presentation at the end of the 1820s and the basis of his reputation in legal philosophy, are full of vitriolic comments on the absurdities of common law thought and the irrationality of a legal system – if system it could be called – developed primarily by piecemeal judicial interventions. Bentham viewed judge-made law as like waiting for one's dog to do something wrong and then beating it (cf. Stein 1980: 70). Austin, however, was not opposed to judicial law-making. What offended him was the total lack of systematic organisation or of a structure of clearly definable rational principles in common law. In his lectures he was determined to map out a rational, scientific approach to legal understanding – a modern view of law which would replace archaic, confused, tradition-bound common law thought but would be able to encompass both legislation and judge-made law.

This aim immediately distinguishes Austin from Bentham. Always the more radical thinker, Bentham has no patience in his writings with the idea that judicial decisions are an appropriate source of law. He pins his faith on the kind of codification Savigny despised. All law should be purposively, deliberately, rationally created by legislative means. As far as possible, law should be expressed in rational, systematically organised codes. Austin also favoured codification and writes extensively in his lectures of its merits and of the absurdity of most of Savigny's objections to it. But he also shows a cool realism about the possibilities. Austin's views on judge-made law, or 'judiciary law' as he prefers to call it, will be discussed later. For the moment it is enough to say that he recognises that judge-made law is an inevitable component of a modern legal system, and that – despite many disadvantages – it has some virtues and is often the only practical means of legal development at certain times and in certain fields. Codification is admirable in theory but, in practice, requires immense legislative skill, juristic knowledge and political vision. What is needed, therefore, is a view of law which can accommodate realistically all these aspects but present them within the framework of the rational, centralised governmental structure of the modern state.

Although the matter is often ignored or underemphasised in commentaries on Austin, it is important to note that he found models of legal scholarship, to help in this task, quite outside Benthamite influences. Austin saw in Roman law – especially as interpreted and developed by continental civil law jurists – the epitome of a rational legal order vastly superior to English common law in its logical organisation. 'Turning from the study of the English to the study of the Roman Law, you escape from the empire of chaos and darkness, to a world which seems, by comparison, the region of order and light' (Austin 1885: 58). The 'extraordinary merit' of Roman law scholarship was in the way scholars had 'seized its general principles with great clearness and penetration, . . . applied these principles with admirable logic to the explanation of details, and. . . thus reduced this positive system of law to a compact and coherent whole' (Austin 1832: 188). By contrast, English law was full of 'useless and misleading jargon' often employed inconsistently (Austin 1885: 686). While distancing himself in his writings from the legal philosophies informing Roman law and, indeed, from that law's actual content, Austin rarely fails to sing the praises of Romanist legal scholarship. He spent several months in Germany, studying the writings of the German scholars of Roman law and German legal philosophy, in preparation for his own lectures.

How important is this in understanding the orientation of Austin's legal philosophy? It suggests that, although he 'was accepted as the heir apparent of Bentham in the special department of jurisprudence' (Stephen 1900: 317) and undoubtedly saw himself, at the time he wrote his lectures, as a disciple (though a critical one) of Bentham, his model of a science of law was not wholly Benthamite. He quoted with approval other writers' praise of the 'scientific method' of the Romanists which had made them 'models to all succeeding ages' (1832: 377). As already indicated, for Austin this method – which could allow the rationalisation of law from many sources, including judicial decisions and custom, as well as legislation – involved identifying general principles, applying them logically to explain detail, and so demonstrating order and coherence in law.

Certainly, Bentham had already supplied many other elements needed. He had recognised the need for a coherent doctrine to guide the rational reform of law and to dispose of common law archaism and had found this in the principle of utility. Utility required that law-making and legal institutions be designed to promote the greatest happiness of the greatest number of people. Utility would replace traditional, self-serving or subjectively moral evaluations with a rational evaluation of the worth of particular practices, institutions and policies in terms of how far they served the common good, measured in terms of maximisation of satisfaction of the actual desires of the greatest possible number of the population. Austin's lectures presuppose the doctrine of utility as elaborated by Bentham and warmly – even fanatically – defend it. But Austin's course was devoted to the theory of law *as it is* (which he called the science of law), not the theory of law as it should or might be (which he termed the science of legislation). Consequently, although several of Austin's lectures directly discuss the principle of utility, it does not occupy the central place in the body of his writings which it does in Bentham's. Bentham's 'expository jurisprudence' (his term for the science of law), upon which Austin drew extensively, was an offshoot of his concern with the working out of the principle of utility in its application to law reform. Thus, the science of legislation (he calls it censorial jurisprudence) is central to Bentham and expository jurisprudence is a necessary basis of knowledge upon which censorial jurisprudence can be pursued. By contrast, Austin is known through a set of lectures devoted to elaborating a theory of existing law. In them he apologetically justifies bringing in the principle of utility as necessary to help to explain why law has taken particular forms (Austin 1832: 59; 1863: 373). In the particular context of Austin's lectures, therefore, the science of legislation is *subordinate* to the science of law.

This, in itself, suggests Austin's less radical view of law as compared with Bentham's, for Austin plainly considered that despite all its defects English common law had often approximated to what utility demanded. Thus, while Bentham sought an instrument to reform the law in numerous respects and found it in the utility principle, Austin sought, above all, a means of rationalising existing law; organising and logically relating its elements; putting it into systematic form; clarifying the reasoning entailed in it; and finding a set of concepts through which it could be 'scientifically' understood. Such a task could be carried out in relation to a particular legal system. But a more fundamental theoretical inquiry – the real foundation of legal science – would be to carry out this task in relation to legal systems generally. Thus, what Austin calls general jurisprudence would be 'the science concerned with the exposition of the principles, notions and distinctions which are common to systems of law' or, at least, mature systems (Austin

1863: 367). In practice, enough illumination of such matters is obtainable, Austin asserts, by concentrating on the writings of his revered Romanist jurists, the modern decisions of English judges, and (with regard to arrangement and systematic organisation of law) the provisions of the French and Prussian codes (1863: 373).

In this programme the influences of the German Roman law jurists and of Bentham seem to come together less uneasily than is often supposed. The three sources of comparison Austin emphasises neatly summarise the three contending forces which needed to be somehow reconciled in contemporary legal thought as he understood it: the untidy raw material provided by common law judicial decisions, the Romanist example of how to rationalise order out of gradually evolved legal doctrine, and the modern experience of systematic codification. But Austin's rigour required him to undertake the preliminary inquiry on the basis of which the exposition of 'principles, notions and distinctions common to systems of law' could be founded as a science. That preliminary inquiry was into the meaning of the ultimate concept of 'a law' itself. Bentham, and before him, the seventeenth century English political philosopher Thomas Hobbes had provided ideas which could be developed for this purpose. In the event, it is this *preliminary* inquiry which has come to be treated as Austin's legal philosophy (cf. Buckland 1949: 3). His contributions to the much broader 'general jurisprudence' have remained relatively neglected.

Positive Law and Positive Morality

From one viewpoint, the most valuable contribution of Austin's legal theory is its attempt to distinguish clearly *law* from other phenomena (for example, moral rules, social customs) with which it could be confused. As has been seen in the previous chapter, classical common law thought did not do this. For Austin, clear thinking about law necessitates such a demarcation of the subject-matter of legal science. Bentham had poured scorn on the way moral notions and legal principles were mixed up in Blackstone's *Commentaries*, the famous eighteenth century treatise on English law (Bentham 1977: 3–33). To Bentham the result seemed thoroughly unscientific, allowing Blackstone to preach moral sermons or indulge his prejudices under cover of stating the law. Thus, when Austin – strongly influenced by Bentham's critique of Blackstone – came to write his lectures it seemed obvious to him that the starting point for the science of law must be a clear analytical separation of law and morality. Such a strategy would in no way imply that moral questions were unimportant (although for Austin, like Bentham, they were mostly to be answered by applying the principle of utility). Indeed, the separation would make clear the independent character of legal and moral arguments and the special validity and importance of each.

So Austin's lectures begin with the assertion that the subject-matter of jurisprudence, as he understands it, is positive law, 'law, simply and strictly so called: or law set by political superiors to political inferiors' (Austin 1832: 9). Immediately law is defined as an expression of power. In its *widest* proper sense a law is 'a rule laid down for the guidance of an intelligent being by an intelligent being having power over him' (Austin 1832: 10). Austin's view of law recognises it, not as something evolved or immanent in community life – as in the implicit common law conception, but as an imposition of power. The lectures then embark on a rather tedious classification, some of which, however, is of the greatest importance in understanding key points of Austin's legal theory. Austin distinguishes laws 'properly so called' from those phenomena improperly labelled law (1832: 10). There are two classes of laws properly so called: divine laws (laws set by God for mankind) – which quickly appear in Austin's jurisprudence to be largely the dictates of utility – and human laws (laws set by human beings for human beings). The most significant category of human laws comprises what Austin calls *positive law*. These are laws set by political superiors acting as such or by people acting in pursuance of legal rights conferred on them by political superiors (that is, acting as the delegates of political superiors in making laws). The term 'positive' refers to the idea of law placed or laid down in some specific way and, as such, could apply to divine law, which Austin conceives as God's commands. But he wants to reserve the term positive law for human laws laid down by, or on the authority of, political superiors – the true subject of the science of law. Thus, the word 'positive' indicates a positing or setting of rules by human creators.

The other category of human law consists of rules laid down by persons having power over others but not as political superiors or in pursuance of legal rights. This would seem to cover numerous rules which the lawyer would not usually regard as law, although Austin has no doubt that the term 'law' can be used here 'with absolute precision or propriety' (Austin 1832: 140). Since he uses the word 'power' in a general sense, it would seem to include the capacity of any authority figures - for example, priests or religious leaders, employers, teachers, parents, guardians or political orators – to control or influence the actions of followers, dependents or those in their charge. Austin clearly regards rule-making in such cases as significant in contributing to shape the attitudes, opinions or moral sentiment of individuals or groups. Indeed, it forms part of what he calls *positive morality*. As morality it is distinguished from positive law; and it is positive because laid down by human beings for human beings. Positive morality also contains another category of rules: those without particular creators but set by the opinion or sentiment of an indeterminate body of people – that is, by public opinion or community opinion. Austin terms these rules without authors 'laws by analogy' – they are not laws 'properly so called', even though we sometimes talk of laws of fashion or etiquette or the laws of honour (1832: 140–1).

Finally, for completeness, Austin mentions one other category of laws 'improperly so called'. Scientific laws are not laws in the jurisprudential sense. They are the regularities of nature which science discovers but which are not laid down as laws. He terms them 'laws by metaphor'. We can say, therefore, that for Austin: (i) the term law is often improperly applied to rules or regularities which are in no strict sense 'legal'; but (ii) the concept of law can properly embrace more than most lawyers would accept. Austin, like many sociologists writing long after him, seems to recognise that rules created 'privately' outside the particular provisions or procedures of the legal system of the state can usefully be recognised as law. On the other hand, (iii) only positive law is the appropriate concern of what Austin considers to be jurisprudence.

From this dissection of the field of rules in the broadest sense what is most important is the establishment of the concepts of positive law and positive morality. As will appear, the interplay between them provides, for Austin, solutions to some of the most serious problems which his critics think they see in the elaboration of his theory of law.

The Coercive Structure of a Law

What then is a law? Like Hobbes before him, Austin defines a law as a species of command. Bentham, as so often, surrounds his basic assertions with a complex, exploratory excursus – in this case on various forms of expression of will – and for various reasons prefers to talk of law as 'an assemblage of signs declarative of a volition' (Bentham 1970: 1, 10). But he, too, essentially treats laws as a species of commands and the thrust of his conception turns out to be much the same as Austin's direct and straightforward characterisation. Again power is made central to law. Thus Austin states: 'A command is distinguished from other significations of desire, not by the style in which the desire is signified, but by the power and purpose of the party commanding to inflict an evil or pain in case the desire be disregarded' (Austin 1832: 14). Thus, the power to inflict punishment (sanction) in case of non-compliance is what makes an expression a command. There is no need for any imperative form. Obviously the nature of the sanction and of the power to inflict it needs further consideration, as does the question of *whose* commands will constitute law.

However, not every command constitutes a rule or law. Austin often uses the words 'law' and 'rule' apparently interchangeably (e.g. 1832: 18–9; 141) but is inconsistent in this since, for example, as has been seen above, he distinguishes moral rules set by public opinion from law strictly so-called. What they certainly have in common, however, is the requirement of *generality*. A particular command – say, a directive issued to a particular government department or administrative agency and requiring that it reconsider a particular case – would not constitute a rule. How much generality is necessary for a law? As Austin notes, generality can be of two kinds: as to acts required or prohibited and as to persons addressed by the command. Generality as to acts indicates that the command refers to a class of actions or situations, not a single, specific action or case. Generality as to persons indicates a class of people, or people generally, as subject to the command – not a particular individual or organisation, or a number of specified individuals or organisations.

It will be seen in later chapters that this question of generality becomes of great importance in relation to the familiar doctrine of the Rule of Law, which usually insists on both kinds of generality. It is highly significant, however, that Austin considers that generality as to acts is the only generality necessary for a command to be a law (1832: 21ff.). Thus, law can consist of rules addressed, for example, to particular individuals, business firms or administrative agencies, as well as rules addressed to the population generally or to specific categories of it. This is one of several aspects of his legal theory which indicate that his view of law is very different from that of many liberal theories. The latter tend to see law as a set of rules whose purpose should be to mark out a general sphere of liberty of the individual guaranteed against the risk of arbitrary state power. Austin, by contrast, sees law as a technical instrument of government or administration, which should, however, be efficient and aimed at the common good as determined by utility.

Law as Government

Since the consequences of this view of law are important to many aspects of Austin's legal theory it is worth commenting further on it before considering Austin's other claims with regard to the idea of law as a species of command. In a sense, law *is*, for him, effective government. Certainly a directive relating to a particular occasion would not be a law. Even here, however, Austin recognises that particular commands issued by a law-making authority may, in practice, sometimes be called laws. The lectures hardly suggest that this incorrect usage raises an important issue of principle for him (Austin 1832: 19; cf. Neumann 1986: 220). When, later, he discusses civil and political liberties, the contrast with liberal theories is made very explicit. Like Bentham, Austin has no patience with the ideas of natural or fundamental rights. There are no rights or laws which are somehow inherent in the human condition, in human nature, or in the very essence of social or community life. All laws, rights and duties are created by positing rules, the laying down of rules as an act of government. Consequently there can be nothing inherently sacred about civil or political liberties. To the extent that they are valuable they are the by-product of effective government in the common interest.

Austin's lectures are generally dry and laden with cold, precise definition and classification. But occasionally a fierceness breaks through; a vehemence that reveals deep feelings normally hidden. The discussion of liberties is one such place: 'To the ignorant and bawling fanatics who stun you with their pother about liberty, political or civil liberty seems to be the principle end for which government ought to exist'. Such liberty 'has been erected into an idol, and extolled with extravagant praises by doting and fanatical worshippers' (1832: 269). But, writes Austin, the purpose of government is to serve the common good. The promotion and protection of civil or political liberties is of value only insofar as it serves that end. Limitation of liberty may in some circumstances be more conducive to the common good than maximisation of it. Austin obviously thinks that the word 'liberty' is a slogan which can easily get out of hand.

Several things follow from this 'governmental' view of law. One is that duties are more fundamental than rights. The individual's ability to make specific claims on others through the legal system is derivative from the law's commands. Austin's command theory of law produces this result analytically. Command and duty are treated as correlative terms: 'wherever a duty lies a command has been signified, and wherever a command is signified, a duty is

imposed' (Austin 1832: 14). We have seen that the threat of
punishment (sanction) is an essential component of the notion of
command for Austin. Duty then becomes the automatic
consequence of being addressed by a potentially enforceable
command: 'Being liable to evil from you if I comply not with a
wish that you signify, I am *bound* or *obliged* by your command,
or I lie under a *duty* to obey it' (1832: 14). Duty thus appears
as a fundamental component or consequence of a law. By contrast,
every right presupposes a duty in someone else. Rights are derivative
from duties. I can claim a right against X because the law has
imposed a duty on him towards me.

Sanctions

Austin's governmental view of law is also reflected clearly in the
emphasis he attaches to punitive sanctions in the structure of a
law. Since sanctions, as has been seen, are essential to the existence
of commands, they are, for Austin, essential to the existence of
laws. There must be 'power and purpose of the party commanding
to inflict an evil' (1832: 14) in case of *non-compliance*. There is
here an important difference from Bentham's legal theory, which
also treats sanctions as essential to law. Bentham (and other writers)
saw no reason why legal sanctions could not include rewards as
well as penalties. Austin, after considering this possibility,
deliberately rejects it. A reward held out for compliance would
indicate a promise or inducement but not a command, on the basis
of ordinary usage of the word, which specifies non-optional conduct.
Thus the idea of law as a species of command necessarily entails
the availability of negative (punitive) sanctions.

Be that as it may, serious doubts can be raised about the direction
in which Austin's view of sanctions pushes his theory. If his idea
is really to maintain a realistic view of modern government through
law, there are good reasons for recognising a whole range of devices
including positive inducements as well as negative sanctions
available to support rules. Terence Daintith has written of
government's powers of *imperium* – much like Austin's coercive
commands – being supplemented or supported by its *dominium*
powers – powers to distribute benefits of many kinds as inducements
to promote compliance with its policies (Daintith 1982). Law's
sanctioning techniques may involve complex combinations of both
imperium and *dominium* (cf. Summers 1971). Nevertheless, if Austin
fails to recognise the variety of forms which power can take, the
stress on coercive sanctions at least keeps the relationship between
law and power firmly in the forefront of attention. It has even

been suggested that Austin's five years of army service coloured his parade-ground view of law as negatively sanctioned command (cf. Rumble 1985: 12–3). But, as will be argued later, a more satisfactory explanation of Austin's outlook on governmental coercion is to be found elsewhere, in his wider view of the nature of society and the state.

Although every law must by definition provide for a sanction, according to Austin's theory, a sanction can be 'the smallest chance of incurring the smallest evil' (Austin 1832: 16). Austin's views on the possible role of sanctions in securing obedience will be considered later but it is important to note that the prominent place which sanctions occupy in his definition of law entails, in itself, no sociological claims about the significance of sanctions in ensuring compliance with law. Such claims are 'foreign to the matter in question' (1832: 16). The role of sanctions in the definition of law is purely formal. Laws, by their nature, provide for sanctions. Sanctions are *analytically* essential to laws, whether or not they are sociologically necessary. Thus, any disadvantage formally specified directly or indirectly by a law as to be imposed in case of non-compliance can serve as that law's sanction. Mere inconvenience or the fact that a transaction or document is rendered null and void by law would count as sufficient sanctions. A sanction can be a further legal obligation. Thus, breach of one law (say, a traffic offence) might lead to a further obligation (to appear in court to answer charges). Breach of that further legal obligation might entail the threat of a direct legal sanction or, perhaps, would render the offender subject to yet another legal obligation. Thus, a chain of obligations is possible. At the end of the chain, however, there must be a sanction (Austin 1885: 444–5). 'Imperfect laws', lacking sanctions completely, cannot be considered laws in the Austinian sense. Similarly, declaratory or repealing 'laws' are not strictly laws since they command nothing (Austin 1832: 26–8).

Sanctions and Power Conferring Rules

The most serious problem for Austin's conception of the relationship between laws and sanctions is usually considered to be that of so-called power conferring rules. These include legal rules which enable people to make wills or contracts, or to enter into other desirable transactions or arrangements which would lack security without legal guarantee (private power conferring rules). They also include rules giving powers to officials (public power conferring rules). A now standard criticism of Austin emphasises that these kinds of rules cannot be assimilated to coercive commands. They often provide facilities for desirable activities. They are not concerned primarily with imposing duties supported by penalties. They *enable* officials or private citizens to act. How can the command conception of law encompass these kinds of rules?

A full attempted defence of Austin must wait until his theory of sovereignty – and especially the concept of delegation entailed in it – has been outlined in the next section. Nevertheless some preliminary remarks can be made here. Austin deals directly with the question of private power conferring rules and clearly does not see it as the problem that later writers have identified. As mentioned above, he includes nullity of transactions as a sanction. Thus, a will executed in improper form will not achieve the intended legal effect since it will be held void in whole or part. A contract made in breach of the Statute of Frauds may be unenforceable. The loss of an expected advantage is the sanction in such cases. Critics have considered that such 'sanctions' are quite different from others Austin recognises (for example, damages, imprisonment or fines) and that to equate them distorts the radically different social functions of 'power conferring' and 'duty imposing' rules (Hart 1961: 38). But it is important to remember that Austin's analytical concern with sanctions is purely formal. The differences in social functions of laws are not pertinent here. Equally, since any disadvantage (the smallest threat of the smallest evil) is enough to constitute a sanction if it is directly or indirectly provided for by law, the difference in the character of sanctions (for example, the nullity of a transaction as against the requirement to pay a fine or monetary compensation) is not *analytically* important either in this particular context (though, of course, it may be of considerable sociological, political or other interest).

Austin's prominent critic H. L. A. Hart, who has stressed the problem of power conferring rules, admits that such rules can be incorporated within an overall framework of law as a coercive phenomenon. The problem Hart identifies is that to force all legal rules into a single coercive model denies the variety of kinds of laws (Hart 1961: 27–41). But it is vital to recognise that Austin's position does not require such a forced distortion. His 'only claim is that the features he indicates are relevant to all laws' (Moles 1987: 66). Austin wishes to stress the coercive basis of law which he considers is reflected in all its rules. There is no suggestion that all rules have the same functions or the same form or the same kinds of sanctions.

Where so-called *public* power conferring rules addressed to legal 'officials' are concerned, the nullity-as-sanction argument may equally apply. The relevant sanction in such cases is likely to be against an official in his 'official capacity', rather than in a personal capacity. Thus, if a judge exceeds his jurisdiction, his decision is liable to be overturned by an appellate court. An improper direction to a jury by the judge in a criminal trial is liable to result in the conviction being quashed on appeal. The legal system as a whole, by providing means of correcting legal errors also provides for indirect sanctions because it enables (professional or social) sanctions of inconvenience, ridicule or lessening of reputation to attach to the official concerned. As has been seen earlier, Austin's 'smallest chance' of 'the smallest evil' encompasses a wide range of possible sanctions. All that is required by the theory is that they be provided for directly or indirectly by the law (a guilty conscience would not count as a legal sanction). It would seem that in cases of public power conferring rules where no direct penalty is attached to an official failing to comply with these rules, the legal nullity-sanction harnesses social sanctions which may be important to someone whose job security, prospects and effectiveness depend significantly on reputation.

In one sense, it is misleading to attach great significance to arguments centring on the sanction of nullity in considering the Austinian view of power conferring rules. The discussion here has done so largely because, given that Austin's critics tend to make so much of this matter, it seems worthwhile to show that Austin's arguments about nullity do have something to be said for them. In fact, however, the nullity sanction would only be relevant, if at all, to that aspect of power conferring rules which imposes *duties* or conditions on the power holder (for example, the duty of the judge not to exceed his jurisdiction, of the administrative official not to act *ultra vires*, or the requirement that the testator sign the will if it is to be recognised as valid). It is absurd to seek sanctions *attaching to the power holder* with regard to the power conferring element itself – that is, the element of *freedom* to act. But Austin's theory enables us to see where, according to his viewpoint, the relevant sanctions lie. It will be recalled that, for Austin, rights in one person (which, in this context, he does not distinguish from powers or liberties) are merely the consequence of duties attaching to other people. Thus, insofar as a rule confers powers on X it is to be understood as a command to all other people concerned to recognise and respect the authority of X. Thus, the relevant sanctions attached to the rule giving X power are those sanctions which support the duty of others to accept X as having authority within the scope of the rule.

It should be added, to complete the Austinian picture, that many procedural rules can be seen as no more than technical devices to make possible the direct sanctioning processes of law. Thus, for Austin, all 'laws or rules determining the practice of courts, or all laws or rules determining judicial procedure, are purely subsidiary to the due execution of others' (Austin 1832: 235). The argument here, as in other contexts, is that strings or combinations of rules can exist, linking obligations to each other, and ultimately connected to some prescribed sanction. Otherwise, laws without sanctions are parts of others which do have sanctions. In fact, a difficult analytical problem is hidden in this kind of thinking: what counts as a single law or rule? Bentham wrestled with the problem of 'individuation' of laws (Bentham 1970: ch 14; cf. James 1973) but Austin largely ignores it. Again, it can be said that for Austin this is a detail. What is essential for him is to demonstrate the structures of power, expressed in complex and interwoven legal forms, to which each crucial element in the legal order is tied by provisions for sanctioning in the event of non-compliance.

Austin's concern with power conferring rules is merely to give them a place within a theory which sets out to portray law (in stark contrast to its portrayal in common law thought) as an expression of modern centralised governmental power. For some later writers – perhaps including Hart – power conferring rules have become a special focus of attention for reasons which do not particularly concern Austin; reasons related to certain liberal legal theories and conceptions of the Rule of Law which will be discussed in Chapter 4. These theories and conceptions tend to stress law's role in marking out areas of guaranteed freedom in life (such as civil or political liberties and economic freedoms). A pre-eminently important matter for them is the freedom or power conferred by legal rules. By contrast, Austin's legal theory emphasises that these areas of freedom are only what the legally directed power of the state defines them to be through the imposition of duties on people. Because law dominates through its coercive force, areas of liberty are merely what law creates and guarantees through this force. Thus, for Austin, emphasis is not on the powers themselves but on the coercive structure which surrounds them and on which they are wholly dependent. Law gives and takes away powers: of people generally, of particular categories of people, or even (given the limited requirement of generality of rules discussed earlier) of specific individuals.

The crucial point is that Austin is not necessarily wrong because he does not share the emphases of these later writers. As the general approach of this book seeks to show, questions in legal philosophy are asked – and made meaningful – in the context of their time and place. Austin answers questions as to how power conferring rules fit within the coercive model of laws and, for *his* purposes, in the context of his theoretical project, the answers are less inadequate than is often claimed.

Sovereignty

Consideration of other criticisms and possible defences of the command theory must wait until its most crucial component – the concept of the sovereign – has been discussed. If law is a type of command, the identity and character of the commanders and what enables them to issue legal commands must be established. If laws provide for sanctions, the authority to impose sanctions must be explained. The theory of sovereignty which Austin adapts from Hobbes' political philosophy and, to a lesser extent, from Bentham's commentaries on Blackstone is intended to serve these purposes.

What makes commands rules is the element of generality in them; what makes rules laws – in the sense of positive laws, the subject of Austin's jurisprudence – is the fact that they are direct or indirect commands of the *sovereign* of an independent political society. These commands are addressed to the members of that society, who are thus *subjects* of that sovereign. Austin writes of the sovereign as a person (for example, an absolute monarch) or a body of persons (for example the lawmakers or electorate of a democracy, or the members of an established ruling elite). It is essential, however, to note that he always means by the sovereign the *office* or *institution*[2] which embodies supreme authority; never the individuals who happen to hold that office or embody that institution through their relationships at any given time (e.g. Austin 1832: 146–7, 261). Austin's sovereign is an abstraction – the location of the ultimate power which allows the creation of law in a society. As will appear later, this point is of the greatest importance, since he has often been criticised for describing sovereignty, and the source of legal authority, in 'personal' terms.

Undoubtedly he felt no need to labour the matter for, in the tradition of political theory which he relies on, sovereignty is explicitly 'abstract'. Hobbes, writing in the context of Cromwellian England, describes sovereignty as the 'artificial soul' of 'an artificial man', the latter being the state or commonwealth. The sovereign

---

[2] For the meaning I attach to the word 'institution' in this context see p 3, above.

is an office, not a particular person or particular people (Hobbes 1962: 59, ch 30). In the seventeenth century, Hobbes transformed English discussion of the authority of the ruler by substituting for the power of the king the abstract notion of the state as expressed in the concept of sovereignty (cf. Hinsley 1986: 142); although, eventually, faced with the difficulty of locating sovereignty in England, he found it (prudently, after the royal Restoration) in the institution of the monarch (Yale 1972: 137–8). No doubt it was Hobbes' image of sovereignty which predominantly shaped Austin's (his admiration for the earlier writer is very clear in the lectures). By contrast, Austin distances himself in important respects, as will appear, from Bentham's tentative and somewhat confusing discussion of sovereignty.

What is the sovereign of an independent political society? Hobbes had defined such a society as one which could defend itself, unaided, against any attacks from without. Austin realistically notes that few if any societies would qualify on this basis. Accordingly, it is the existence of sovereignty which defines independence, assuming the society is of a certain minimum size (Austin 1832: 198, 207–8, 213). Political independence and sovereignty are correlative terms. Sovereignty exists when two conditions are satisfied: first, the bulk of the society are in a habit of obedience or submission to a determinate and common superior (whether an individual or a body of individuals) and, secondly, that individual or body is not, itself, in a habit of obedience to a determinate human superior. The idea of a habit of obedience introduces a factual, indeed sociological, criterion of the existence of sovereignty and, in this, Austin follows Bentham rather than Hobbes. Hobbes founded the existence of sovereignty in an assumed 'social contract' by which individuals could be thought of as joining together to form a society and entrusting the absolute power of government to a sovereign who would provide peace and physical protection for them. The 'war of all against all' which would exist without government would be replaced by the domination of the sovereign to whom all are subject. But this analysis presupposed that individuals have natural rights which, by the social contract, they agree to forego so as to institute a sovereign power over them. As has been seen earlier, neither Bentham nor Austin was prepared to accept ideas of natural rights, treating them as irrational dogma. Thus Bentham, and Austin following him, discard Hobbes' social contract basis of sovereignty and replace it with the idea of a factual basis of sovereignty in actual habitual obedience. One consequence of this is that while Hobbes' social contract gave the sovereign the right to rule, both Bentham and Austin deny that it makes any sense to talk of a right in this context (see Hart 1982: 221; Austin 1832: 277-8). The existence of sovereignty is merely a political fact, not a matter of right and wrong.

On one view, the 'weak side of the "Austinian analysis" is this transference of a legal conception to a sociological problem' (Stephen 1900: 329) and certainly the grounding of the ultimate authority to create law in a sociological consideration stores up problems for normative legal theory. Nevertheless, it is easy to see here the utilitarian attempt to be realistic, to avoid dogma and abstract talk about arbitrarily assumed natural rights, and to avoid sanctifying authority. Austin cannot resist speculating on *why* people might habitually obey but for the moment that matter can be left aside. Like the sociological question of how far state sanctions induce compliance with law, it is not important to the *analytical* issue of the location of sovereignty. All that is necessary for the latter is the fact that habitual obedience by the majority of the population exists. Where there is no such obedience there is either anarchy (no recognised sovereign at all) or revolution (the population is divided into groups rendering habitual obedience to different authorities).

Some Characteristics of Austin's Sovereign

Two important characteristics of the Austinian sovereign have already been noted. It must be common (that is, only one sovereign can exist in any single political society; the sovereign is, in that sense, indivisible although it can be made up of several components). And it must be determinate (that is, the composition of the sovereign body or the identity of the sovereign person must be clear). A further characteristic has produced more controversy than any other aspect of Austin's conception of sovereignty. This is that *the sovereign is illimitable by law*. This follows directly from Austin's definition of law. Every law is the direct or indirect command of the sovereign of an independent political society. But a sovereign cannot issue enforceable commands to itself – or at least, even if such an idea is conceivable, the sovereign can abrogate them at any time. And no laws other than the sovereign's own commands can exist to bind it. 'Supreme power limited by positive law, is a flat contradiction in terms. . . Every supreme government is legally despotic' (Austin 1832: 254, 271).

Many critics have considered that Austin's view of sovereignty conjures up the image of a despotic monarch – an archaic and wholly inappropriate way of thinking upon which to found an analysis of the authority of law in modern Western societies. But if we look more closely this is not necessarily so. First, Austin does not suggest the sovereign is free of limitations but only legal limitations. Thus positive morality (reflected in public opinion, widespread moral or political expectations, and ultimately the threat of rebellions) may provide important constraints. Secondly, most of Austin's discussions of sovereignty relate primarily to the conditions of representative democracies (especially Britain and the United States). Thirdly, Austin's concept of delegation by the sovereign, which will be considered below, is used by him to express the possibility (which has become a reality in most complex modern industrialised societies) of very extensive dispersion of legislative, adjudicative and administrative authority within the overall hierarchical framework of a centralised state.

Nevertheless, it is widely considered that Austin's conception of an indivisible and legally illimitable sovereign quickly runs into the most serious analytical difficulties. The problems seem to begin as soon as one seeks to identify the sovereign in particular societies. In orthodox British constitutional law the sovereign is said to be the Queen in Parliament: that is, the sovereign is made up of the monarch and the two houses of Parliament. Constitutional law supports the claim that such a sovereign is legally illimitable. Parliament cannot bind itself or its successors by legislation[3]. Since the House of Commons is the representative of the electorate, however, Austin locates sovereignty in the monarch, the House of Lords and the electorate of the Commons (Austin 1832: 230–1).

Many critics have seen this as either problematic or utterly misleading. In particular, Austin has been seen as confusing legal and political sovereignty (Dicey 1959: 76; Buckland 1949: ch 9). Popular sovereignty may well reside in the electorate, but for legal purposes surely Parliament is sovereign. In fact, there is no confusion. Austin does not write of *legal* sovereignty or treat sovereignty as supreme legal competence. As C.A.W. Manning points out, Austin's sovereignty is not a legal but a pre-legal notion. It is 'the logical correlate of an assumed factual obedience' (Manning 1933: 192, 202). In modern terms, we can say it is the locus of legitimate ultimate political authority. It is not 'a specified organ or complex of organs, but. . . that individual or collectivity at whose pleasure the constitution is changed or subsists intact' (Manning 1933: 192). But if this is so how can the electorate as subjects

---

[3]   E.g. *Vauxhall Estates Ltd. v Liverpool Corporation* [1932] 1 KB 733; *Ellen Street Estates Ltd. v Minister of Health* [1934] 1 KB 590.

be in a state of habitual obedience to themselves as sovereign? The answer is that the members of an independent political society *as individuals* can be in a state of habitual obedience to a sovereign which is the abstract institution defined as monarch, Lords and the *collectivity* represented by the electorate of the Commons. The distinction between the subject population and the electorate forming part of the sovereign (and made up of essentially the same people) is a distinction between subject individuals and a sovereign collectivity. There is nothing incoherent in claiming that the individual is subject to the authority of the collectivity as an institution, or that the collectivity as a whole retains authority because the bulk of individuals continue to accept its authority.

What of the case of written constitutions and those where the distribution of governmental authority is especially complex; as, for example, in federal systems? Austin considers at some length the location of sovereignty in the United States to illustrate his approach. The sovereign must be a person or body of persons, but the ultimate authority of the American polity appears to be *a document* – the Constitution. Where then does sovereignty lie. Of course, in the Austinian analysis it must lie with that body of people that has ultimate authority to alter the Constitution (Austin 1832: 250–1). The Constitution itself provides in Article 5 that amendments to it must, to be valid, be ratified by the legislatures of (or conventions in) three quarters of the states. Again, in an Austinian analysis, where representatives are involved, it is the electors of these representatives who form the sovereign body.

Critics note that the Austinian sovereign in such a context is 'a despot hard to arouse', 'a monarch who slumbers and sleeps', since constitutional amendments are rare (Dicey 1959: 149). But this situation matters only if we are seeking (as Austin is not) a legal sovereign – that is, an active, ultimately authoritative lawmaker. By contrast Austin is identifying only the location of ultimate authority underlying the constitutional order; the institution which is recognised as having authority to confirm or amend that order. Suppose that in a political society with a written constitution there is no such institution; no means of constitutional amendment. Sovereignty would then seem to lie in those governmental and legislative institutions which the constitution recognises as ultimately authoritative, since nothing capable of changing their authority stands behind them. In an Austinian view, however, sovereignty resides in these authorities not *because* of their designation by the constitution, but because the authorities so designated are themselves habitually accepted[4].

Must the Sovereign be Legally Illimitable?

We have noted that Austin insists that by definition the sovereign cannot be subject to legal limitations. Blackstone (1809 I: 49) had earlier claimed that in every legal system there is a supreme, absolute and unlimited legislative power. Bentham, however, thought differently. While claiming that there are no *a priori* theoretical limits on sovereign power, he nevertheless considered that legal limits on such power were practically possible. Like Austin, he grounds the existence of sovereignty in the fact of habitual obedience. Hence he sees the possibility of *conditional* habitual obedience; that is, obedience might be habitually rendered to sovereign acts *within certain limits*. The 'obedience of the governed is susceptible of every modification of which human conduct is susceptible: and the rules which mark it out, of every diversity which can be clearly described by words' (Bentham 1970: 69; cf. Bentham 1977: 489).

[4]   Consider a further problem arising in a full parliamentary democracy in which, in Austin's terms, the electorate alone is the sovereign. The parliament may pass legislation altering the composition of the electorate (for example, by enfranchising people who previously had no legally recognised right to vote). This seems to be a case of the sovereign purporting to alter itself by law. Yet, for Austin, the sovereign is above law; its creator, not the creature of law. Can Austinian theory be applied to explain such a situation? Austin himself provides no satisfactory solution but the matter could be argued as follows. The legislation changing the composition of the electorate is certainly law (as the sovereign's command). The issue is as to whether it is, in itself, effective to alter the sovereign. Austin must say it is not, for the sovereign's identity depends not on law but on recognition by the bulk of the population. The identification and limits of the sovereign and its authority are essentially governed by what Austin would term positive morality. But the new electoral law does, at least, have the authority of law and as such may strongly influence positive morality towards the acceptance of a redefined sovereign. Obviously the legitimacy of future law which claims authority as the commands of the redefined sovereign depends, on this analysis, on popular acceptance of the redefinition, not on the fact that the redefinition has been enshrined in law. If the redefinition of the sovereign is accepted, however, the redefining law will, no doubt, be treated as legally expressing the new understanding of sovereign authority.

This is plausible, but seems to run into problems when it is suggested that the limitations on sovereign power are *legal*. In *Of Laws in General* Bentham does suggest this by terming some of these limitations *leges in principem* (1970: 64). But where does their legal quality come from? He recognises that *leges in principem*, like all other laws, must derive from the sovereign but his explanations of how the sovereign can bind itself are far from satisfactory, relying on suggestions about the invocation of external pressures of popular opinion, religious or moral sanctions, or international relations (Bentham 1970: 67-70). For Austin, of course, these kinds of sanctions are characteristic not of law but of positive morality. It is by no means apparent how Bentham's *leges in principem* acquire their legal character. His apparently inconclusive discussion seems motivated here primarily by the desire to recognise clearly the variety of constitutional structures which do indeed distribute authority within states in complex ways – for example, through federal arrangements, provision for judicial review of legislation, entrenched constitutional clauses, or the explicit separation of governmental powers.

Austin's simpler and clearer conception of legally unlimited sovereignty is not incapable of dealing with these complexities. It has been seen that for Austin the sovereign is always an institution – for example, the monarch, not the person who is king at any given time; the body which can change the constitution, not the particular individuals who may form that body. How is the institution defined or identified? It would seem that two kinds of rules may do this: rules of positive law and rules of positive morality (for example, public opinion expressed in customary, moral or other rules, conventions or expectations). Only positive morality can actually bind the sovereign so as to fix its institutional character. Positive law cannot do this since the sovereign can alter this law at will. But even if it does not bind the sovereign it can have the status of law if commanded by the sovereign and addressed to any *part* or agent of the sovereign body (for example, to the British parliament – perhaps defining its procedures; to judges – perhaps specifying jurisdiction; or to the monarch within a constitutional monarchy – perhaps defining the monarch's powers as well as the right of succession to the throne). Positive law can bind each part of such a sovereign body as 'the Queen in Parliament' since each part is not itself sovereign.

Nevertheless, the considerations which fix the nature of sovereignty in general in a particular political society must be founded in positive morality, not law. Sovereignty is, as has been seen, a pre-legal concept. In an Austinian view no law can confer or validate sovereignty. Austin asserted that much of constitutional 'law' must, in fact be merely positive morality for this reason. This is a much less unrealistic view than has often been claimed, once it is appreciated that, on the basis of the arguments above, laws directed to distinct parts of the sovereign body (or, perhaps more accurately, distinct institutions through which sovereignty is expressed) can certainly be accepted as laws in Austinian terms, even though they cannot bind the sovereign as a whole.

The acceptance of the sovereign as an institution seems to remove much of the difficulty which has been thought to exist for Austinian attempts to explain the persistence and continuity of laws (cf. Hart 1961: 50–64). Laws can remain in force as long as the institutional sovereign remains, perhaps for centuries. Equally, the problem of succession to authority (for example, how one king succeeds another in a recognised line of succession) and the continuity of laws which accompanies it may be explained in Austinian terms by the existence of rules of positive morality or of positive law as described above. Where sovereignty appears to reside entirely in a single person such as an absolute monarch it would seem that that the rules governing succession to the throne can only be rules of positive morality. But Austin would consider this a wholly realistic view of the matter. Whatever may be written in 'legal' form (as statutes, for example), succession in such a situation depends on political loyalties, traditional beliefs, and ideological notions which only a most narrow-minded jurist could try to reduce to purely 'legal' determinants of succession.

This defence of Austin is far from claiming that law *must* be interpreted in something like his terms. He offers only a particular partial perspective which emphasises a certain relationship between law and the modern state, viewed in terms of sovereign power. Writers who have argued forcefully against his interpretation have usually wanted to see the legal system as being governed by rules, even in its highest regions of authority, rather than – as Austin's theory so starkly claims – governed by *people*, mere human decision-makers with all their frailties and potential for arbitrary or tyrannous exercise of power. As noted earlier, Austin's theory is not a theory of the Rule of Law – of government subject to law. It is a theory of the 'rule of men' – of government using law as an instrument of power. Such a view may be considered realistic or merely cynical. But it is, in its broad outlines, essentially coherent.

The Judge as Delegate of the Sovereign

The concept of *delegation* of sovereign power is fundamental to Austin's thinking. It is obvious that the theory of sovereignty applied to modern conditions must entail such delegation among numerous agencies, empowered to transact the business of the state in one way or another. Indeed, the idea of delegation in this sense is the element necessary to complete the discussion of power-conferring rules which was begun earlier in this chapter. The sovereign, in Austinian terms, delegates legislative and administrative functions to many institutions – including, significantly, the judiciary. Equally, law-making power is delegated to private citizens who exercise it, for example, in the creation of contracts according to terms chosen by the contracting parties, but which the sovereign's institutions will enforce (cf. Bentham 1970: 22ff). Each dispersion of sovereign power in this way is a delegation, not a release of it. Each legitimate exercise of such power to create legal obligations (for example, when a court lays down a new rule in a case or when an official establishes a rule on the basis of statutory authority conferred on him) must be treated as an exercise of the sovereign's power of command. Hence, insofar as such an act is not revoked or invalidated by higher authority representing the sovereign, it can be considered a *tacit command* of the sovereign (Austin 1832: 31-2; 1885: 642).

Many critics have claimed that this notion of tacit command – which is present also in the theory of Hobbes (1962: 248) – is unrealistic as regards law-making through judicial decisions (e.g. Maine 1875a: 364–5; Rumble 1985: 112). Are not judges independent in such democracies as, for example, Britain and the United States? How can they be considered mere delegates of some other authority? The difficulty again arises from treating Austin's sovereign as a legal sovereign – an ultimate legislating institution. Thus, the legal doctrine of parliamentary sovereignty in Britain – which recognises Parliament as the highest law-creating authority – does not, of course, entail that judges are delegates of Parliament. Austin's theory does not, however, suggest that they are. It claims merely that they must act as representatives of the constitutional order of which they are a part. In Austinian terms that constitutional order is the consequence of the pre-legal sovereign authority embodied in monarch, Lords and the electorate of the Commons.

Logically, it would seem to follow that delegation of sovereign power, insofar as it is accomplished by law, must itself be accomplished by means of the sovereign's commands – whether as specific requirements for action or prohibitions imposing limits on action, whether addressed to holders of an office or to those people who are to be subject to the power of the office-holder, and whether express or tacit.

Many important consequences follow from Austin's way of looking at the distribution of political and legal authority in the state in this way. For example, his view of the judge as delegate of the sovereign entails a straightforward recognition that judges *legislate* no less than do legislatures. Judges make law insofar as their decisions embody what can be considered to be the sovereign's tacit commands. Austin's carefully expressed views on judicial law-making have often been misinterpreted and are certainly very different from Bentham's. Bentham sought a rational, codified legal system which would make not only judicial law-making but probably also judicial interpretation of law unnecessary and inappropriate. The role of the judge would be to decide cases not by appeal to legal precedent but by following the demands of utility in the particular case, and seeking to reconcile differences between the parties where possible (Postema 1986: ch 10). Judicial decision-making would thus be radically separated from the rational code structure of the law itself. Such a position follows from Bentham's conviction that rational law could only be constructed through purposive legislation, not by judicial pronouncements inspired only by the accidents of litigation. As Bentham's recent interpreter Gerald Postema admits, it is hard to construct a coherent theory of the place of the judiciary in the legal order from such ideas (Postema 1986: 453–9).

Austin is the model of cautious moderation beside Bentham's radicalism. But he does claim that judges 'of capacity, experience and weight' have generally been insufficiently active in developing the law (Austin 1885: 646–7). He argues against the idea that judicial law-making (or, as he calls it, 'judiciary law') is arbitrary or undemocratic, taking as his primary point that judiciary law is no different in this respect from any other form of subordinate legislation and, in all such situations, positive law and public opinion must provide the necessary safeguards. The most radical theme which emerges is that insofar as judges make law there is no reason to treat their law-making role as necessarily and essentially different from that of other delegates (officials, administrators, boards and committees) of the sovereign entrusted with rule-making functions. Thus, Austin's criticisms of judiciary law are entirely technical ones. It tends to be made in haste; it is inevitably established *ex post facto*; it 'exists nowhere in fixed or determinate expressions'; it tends to be vague and inconsistent; its rules are 'never or rarely comprehensive'; there is no clear test of its validity; its existence tends to make accompanying statute law 'imperfect, unsystematic, and bulky' (Austin 1885: 649–59). Hence code systems are, as Bentham had argued, better than common law systems. But, whereas Bentham rests the matter squarely on unshakeable assumptions about where perfect legal rationality resides and would, it seems, like to sweep away the law-making judge into the museum of archaic curiosities, Austin painstakingly weighs up the practical considerations and on balance confirms the purely technical virtues of codification and legislation.

Austin's Theory of the Centralised State

Austin's view of the judge as essentially just one variety of state functionary among many others leads us into a wider consideration of his image of the modern state. Austin's political and social theory is ignored in most jurisprudential discussions of his work, yet it provides the essential context in which his concept of delegation of sovereign power is given significance. In his early political writings he made clear his belief in the virtues of political centralisation. Austin's top-down image of law reflects a top-down image of the polity. Like the other major nineteenth century writers discussed so far in this book he was far from from being a democrat (though Bentham, towards the end of his life, came to advocate a kind of democratic government: see Dinwiddy 1975). Austin viewed government as a matter of rational management to be guided by principles of utility. As such – and rather like Maine – he viewed it as a matter for experts. John Stuart Mill wrote that after Austin's return from Germany in 1828, 'he acquired an indifference, bordering. on contempt, for the progress of popular institutions' (quoted in Dicey 1905: 163). As time went on, his views became increasingly conservative and in his last published writings he polemicised against any constitutional reforms which would extend democracy.

These views should be understood in the context of the intellectual climate of his times. At the time Austin wrote his lectures his view of government was undoubtedly elitist in the most literal sense. The real security for good government would be not popular participation but an enlightened population, which, understanding the rational principles which governing elites should follow, would not obey government blindly but on the basis of a critical recognition of its rational purposes. Both John and Sarah Austin believed fervently in the need for universal education, which would make it possible for the broad population to distinguish sound policy and scientific principles (for example, of political economy) 'from the lies and fallacies of those who would use them for sinister purposes, and from the equally pernicious nonsense of their weak and ignorant well-wishers' (Austin 1832: 66). While most ordinary subjects lacked both time and inclination to master the knowledge that would make acquiescence in government a *fully* rational affair, Austin considered that they could learn at least the 'leading principles' of those matters (such as social ethics and economics) which concern government, and 'if they were imbued with those principles, and were practiced in the art of applying them, they would be docile to the voice of reason, and armed against sophistry and error' (Austin 1832: 65). Thus, Austin's view of the bases of obedience is not like that of Maine who, as noted in the previous chapter, saw the role of reason as strictly circumscribed and emphasised the irrational, customary foundations of the acceptance of authority.

All this suggests that to see Austin's view of law (as commands supported by sanctions) as much like a view of mere orders backed by threats (such as those of a gunman pointing his gun at the person addressed) is misleading (cf. Hart 1961: ch 2). The relation between sovereign and subject is far more than one founded on coercion. The habit of obedience to the sovereign is, according to Austin, rooted in custom, prejudices and 'reason bottomed in the principle of utility' – that is, a recognition of the expediency of government (Austin 1832: 300). In a soundly educated people, reason would play a most important role. Equally, when we consider the significance of the sanctions attaching to law in actually securing obedience to law, Austin notes that fear of state (legal) sanctions is not likely to be more powerful as a deterrence against deviance than is 'the fear of public disapprobation, with its countless train of evils' (1832: 69). In forming moral character the latter is far more significant than the former.

Thus, Austin's image of the centralised state, making extensive use of coercion through law in the matter of government, is also an image of a state which can be based on reason; guided in governmental activity by utility, and securing the allegiance of subjects to the sovereign ideally through their rational understanding, not prejudice, fear or blind habit. Nevertheless, Austin considers that it must realistically be recognised that populations are kept largely unenlightened by their rulers. Hence much government, in fact, relies on irrational, habitual acquiescence by the population. Universal education is thus the Austinian prescription for a sound and enlightened polity.

A need for acquiescence in a centralised source of state authority in the sovereign goes along with the need for extensive delegation of sovereign powers, as has been seen. Austin praised the institutions of local government and recognised the appropriateness of judicial law-making and extensive rule-making in administrative contexts. Nevertheless, in his writings on the virtues of centralisation he insists that none of this delegation must be allowed to defeat the central co-ordination of government by which rational utilitarian policies can be consistently brought into effect.

In later life, Austin changed many of his political views, replacing much of his optimism about the prospects for rationality in politics and social organisation with a Maine-like pessimism. Centralisation seemed less attractive to him with his fading belief in the potential of government to direct society rationally, and with a growing fear of its control by despots or mobs (Hamburger and Hamburger 1985: 185–6). Most fundamentally, Sarah Austin tells us that her husband decided some time after 1832 that 'until the ethical notions of men were more clear and consistent, no considerable improvement could be hoped for in legal and political science, nor, consequently, in legal or political institutions' (Austin 1885: 16). Apparently, education remained the key to advance but the struggle was now seen as a far harder one than had originally been envisaged; perhaps, indeed, an impossible one.

Austin's late and profound pessimism should not affect the assessment of the ideas contained in his lectures. It should alert us only to the fact that his 'timeless' concepts of 'sovereign', 'command', 'sanction' and 'habitual obedience' are not formulated in isolation from specific political conditions. Like most elements of normative legal theory they are conceptual reflections of a particular time and place, transformed in a way that gives them the potential to speak to other generations in other legal conditions. In Austin's case, however, these concepts are formulated with a clear awareness of the sociological questions they entail. This dimension of his thought has been almost totally ignored by his critics in the field of normative legal theory.

Austin and the Legal Profession

Austin's legal philosophy, like Maine's historical jurisprudence with which it was effectively contemporaneous, reflected the political conditions of a state gradually forming modern capacities for deliberate direction of economic and social life. But it was far more influential on professional legal thinking, in the long run, than was Maine's work. Austin explicitly addressed his work to lawyers.

His concern for systematisation and rationalisation of legal doctrine was noted at the beginning of this chapter. He seemed to offer a means of working towards the neat and 'scientific' organisation of professional legal knowledge which historical jurisprudence and the common law tradition apparently could not provide. Austin wrote of the possibility of supplying a 'map of the law' for the newcomer student; a map based on broad rational principle and demonstrating the structure of a legal system (Austin 1863: 379). His theory of law and sovereignty seemed to show how even the most basic notions of law could be explained in terms of their logical structure and their unifying authority. Thus, when the second edition of Austin's *Province of Jurisprudence Determined* was published it 'was immediately welcomed as the only English work which offered a methodology for the scientific textbooks on English law required by the new courses' in legal education beginning in the universities and the Inns of Court (Stein 1980: 85–6). Austin's jurisprudence, whatever its faults, showed a serious attempt to analyse the character of law without appeal to the vague, romantic images of common law thought. It seemed to offer a theory for the times which would explicitly recognise the modern dominance of legislation, the active law-making of the modern state, and the idea of law in flux as a purposive human creation.

But, it may be suggested, Austin's most important professional contribution was to show, at the same time, that despite the potential changeability of law and the fact that political powers – not judges – now made the running in legal development, law could still be considered a unified field of professional knowledge. Austin's jurisprudence, as has been seen, clearly distinguishes law from morality. It asserts also that custom is not law unless adopted as such by the courts (that is, by the sovereign's tacit command). It marks out the field of law – the province of the lawyer's concerns – with a rigour which is quite impossible within the framework of classical common law thought. Thus, intellectually-minded lawyers could see that Austin might be offering the basis for elaborating legal knowledge as a well organised subject respectable within the environment of university education and as the special learned expertise of a modern profession of lawyers. Law would be 'neither a trade, nor a solemn jugglery, but a science' (Pollock quoted in Sugarman 1986: 36).

Austin's work left unanswered questions about the nature and method of this science which, as will be seen in the next chapter, have troubled later writers. However, the professional considerations to which his work relates explain, to some extent, why it is the theory of law and sovereignty in *The Province*, and not the broader elements of Austin's 'general jurisprudence' developed in the other lectures, which has attracted continuing attention. While the latter lectures dwell on the substance of law – the notions common to mature systems of law such as 'property' and its numerous aspects and categories – the theory of *The Province* is primarily concerned with the form of law and the structure of legal authority. Perhaps, it can be suggested, professional knowledge of law in an era of continuous legal change promoted by the directive, legislative activity of the state, could only be unified around ideas about the form and structure of law, and not around ideas about law's substantive content. The content of law was not only potentially in constant flux, but was beyond lawyers' control (unlike the situation in earlier eras when judges both explained and controlled legal development). It was the result of political considerations which could not themselves easily be brought within the professional knowledge field of lawyers.

Of course, these political considerations intrude into Austin's lectures in *The Province* in those passages where he discusses the principle of utility. But it has been noted earlier in this chapter that Austin's emphasis is always on rationalisation of law as it is – as a lawyer or law student needs to understand it. The 'science of legislation', which had been fundamental to Bentham, is portrayed by Austin as something for the ordinary student to avoid. There are passages in Austin's writings where his caution proscribes any flights of the imagination. He explains (1863: 374) that a teacher might properly occasionally spice his exposition with references to issues of legislative policy but should do so only on matters 'which do not try the passions'. And there is always a need for a narrow focus, for limiting the range of what is studied. Most people must be content with putting together no more than the limited package of knowledge they need for immediate practice. 'I am sorry it is so', he writes (1863: 388).

This is a far cry from Bentham's urgent commitment to legal reform and to a legal science which would continually serve the needs of legal improvement. But Austin's outlook pointed the way towards what has been called the expository tradition in legal education and scholarship. It suggested that a viable science of law could be built around the task of rationalising law as it is without much concern for how it ought to be, even in the modern era of never-ending legislative change.

On the other hand, the elements of Austin's theory discussed in this chapter also explain some primary reasons why it evokes so much hostility among many writers concerned with normative legal theory today. Discussion here has tried to suggest that it may be not the general logic of Austin's jurisprudence which is primarily at fault, for many of the matters which critics have most strongly emphasised were well understood by Austin and dealt with by him in the context of his theory. A main – if usually unstated – reason for condemnation of Austin may be that the emphases of his thought seem *politically* inappropriate. Austin's theory, as has been seen, does not deny the possibility of constitutional controls on government. But, as an optimistic utilitarian at the time he wrote his lectures, he, like Bentham, saw strong government as a virtue as long as that government was guided by the rational principles of utility. The theory of sovereignty and the political theses of centralisation and delegation which inform and fulfil it are inspired by this opinion. Equally, Austin's lack of an overriding concern for the value of liberty except as part of the utilitarian calculus of advantages offends modern sensibilities. The apparent reduction of judges, in Austin's portrayal, to merely one type of rule-creating or rule-interpreting state official among others also rankles, as does the related lack of patience with orthodox theories of the separation of governmental powers. Finally, Austin's view of international law (which will be left for comment until the next chapter) as positive morality rather than law seems inappropriate in a modern world of increasingly intricate international ties.

These political and constitutional matters seem specially relevant for lawyers' professional outlook and concerns and the different view of them in some post-Austinian normative legal theory will be considered in the next chapter. The concern of discussion here has been to suggest that, interpreted in its own context and in terms of its own emphases, Austin's jurisprudence remains a valuable contribution to normative legal theory and one which grasped the problem of recognising realistically the phenomenon of centralised modern state power in a way that classical common law thought seemed wholly ill-equipped to do.

4   Analytical Jurisprudence and Liberal Democracy: Hart and Kelsen

Although Austin's legal theory may still have much to teach, given its serious attempt to view law realistically as an instrument of state power, it is obvious that much has changed since he wrote. The confident utilitarianism that emphasised social benefits to be brought about by rational government and rational law was typically also an unashamedly elitist view of government. It was seen in Chapter 3 that the virtues of democracy do not enter into Austinian calculations. The limitation of governmental power is not viewed as an especially important concern. Liberty is seen as a by-product of rational government, rather than as potentially threatened by state power. The doctrines of the Rule of Law and the *Rechtsstaat* – the state defined by and subject to law – are not reflected or prefigured in Austin's legal philosophy to any notable extent. Constitution building and the careful legal separation of governmental powers – matters which were of considerable importance to Bentham – play little part in Austin's thinking in his lectures. In the modern Anglo-American world, however, all of these matters are regarded as politically of great importance. They are also, typically, matters of serious professional concern to lawyers. Thus, it is not necessarily only the defective logic of earlier legal philosophy which has inspired different approaches in the literature to be considered in this chapter. These newer writings may also reflect different concerns from Austin's, different fears, different political experiences and a changed social (and legal) environment.

This chapter is concerned with the work of two writers both of whom can be seen, in terms of the theses of this book, as trying to transcend – in radically contrasting ways – the approach to legal philosophy adopted in Austin's lectures. One of them, H.L.A. Hart – Professor of Jurisprudence at Oxford University from 1953 to 1968 – explicitly builds his ideas in normative legal theory on a critique of Austin's jurisprudence. Of Hart's work it has been appropriately said that it 'provides the foundations of contemporary legal philosophy in the English-speaking world and beyond' (Hacker and Raz eds. 1977: v). The other major writer to be considered here is the Austrian Hans Kelsen, perhaps the most illustrious and widely discussed figure in twentieth century legal philosophy. Kelsen originally developed his theories in a continental European tradition without reference to Austinian thought, but arrived at positions which he himself recognised as having an affinity with Austin's analytical jurisprudence. Thus he wrote in the 1940s, three decades after having laid the foundations of what has become known as the 'pure theory' of law, that this theory 'corresponds in important points with Austin's doctrine' (Kelsen 1941b: 271). 'Where they differ, they do so because the pure theory of law tries to carry on the method of analytical jurisprudence more consistently than Austin and his followers' (Kelsen 1945: xv).

Kelsen's willingness to recognise these parallels is generous. His work is far wider in intellectual scope than Austin's and, outside the Anglo-American world, has been much more influential. It is based on a rigorous epistemology and a sophisticated philosophical view of the nature of legal theory – matters which Austin never seriously addressed in any comparable fashion. Kelsen's writings demonstrate his familiarity with literature in such fields as psychoanalytic theory, political and social theory and anthropology, as well as law and philosophy. Hart's normative legal theory does not show a comparable range. As will appear, it was constructed primarily in conscious reaction to Austin's jurisprudence, and has since been refined and revised largely in the context of commentary on and criticism of Bentham's normative legal theory. Given the contrasting intellectual contexts of Hart's and Kelsen's work it is interesting that, while Kelsen draws significant parallels between his own and Austin's work despite fundamental philosophical differences, Hart asserts unequivocally the need for 'a fresh start' and a total rejection of Austin's jurisprudence ('the record of a failure') in order to advance legal philosophy (Hart 1961: 78).

Kelsen's legal theory was shaped in a legal and cultural environment significantly different from that of the Anglo-American common law world. His ideas are relevant to this book insofar as they have had a significant impact on legal thought in the Anglo-American context but also because they help to put Hart's work into a broader intellectual perspective in two ways. First, parallels between Hart's and Kelsen's ideas help to show how themes in Hart's jurisprudence may reflect wider political concerns about modern law which are not confined to the Anglo-American tradition. Secondly, a consideration of Kelsen's methods of constructing his legal philosophy – methods which are radically different from Hart's – helps in evaluating ideas about the nature and appropriate methods of normative legal theory which are often taken for granted in the Anglo-American context, but not necessarily shared outside it. Indeed, the root of the most fundamental difference between Hart's and Kelsen's theoretical approaches is in two different ideas of the very nature of theory itself. It will be necessary to outline the contrast between these ideas about theory before proceeding further.

Empiricism and Conceptualism

The contrast emerges clearly from recent discussions of Austin's work. Quite apart from any particular merits or demerits Austin's jurisprudence has in clarifying the nature of modern Western law, it has apparently left a deep ambiguity at its core; one which continues to puzzle later writers. The ambiguity relates to Austin's aims and methods of analysis.

One view claims, in essence, that Austin's purpose was to produce in his general jurisprudence a systematic and orderly account of the key components of modern legal systems. Austin's concern was empirical in the sense that he wished to represent or describe in theoretical terms the reality of actually existing legal systems, identifying elements common to these modern systems of law and organising them into a body of scientific knowledge. Thus, Austin sought, in W. L. Morison's words, 'to represent law empirically, as something we can readily understand in terms of observable occurrences' (Morison 1982: 2) – observable at least, for example, in the form of actual statutes, judicial decisions and instances of other official action, and the habitual behaviour of subjects. So Morison argues that 'all the evidence indicates that when Austin made general factual statements about independent political communities, he believed them to be universally true' (Morison 1958: 231). They could be tested for their truth against the circumstances of particular legal systems. The idea that theory is, in some such way, a direct representation of empirical reality, with its concepts derived from observation of and generalisation about that reality and so corresponding with it and testable for truth against it, will be called here *empiricism*.

There is, however, another view of theory which, in fact, has been more widely attributed to Austin by recent commentators on his work. It can be explained as follows. Empirical reality – the world of objects and experiences 'out there' – does not, in fact, present us with evidence which we can merely package together or generalise about to arrive at scientific truth. Concepts need to be formed in advance – *a priori* – in order to organise empirical evidence. The previously established concepts not only determine what is empirically relevant but also reflect a view of why it is relevant. Thus, theory aiming at a scientific explanation of any object of knowledge cannot take its concepts from observed experience but must deliberately *construct* concepts as a means of interpreting experience, of *imposing* order on it. A theory is not an attempted representation of observable reality but an intellectual construction – a logically worked out model – which can be used to organise the study of what can be observed in experience. This idea of the nature of theory will be termed here *conceptualism*.

Thus, Julius Stone, rejecting the view of Austin as an empiricist, argues that he should be understood as a conceptualist, 'presenting an apparatus for seeing as clearly as possible the aspect of a legal order with which his analytical system was concerned'; he 'sought the starting-points which would enable him to construct definitions and classifications on the basis of which he could, to a maximum extent, show the logical inter-relations of the various parts of the law to each other, and the subordination of the less general to the more general parts' (Stone 1964: 68, 69). Whereas an empiricist view would say that a theory's truth can be tested in the light of experience, a conceptualist would claim that it is usefulness, not truth, which is the issue. Do the ideas of the theory make it possible to interpret and organise what we know about actual legal systems in a clearer and more illuminating fashion?

Ultimately the methods-debate around Austin's legal philosophy is unfruitful since there seems good reason for an uncommitted reader of his lectures to conclude not only that Austin did not recognise the conceptualism-empiricism dichotomy but also that he wrote in ways which will support either interpretation of his theoretical methods. Nonetheless, the matter is important for at least two reasons. First, some of those writers (notably Hart) who in various ways follow the empiricist approach to theory also tend to see Austin as an empiricist, and this interpretation seems to go along with an emphasis on Austin's theoretical indebtedness to Bentham and an underestimate of other influences on him. Austin's methodological ambiguity may, however, reflect the odd mixture of influences which shaped his jurisprudence: that is, on the one hand, Bentham's 'pseudo-realistic mystery-dispelling analytical technique' (Manning 1933: 212), empiricist in orientation and, on the other, continental Roman law scholarship. In the latter tradition the deliberate construction of abstract legal concepts by jurists to organise the empirical detail of legal doctrine was an admired skill. Such an outlook on law seems compatible in various respects with a conceptualist view of theory. But this possible pull towards conceptualism in Austin's thinking tends to be ignored in the common view of him as merely a disciple of Bentham.

Secondly, an excessively empiricist view of Austin may make it harder to appreciate the character of some of the key concepts he uses. Thus, Hart's apparent failure to recognise the 'abstract', institutional character of Austin's sovereign may result from a too literal, empiricist interpretation of Austin's claim that the sovereign is a person or body of people. The tendency may be to assume that Austin's concept must directly represent something observable (for example, an individual person who is king) rather than operating as a means of conceptualising the ultimate authority by which positive law is made (for example, the institution of monarch). Equally, an excessively empiricist interpretation may be at the root of the common tendency of Austin's critics to seek the sovereign (and inevitably not find it) in sources of legal authority existing *within* actual legal systems (as elements of constitutional structure which a lawyer can recognise), rather than in an abstract institution 'standing behind' the constitution and legal system and presupposed by it.

However that may be, the empiricism-conceptualism dichotomy in normative legal theory is important. A tendency to adhere to one approach rather than the other pushes legal theory in distinct directions. Each tends to lead to different kinds of concepts being used and certainly to different ways of evaluating these concepts. Kelsen's legal philosophy exemplifies a sophisticated and rigorous elaboration of an avowedly conceptualist approach to normative legal theory. On the other hand, Hart's 'fresh start' in legal philosophy built from his criticisms of Austin is best seen – so this chapter argues – as an attempt to adopt empiricist methods more satisfactory than those which he attributes to Austin.

Hart's Linguistic Empiricism

Most English legal philosophy was empiricist (in the particular sense used above) in orientation between the time when Austin's jurisprudence became influential (from the 1860s) and 1953 when Hart was elected to the Oxford chair of jurisprudence. Its dominant approaches had come to be called analytical jurisprudence. They adhered to Austin's view that law and morality should be kept analytically separate and that the appropriate subject of jurisprudence was positive law. Analytical jurisprudence thus viewed law as a human creation established through political power. A primary object of analytical jurisprudence was to clarify the meaning of legal concepts, to try to establish what such concepts represent or refer to. The idea of corporate personality, for example, although fundamental to legal thought, seemed puzzling. What does the concept of 'corporation' represent? Does it refer to a real group entity? Is it just a kind of legal shorthand form used to refer to a complex of legal rules defining certain relationships between individuals linked in some common enterprise? In an empiricist perspective, concepts arise from and represent some observable reality. Analytical jurisprudence concerned itself, therefore, with trying to discover the meaning of concepts such as possession, ownership, intention, legal personality, right and duty, generally by trying to ascertain what actual legal state of affairs each of these terms necessarily referred to.

It may be supposed, with hindsight, that an important reason why English legal philosophy generally declined in influence and interest as far as lawyers were concerned in this period was that the English empiricist approach to analysis of legal concepts appeared increasingly unrealistic and fruitless. The endless debate on the nature of corporate personality, for example, sought to fix the meaning of the concept without adequate reference to the immense variability of the circumstances in which it could be invoked, and of the legal consequences which could follow from it. In the United States, some jurists tried to develop an approach to analytical jurisprudence which showed elements of the conceptualist, as opposed to empiricist, outlook. Wesley Hohfeld, who taught at Stanford and Yale Universities before his premature death in 1918, analysed a set of 'fundamental legal conceptions' – rights, duties, privileges, 'no-rights', powers, liabilities, immunities and disabilities – as what he called the lowest common denominators of law. While some of these concepts were obviously taken directly from lawyers' established usage, Hohfeld's development of them was a creative one. The concepts were rigorously defined theoretical constructions which, whether or not actually reflected in existing judicial practice in the way he described them, were intended by him to organise and clarify legal reasoning by giving it a more precise set of conceptual distinctions. Thus, analytical jurisprudence in this form was intended to aid clarification of law by devising concepts as a 'logical frame built according to specifications drawn from an actual body of law' (Stone 1964: 138).

The value of Hohfeld's work is perhaps especially in a kind of limited reconciliation between conceptualism and empiricism. It combined a deliberate, creative development of illuminating concepts – with their logical relationships precisely worked out – and an insistence that the concepts should relate directly to and be grounded in actual judicial reasoning as expressed in reported cases. Some other American writers, notably Albert Kocourek of Northwestern University, took a more clearly conceptualist approach to legal analysis (Kocourek 1928: 228, 234, 236), inventing such new organising and interpretive concepts as 'ectophylactic', 'zygnomic' or 'mesonomic' relations and 'autophylaxis'. The danger of such an approach – a danger which Hohfeld largely avoided – is that its conceptual originality can seem as far removed from actual practical legal reasoning as does excessively broad empiricist generalisation about the meaning of lawyers' notions.

Hart's very influential inaugural lecture (Hart 1953) was clearly intended to mark a sharp break with all of these previous tendencies in analytical jurisprudence and to call in aid new resources for a more realistic analysis of legal concepts. In the lecture Hart presents the futility of the corporate personality debates as one of several reasons why new methods are needed. Legal words, he explains, must be understood in the context of whole sentences in which they play their characteristic role. They cannot be defined in isolation as if they represented some specific entity. Their use presupposes the existence of an entire legal system and that particular rules are valid within it. Furthermore, legal statements may have a different status in different contexts; for example, a statement's status when made by a judge in the course of deciding a case in court may be wholly different from its status when made outside the courtroom in various situations. Equally, legal concepts do not necessarily relate to a uniform, invariable set of circumstances, because legal rules may attach the same legal consequences to a variety of factual situations.

The viewpoint of Hart's lecture suggests an attack on empiricism because concepts are no longer to be seen as representing anything in a one-to-one fashion. The meaning of a legal concept, according to this view, cannot be defined as if the concept represented some invariant state of affairs. But, in fact, Hart institutes a new kind of empiricism in place of the old; an empiricism grounded in the linguistic philosophy associated especially with Ludwig Wittgenstein at Cambridge University and J.L. Austin (not to be confused with the jurist John Austin) at Oxford. Hart brought to jurisprudence the methods and enthusiasms of English linguistic philosophy. When appointed to the Oxford chair of jurisprudence he had no law degree but had practiced at the Chancery Bar and then, after the 1939-45 war, taught philosophy at Oxford for seven years. During the latter period he became closely involved with the Oxford development of linguistic philosophy, sometimes termed 'ordinary language philosophy'. Hart has said of this that it was 'inspired by the recognition of the great variety of types of human discourse and meaningful communication, and with this recognition there went a conviction that longstanding philosophical complexities could often be resolved not by the deployment of some general theory but by sensitive piecemeal discrimination and characterisation of the different ways, some reflecting different forms of human life, in which human language is used' (Hart 1983: 2). Linguistic philosophy, in this form, focussed not on the meaning of words in some definitional manner, but on clarifying the way in which words are used in various linguistic contexts. The method could be used to illuminate 'the discourse of everyday life' or of any intellectual discipline – such as law – where a failure to appreciate its distinctive character and its differences from other discourses might result in 'perplexity or confusion' (Hart 1983: 3).

Three insights from this kind of philosophy have been especially important in the development of Hart's normative legal theory. First, language has many meaningful forms apart from empirical description or the statement of logical propositions. A significant characteristic of legal language is its 'performative' aspect, 'where words are used in conjunction with a background of rules or conventions to change the normative situation of individuals and so have normative consequences and not merely causal effects' (Hart 1983: 4). The point here is that words used in legal contexts can actually change legal situations and all the expectations which attach to them. For example, when a contractual offer is accepted by the offeree the legal relationship between offeror and offeree is fundamentally changed. And this function of language applies not just to law. Words said in a christening ceremony, or in the making of vows, are also performatives. They change expectations, obligations and relationships through their use in a specific context.

A second important insight from linguistic philosophy is that of the 'open texture' of language. As will appear, this is basic to Hart's ideas on judicial decision-making and legal interpretation. Linguistic philosophy could not admit a *general* indeterminacy of language, otherwise philosophical study of its meaning in use could not proceed. Within specific contexts linguistic meaning is asserted to be, potentially, definitely ascertainable. At the same time, however, language has a 'porosity' or partial indeterminacy so that the relationship between the core of certainty and the penumbra of uncertainty in even the most precisely stated rules requires philosophical examination.

Thirdly, perhaps the most important claim of linguistic philosophy, as far as Hart's legal theory is concerned, is that the 'elucidation of the multiple forms and diverse functions of language'

(Hart 1983: 3) is assumed to be capable also of illuminating the social context in which language is used. This claim about the social insights to be gained from linguistic analysis is one which Hart does not hesitate to make. Thus, 'the suggestion that inquiries into the meaning of words merely throw light on words is false. Many important distinctions, which are not immediately obvious, between types of social situation or relationships may best be brought to light by an examination of the standard uses of the relevant expressions and of the way in which these depend on a social context, itself often left unstated' (Hart 1961: vii).

How then would analysis proceed on such a basis? Instead of asking what the legal term 'corporation' designates we should 'characterise adequately the distinctive manner in which expressions for corporate bodies are used in a legal system' (Hart 1953: 42). And this is – although Hart never calls it such – a new kind of empiricism because what is required is 'a close examination of the way in which statements e.g. of legal rights or of the duties of a limited company relate to the world in conjunction with legal rules' (Hart 1983: 3). It is, thus, necessary to examine the actual conditions under which such statements are regarded as true. The observable reality which legal statements represent is not a range of identifiable entities which are referred to by words such as 'corporation'. It is the reality of the linguistic practices of people living within a legal system and orienting their conduct and expectations in relation to it. In the 1953 lecture there could be little doubt that Hart was thinking of lawyers' practices. The emphasis on actual judicial and legal professional usage in all its variety and complexity seemed to breathe a healthy realism into legal philosophy.

The idea of 'performatives' entails, however, that statements can be practices in themselves. One can 'do things with words' in J.L. Austin's phrase; 'words are also deeds' as Wittgenstein put it (cf. Hart 1970: 275). Thus, Hart's form of linguistic philosophy does not necessarily claim to be concerned with words or statements as *representations* of a social reality. The statements *are*, in themselves, the social reality. They constitute it. Adopting this viewpoint it is not difficult to slip into the position of arguing that philosophical analysis of ordinary language use amounts to a kind of empirical explanation of aspects of social life. Thus, Hart claims in the preface of his most important work in normative legal theory, that the book is not only an essay in analytical jurisprudence but also in 'descriptive sociology' (1961: vii). This controversial claim must await evaluation later. For the moment it is enough to note that Hart's legal philosophy firmly rejects conceptualism (see e.g. Hart 1970: 271, 274) and seeks to find its concepts in the actual linguistic practices of lawyers, judges and citizens.

The Character of Rules

Given what has been said above about Hart's methods it is unsurprising that he rejects any attempt, such as Austin's, to define 'law' or 'a law' and seeks instead a concept of law which treats it as a complex of social practices. He makes no attempt to specify these practices exhaustively in a definitional manner. His concern is, apparently, only to try to clarify those which seem central to the way law is generally perceived. They are to be identified primarily by studying distinctive linguistic practices typically associated with law in ordinary usage.

These methods of proceeding are obviously very different from Austin's. Instead of defining a set of concepts (command, sanction, sovereign, habitual obedience) and exploring their relationships, Hart takes certain distinctions which seem to be drawn in everyday language, and then considers their implications. The starting point is to identify the idea of a 'rule' as the central idea in ordinary discourse about law. Hart's method of doing this is through a critique of an Austinian model of law, which concludes that Austin's failure to examine the concept of rule and to make it central to his jurisprudence was the root cause of the inadequacies of his view of law (Hart 1961: 78). Austin's supposed inability to explain the continuity and persistence of law is traced to his inadequate acknowledgement that the sovereign is itself defined by rules, acquires and exercises authority through them and can be limited by them. The problem of power-conferring rules and the difficulty of assimilating them to commands are held to show that Austin's jurisprudence was incapable of recognising the variety of types of legal rules. Equally Austin's tracing of the source of all law to the sovereign's command is considered to ignore the fact that customary law and judge-made law may arise from and derive independent authority from sources different from that of legislation.

In Chapter 3 it was suggested that at least some of these criticisms of Austin may be misguided. Nevertheless they are important in Hart's major work *The Concept of Law* as the device by means of which the concept of 'a rule' is installed as the self-evidently appropriate starting point for an ordinary language analysis of the nature of law. As will be seen in later chapters, it is certainly possible to argue that law is best analysed theoretically as something other than, or at least something involving much more than, a set of rules. Nevertheless, the lengthy attempt to demonstrate the inadequacies of a version of the command theory in the first four chapters of Hart's book (taking up a third of its text) provides a kind of tableau in which the terms of debate are set and in which the missing element of rules emerges to solve most difficulties.

In ordinary language we often talk of doing things 'as a rule', that is habitually: 'I play my saxophone at weekends, as a rule'. When the word 'rule' is used in other types of statement, however, it is often accompanied by expressions such as 'should', 'ought to', 'ought not' which suggest something other than the regularities of habit: 'You shouldn't make so much noise late at night. There are rules of law about causing a nuisance'. Words such as 'should' and 'ought' are normative terms; that is, they imply evaluation, criticism, or judgments regarding behaviour and not merely description or prediction as do words indicating merely habitual behaviour. The fact that my habitual saxophone playing can also be interpreted normatively – here, in terms of its conformity or lack of conformity with legal rules about nuisance – illustrates the point that events, activities and occurrences can be spoken about in two radically different ways. They can be discussed in *predictive* terms (Am I so attached to my saxophone that I shall keep on playing it whatever happens? Will the neighbours actually sue? In practice what kind of sanction is usually imposed on people who disturb the neighbours at three o'clock in the morning?). Or these matters can be discussed in *normative* terms (Do the neighbours have a legal right to complain? According to law, ought the nuisance to stop? What order can a judge properly make if the nuisance continues and the case comes to court?)

Normative language about rules thus entails evaluations, judgments about what is proper or right according to the relevant rules, or criticism of deviations from the rule. Such deviation is considered good reason for criticism by those who accept the rule which has been broken as legitimate. Words such as 'ought' and 'should' are commonplace in normative statements. But they have no place in purely predictive statements. In the later cases it is not a matter of what 'should' or 'ought to' be done, but what 'is' or what 'will be' the situation (Will the noise stop? Will the neighbours sue? What penalties are the courts in practice imposing?).

This linguistic distinction between normative and predictive language is fundamental to Hart's concept of law. Insiders within a legal order, people who understand and act upon the normative content of the law, can reason critically with legal rules. They have an 'internal' view of the rules, or view the rules in their 'internal aspect'. Equally it is possible for people to adopt a purely external or predictive view of aspects of the legal order ('It's sensible not to drive at 80 miles per hour along Mile End Road. It is very likely that you will be stopped by the police if you do'). One of the most important characteristics of rules, in Hart's analysis, is that they lend themselves to both an internal and external understanding. The internal view of rules obviously involves a certain specific mental attitude – a critical, reflective attitude to one's own conduct and that of others in the light of the rules (Hart 1961: 56) – but Hart insists that it is not equivalent to a psychological feeling of being bound by the rules. A person enthusiastically engaging in tax evasion may understand perfectly well that his activities are wrong in law and, indeed, may be well versed in the relevant rules and their legal meanings. But he may feel no compulsion to obey the law as long as he can avoid detection. Beyond this insistence on what the internal view or aspect of rules does *not* entail, Hart does not offer much further clarification of its nature.

Sociological Drift

Hart's distinguishing of the two aspects of rules is important for several reasons. One is that it marks a serious attempt to break with Austin's methods. As has been seen, Austin tried to identify the field of law by defining essential elements of law as rigorously as he could in contradistinction to moral ideas or to matters 'improperly' termed legal. The field of law is marked out in descriptive fashion. Hart, however, avoids marking out the legal field as such but, instead, distinguishes between the states of mind (with regard to legal rules) of 'insiders' of the legal system and 'outsiders'. The outsiders (adopting an external view of legal rules) might be not just those calculating in purely predictive terms their practical chances of avoiding punishment or gaining some benefit, but also, for example, behavioural scientists only concerned with studying the patterned behaviour of people and unconcerned with their critical, reflective attitudes to rules. Hart argues that lawyers, judges and other legal officials must, however, take an insider's internal view of at least those rules which regulate their own official activities within the legal system. Many ordinary citizens may similarly take an internal view of some or all legal rules. People presumably may be insiders or outsiders in different circumstances or on different occasions or with regard to different legal rules.

Even before looking at the way this dichotomy is further developed in Hart's concept of law some odd features of it can be noted. The opposition Hart initially develops is between habits and rules. But it is not made clear what kinds of entities are being compared. It may be that Hart's method of linguistic philosophy prevents this (concepts only have meaning in use) but since the concept of a rule is being treated as fundamental it is surely appropriate to ask what this concept means in general use. Presumably the only way of treating habits and rules as directly comparable is to view both as impulses or motivations towards action (habits give rise to habitual behaviour; rules inspire rule-governed behaviour). Rules are, it seems, therefore, understood by Hart only in terms of their social functions or potential social effects.

That this is the way Hart views them seems to be confirmed by what he says about the concept of obligation. The idea of obligation presupposes rules though some rules (for example, those relating to etiquette or grammar) are not spoken of as imposing obligations (Hart 1961: 84). Obligation-imposing (or duty-imposing) rules are distinguishable from others, according to Hart, in three ways. First, in the case of obligation-imposing rules 'the general demand' for conformity is insistent and great social pressure is brought to bear against actual or potential non-conformity with them. Second, these rules are considered important as 'necessary to the maintenance of social life or some highly prized feature of it'. Third, compliance with them is thought of as characteristically requiring some sacrifice; duty and interest often being in conflict (1961: 84–5). The most interesting aspect of these distinguishing marks is that all relate to ideas about the relationship between the rules and the social conditions in which they exist. They are concerned with assumptions about the social function or effects of the rules or of compliance or non-compliance with them.

Thus, Hart's legal philosophy identifies the fundamental component of law, obligation-imposing rules, not by organising the familiar material of legal study in terms of concepts such as command and sovereign, but by speculating about widely held attitudes to various kinds of rules. This is, it must be said, not descriptive sociology (cf. Hart 1961: vii), which should presumably be based in substantial empirical study. It is speculative philosophy not grounded in any consideration of actual social conditions. The conceptualisation of obligation-imposing rules does not explain or even consider the conditions under which general agreement on the matters indicated might exist in a society; or, if agreement does not exist, which members of a population must hold the views specified; or what kind of evidence would be appropriate and sufficient to enable us to reach conclusions about these matters.

The root of the problem is this: Hart seeks to provide a general explanation of the character of law on an empiricist basis – in other words, the concepts which he seeks to link theoretically are to be drawn from actual experience or observation of law. But he rejects the idea that legal doctrine itself provides the empirical materials for theory, because there is no necessary fixity of meaning of legal ideas. They do not necessarily represent anything consistently so theory cannot concern itself exclusively with their meaning and the logic of their relationships in legal doctrine. Therefore, the empirical reality to be reflected in theory is the reality of people's (linguistic) practices – the way they talk and think around notions such as 'obligation'. But this should involve actually finding out how people talk and think and such an inquiry is not normative legal theory but sociology or social psychology. As long as empiricist approaches in normative legal theory were satisfied with analysing legal doctrine (the concept of 'corporate personality', for example) as the relevant empirical reality (asking what is a 'corporation'), they did not lead normative legal theory's inquiries into a study of society at large. But Hart's empiricist approach leads in just such a direction. There is a kind of sociological drift (but no serious sociology) in Hart's normative legal theory. It will be necessary to return to this matter after considering further claims he makes about the nature of legal rules.

The Structure of a Legal System

In Chapter 3 it was noted that Hart insists that Austin's command theory cannot accommodate satisfactorily the existence of power-conferring rules in a legal system. These cannot, in his view, be treated as having essentially the same character as duty-imposing rules. Both kinds of rules are present in a legal system and the distinction and relationship between them becomes the central idea of Hart's concept of a legal system. In a simple society it might be possible to maintain social order solely through duty-imposing rules such as rules restricting violence, protecting property, or punishing deceit. Such duty-imposing rules Hart terms *primary rules*. A regime of primary rules alone could maintain itself in practice only if the vast majority of people subject to these rules viewed them from an internal perspective, in the sense discussed earlier; that is, normatively as guides to conduct, rather than merely predictively. Any such regime, however, is subject to obvious defects.

First, the primary rules will not constitute a system but merely a set of separate standards, so doubts as to how the rules relate to each other or how far they extend cannot be resolved. They suffer from the defect of uncertainty. Second, they have a static quality since no means are available for changing them in deliberate fashion, either generally or in their applicability to particular individuals. Third, there is no means of establishing conclusively when a violation of the rules has occurred or of systematically enforcing them.

Behind this fictitious idea of what Hart terms a pre-legal society can be sensed not only a vision of some simple changeless society which an anthropologist might discover but also, perhaps, the image of unguided, culturally determined legal evolution suggested in classical common law thought, as discussed in Chapter 2. Such an image has no conception of law as *positive*, deliberately created and so subject to human interpretation and development. This conception of doctrine as subject to positive development, which Austin found in the idea of sovereignty, Hart finds in a further set of rules beyond the primary duty-imposing rules. Their introduction or evolution marks, for Hart, the transition from a pre-legal to a legal order.

These *secondary rules* are generally portrayed as parasitic on primary rules, power-conferring rather than duty-imposing, and of three kinds which correspond with the three major defects of a regime of primary rules alone. Thus, the secondary *rule of recognition* is the simplest remedy for the uncertainty of the regime of primary rules. It specifies what particular features a rule must have to be recognised as a rule of the society. The rule of recognition may be simple or complex. An example of a complex one could be that rules are to be recognised as rules of the society if created through a certain legislative procedure, or declared by a judge in certain conditions, or supported by long customary practice. The limbs of such a complex rule of recognition could be hierarchically ordered so that the limb recognising legislative rules takes priority over those recognising customary rules and rules declared in judicial decisions. Secondly, *rules of change* remedy the static quality of a regime of primary rules because they regulate procedures for creating or changing other rules or altering their operation. For example, they include rules governing the composition and procedures of a legislative body, as well as rules allowing individuals to alter their own legal circumstances: for example, by making wills or contracts. Finally, *rules of adjudication* are necessary to remedy the inefficiency in operation of a regime of primary rules. They specify means by which a final authoritative decision can be reached as to whether in a particular case a primary rule has been broken. These rules specify who has the authority to adjudicate and the procedures to be followed. They specify, for example, the jurisdiction and procedures of courts and the qualifications of judges.

When a close look is taken at the secondary rules, as Hart discusses them, considerable uncertainty is seen to surround their nature. They are identified originally as power-conferring in contrast to the duty-imposing primary rules. Hart has, however, now admitted in effect that the rule of recognition can be duty-imposing or power-conferring depending on how it is viewed (Hart 1982: 258–9). Other writers have noted more generally that the distinction between primary and secondary rules is not necessarily consistent in Hart's discussions. As well as the distinction between duty-imposing rules and power-conferring rules it may be a distinction between 'non-parasitic' rules – that is, ones which can in principle exist as meaningful social standards quite apart from any systematic relationship they may have with other rules – and 'parasitic' rules which have meaning only in relation to others; or between rules concerning actions involving physical movement and change and others leading to the creation or variation of obligations. These varied distinctions are not necessarily mutually consistent. Several commentators have noted that secondary rules are not necessarily power-conferring (MacCormick 1981a: 106; Raz 1980: 199). Hart himself has suggested that most lawyers would accept the view that with regard to rules relating to the power to appoint judges there are two relevant types of law, one fixing the *duties* of judges (and their powers) and the other conferring on some person the *power* to appoint them (Hart 1972: 215). The conferring of powers and the determination of duties are thus (as Austin well understood) typically intertwined. One commentator has suggested that 'there is simply no such thing as the distinction which we may understand Hart as having made between primary and secondary rules' (Sartorius 1966: 167). Hart himself has referred to his 'own previous inadequate approach to the subject' and admitted that *The Concept of Law* contains 'no close analysis either of the notion of a power or of the structure of the rules by which they were conferred, save to insist that they were different from rules which imposed obligations or duties' (Hart 1972: 196).

This is, if taken at face value, extremely puzzling. Austin's failure to put the distinction between power-conferring and duty-imposing rules in a central place in his theory is the focus of some of Hart's fiercest attacks on him. Yet the distinction remains vague and undeveloped in Hart's major work on normative legal theory. Hart accepts that some such distinction as he makes has long been recognised; but 'perhaps my claim that this distinction could throw light on many dark places in jurisprudence was novel' (Hart 1965: 358). Yet no rigorous analysis is offered to cast that light. As Hart's sympathetic critic Neil MacCormick remarks, given 'the centrality of this topic to Hart's theory of law, it is regrettable indeed that such vagueness and imprecision attends his distinction' between primary and secondary rules (MacCormick 1981a: 106).

What explains this vagueness at perhaps the most fundamental part of Hart's legal theory? The explanation is surely that the need to distinguish primary and secondary rules is not dictated by considerations of analytical rigour in normative legal theory but by a *political* concern to emphasise aspects or perhaps ideals of law which Austin was thought to have underemphasised. Joseph Raz hints at the truth in asserting that the 'fundamental reason which moved Hart to adopt his doctrine of the rule of recognition' is his assumption that the answer to the question of whether a legal rule is valid must be found in a criterion of validity provided by *some other* rule (Raz 1980: 199–200). Putting it another way, Hart's legal theory portrays law as a self-regulating system of rules. The rule of recognition and the other secondary rules are seen as governing the entire process of production, interpretation, enforcement, amendment and repeal of rules within the legal system. In contrast to Austin's picture of a legal order as the expression and instrument of all-too-human political power (the power of the sovereign and its delegates), Hart's image of law is that of a system in which rules govern power-holders; in which rules, rather than people, govern. What is, indeed, implied here is an aspect of the deeply resonant political symbol so obviously missing from Austin's jurisprudence – the symbol of the Rule of Law, a 'government of laws and not of men' (cf. D'Entreves 1967: 69ff).

The concept of secondary rules can be seen, therefore, as an attempt to devise an analytical category which can serve as the umbrella under which an appropriate emphasis can be given to power-conferring *functions* of legal rules. These secondary rules, insofar as they are 'public' in character, are the ones which typify the modern constitutional state (*Rechtsstaat*) in which the powers of officials are not arbitrary but defined by rules of law. Equally, rules conferring 'private' powers (such as rules governing the making of wills, contracts and other transactions and arrangements) allow individuals to adjust their personal legal positions in deliberate, freely chosen and purposive action. These rules mark an individual's autonomy as a *citizen* within the legal order, participating in it as a member of a legal community. To make use of such private power-conferring rules the individual presumably must be a legal 'insider', someone who adopts an internal view of the rules. Thus, while the stress on public power-conferring rules builds the normality of the ideal of the Rule of Law – in the sense of government subject to law – into Hart's theory, the parallel stress on private power-conferring rules builds into it the normality of the ideal of autonomous citizenship, a very different perspective from that entailed in Austin's notion of subjection to a sovereign and undoubtedly a much more attractive one, politically, in a modern democracy.

The Existence of A Legal System

The rule of recognition of a legal system, according to Hart's concept of law, determines which other rules in the system are valid as law. It does this, of course, insofar as it is, itself, recognised or presupposed as a valid rule. One minimum condition, therefore, for a legal system to be in existence is that the rule of recognition and the other secondary rules are accepted as binding by those persons (whom Hart calls 'officials') having the task within the legal order of creating, changing, interpreting, applying, enforcing, or advising on legal rules. This acceptance is essential because the secondary rules are the means by which the legal system governs the fulfilling of these tasks. It follows that the officials must adopt an internal view (in Hart's sense) of the secondary rules. They must view them as meaningful guides for their own conduct and that of others. The other minimum condition for a legal system to exist is that citizens, in general, regularly obey the primary rules. It is not necessary that they should view the primary rules from an internal viewpoint. Obedience merely because of the fear of punishment would be sufficient. Thus, for a legal system to exist there must be general obedience to the primary rules, coupled with an acceptance by officials of the secondary rules from an internal viewpoint.

As some critics have pointed out, it is not entirely clear what Hart intends to convey by this claim about the minimum conditions of existence of a legal system (cf. Campbell 1988: 11–2). The claim does, however, seem to be important insofar as it links, like a buckle, the two fundamental oppositions (primary as against secondary rules; internal as against external aspects of rules) around which the whole of his normative legal theory revolves. But the giving of sociological hostages to fortune seems even more pronounced here than in the instances of sociological drift noted earlier in relation to Hart's theory. One writer refers to Hart's claims about the necessary attitudes of officials as a 'bizarre piece of prescriptive psychology' (Goodrich 1983: 260). A point reiterated frequently by Hart's more sociologically oriented critics since the first publication of his theory has been that to describe officials' views of the secondary rules in terms of a Hartian internal attitude is highly inadequate to represent the complex reality of official motivations (e.g. Hughes 1962). A defender of Hart might insist that the idea of the internal aspect of rules is intended not to represent the complexities of official compliance with secondary rules but merely to establish an analytical distinction between the discourse of 'insiders' and 'outsiders' in relation to a rule system. That those who understand rules 'internally' can reason with them in particular ways, using normative language which makes their discourse significantly different from that of outsiders is what is important here; motivations for obedience to the rules, and whether or not citizens or officials approve or disapprove of them, are wholly different matters.

Hart's Hermeneutics

Up to a point this is a plausible answer. Hart uses his internal-external distinction to assert that law cannot be explained adequately in purely behavioural (external) terms. The essential distinguishing character of rules is that they can be understood in normative terms (from an internal aspect). Law is to be understood not through any purely behavioural social science (observing and measuring behaviour) but by entering its mode of discourse and its ways of reasoning. This kind of empathetic understanding is sometimes referred to as *hermeneutic* understanding. There is, however, an ambiguity in Hart's original presentation of the internal and external aspects of rules. In order to understand rules from an internal standpoint must one actually be a committed insider within the legal system; that is, someone who personally accepts the rules as guides to conduct? Is the only other possible position that of the external observer who does not even recognise the normative character of legal rules? Or can one be an 'outside' observer (not actually, oneself, committed as a citizen within the legal order) who can nevertheless interpret and understand the rules, *as if* personally accepting them as guides to conduct?

Neil MacCormick, in a valuable analysis of Hart's ideas, has suggested the need for a third position, between the strict internal and external views of rules, to take account of the situation of an uncommitted observer who can nevertheless interpret law normatively and make what Raz has called 'detached statements' (Raz 1980: 236); that is, normative statements entailing no personal normative *commitment* to the legal system to which they relate. MacCormick (1981a: 38) terms this third position the hermeneutic point of view. Various passages in *The Concept of Law* might suggest that Hart assumed all along that the internal view of rules was one which could be understood by a hermeneutic observer (a legal theorist, for example) as well as by an official or citizen personally adopting the rules as guides for his and others' conduct (e.g. Hart 1961: 87). Yet Hart has recently recognised Raz's distinction between committed and detached statements as an important supplement to the ideas expressed in *The Concept of Law* (Hart 1982: 153–5). Further, he has adopted MacCormick's proposed third point of view as well as the term 'hermeneutic' to describe it (1983: 14).

These apparent concessions on Hart's part are significant. In 1961, when *The Concept of Law* was published, he saw, as the chief theoretical enemies which the idea of the internal aspect of rules was intended to address, all views of the legal system which tried to describe law (and especially judicial decision-making) in behavioural terms, that is from a viewpoint emphasising only the external aspect of rules[1]. The idea of the internal aspect entailed an insistence that a purely behavioural description of law was wholly inadequate. Yet Hart has always assumed that a descriptive account of the nature of law is possible (even, as noted earlier, a 'descriptive sociology'); the point being, however, that such a description must focus on law as having both internal and external aspects. Linguistic philosophy would provide the key to an understanding of the internal aspects. In 1961 it was perhaps not necessary to point out that a legal theory entailing understanding of the internal aspect of rules (the insider's perspective) could nevertheless be 'detached', uncommitted and concerned only with description, as regards the normative meaning of those rules. The only kind of analytical detachment Hart felt it necessary to argue for explicitly was the one Austin had insisted on: the analytical separation of law and morals – a matter to be considered in more detail in the next chapter. Recently, however, various writers and especially the American jurist Ronald Dworkin, have challenged the assumption that normative legal theory should aim at 'detached', objective description of law. An internal view of legal rules – that is, participation in the enterprise of legal interpretation – is viewed

---

[1]   Some main types of theory which Hart interprets as adopting this viewpoint on law are discussed in Chapter 7, below.

in these post-Hart theories as providing, in itself, knowledge of the nature of law. The only view of rules to be taken account of by the legal theorist thus becomes the internal view.

Dworkin's theses will be considered in Chapter 6. For the moment it is enough to recognise that the legal theory Hart advocates must now fight on a different front from that which existed when *The Concept of Law* was first published. The challenge to his approach now comes not from writers who advocate exclusive emphasis on the external (behavioural) aspect of law since it would be hard now to find any influential jurist (if ever there was one) who seriously argues that law can be understood in purely behavioural terms. The challenge which Hart now recognises is from theories which put exclusive emphasis on the internal (normative) aspect of law (cf. Hart 1987). Hence his need to make explicit what was always implicit in his thinking: that the hermeneutic point of view (the view appropriate to a Hartian legal theorist) is not identical with the committed internal view of a participant in the legal system. The legal theorist is not simply engaged in legal reasoning, but tries to *describe* and *objectively explain* the nature of legal reasoning. Hart's theory is most interesting and praiseworthy, indeed, for the balancing act it tries to sustain: the insistence that legal theory must be simultaneously 'inside' and 'outside' the law as a system of ideas. In Hart's approach, normative legal theory adopts the perspective of the legal insider, but it does so only in order to enable an objective, detached view of legal activities to recognise fully the normative character of law.

Judicial Decisions and the 'Open Texture' of Rules

Unfortunately, this favourable image of theoretical balance is not the one with which we can leave a discussion of Hart's concept of law. The defence that his various major categories and distinctions are purely analytical and therefore immune from sociological critique (cf. Hacker 1977: 12) is unsupportable. This is because Hart's method, as has been seen, is founded on the claim of linguistic philosophy that analytical categories and distinctions are to be given meaning only in the context of actual linguistic usages which themselves reflect social practices. Hart's empiricist method entails that concepts reflect social practices. What becomes important then is to ask how successfully conceptual analysis, in illuminating linguistic practice, helps reveal aspects of social reality. Adopting this yardstick it must be recognised that Hart's minimum conditions of existence of a legal system and the claims about officials' attitudes to secondary rules are ultimately sociological claims about the way people think and behave. Hart's minimum conditions of existence of a legal system are actually hypotheses about the sociological conditions under which a legal system maintains legitimacy or acceptance. These matters are addressed with a wealth of historical detail and empirical illustration in some of the most influential writings in the history of sociology[2]. In Hart's writings, however, they remain at the level of brief, highly generalised, and empirically unsupported philosophical speculation.

Again, therefore, it seems that Hart's empiricism directs him towards inquiries beyond the scope of normative legal theory. A further example of this tendency can be seen in his analysis of judicial decision-making and the 'open texture' of rules. Hart adopts the philosopher Friedrich Waismann's idea of the porosity or open texture of concepts to try to analyse the degree of certainty with which rules can be interpreted and applied. In considering the task of judicial decision-making this must be a vital concern for any theory such as Hart's which treats law as, in essence, an affair of rules. Surely, insofar as judges through their interpretations of law develop *new* law they cannot be *bound* by pre-existing rules? Rules may govern the means by which judicial law-making proceeds (for example, rules of precedent or jurisdiction) but the substantive content of judge-made law, by definition, is not covered by rules predating the relevant judicial decisions. Thus, Hart's theory admits that judges in certain circumstances may and do exercise *discretion* in legal interpretation. Existing rules plus judicial discretion are, therefore, the ingredients of judge-made law.

It then becomes essential to determine the relationship between rule and discretion. If it were to be admitted that judicial discretion is very extensive, or unpredictable, the model of law in terms of rules would collapse. Hart's empirical orientation forces him to recognise that rules are often, in practice, open to widely varying interpretations. But a theorist not wedded to the idea that rules are the central element of law might suggest that legal rules are effects or consequences of judicial or other official decisions, rather than the reverse. Thus, for Austin, as has been seen in Chapter 3, law consists, strictly speaking, not of rules but of commands, and judicial decisions are a species of delegated sovereign commands. Whether these decisions embody wide or severely limited discretion they can be seen as having a uniform character. Discretion is not a fundamental problem for Austin in the way it tends to be for a model of law in terms of rules.

[2]   See Weber 1978: Part I ch 3, Part II chs 10, 11, 14, 15.

Hart tries to solve the problem of maintaining the centrality of rules in his concept of law by identifying two components of them – a 'core' of settled meaning and a 'penumbra' of uncertainty (Hart 1958: 63–4). The 'life of the law consists to a very large extent' in guidance by 'determinate rules' (1961: 132). But in penumbral cases 'it is clear that the rule-making authority must exercise a discretion, and there is no possibility of treating the question raised by the various cases as if there were one uniquely correct answer to be found, as distinct from an answer which is a reasonable compromise between many conflicting interests' (1961: 128).

As with the question of whether legal theory should view law 'internally' or 'externally', Hart seeks a balanced mid-position on the question of interpretation. Law is neither the 'noble dream' of a consistent, complete set of rules whose meaning is ultimately conclusively determinable; neither is it the 'nightmare' of rule-free judicial discretion (Hart 1977). But this 'reasonable' position betrays the tension between Hart's analytical objectives and the empiricist manner in which they are pursued. His analytical model impels him to put rules in centre position in his theory. Consequently the core of certainty in them is strongly emphasised in *The Concept of Law*: the result of the English doctrine of precedent has been to produce a set of rules 'of which a vast number. . . are as determinate as any statutory rule'; the operations of courts are 'unquestionably rule-governed. . . over the vast, central areas of the law' (1961: 132, 150).

On the other hand, what determines the areas of core and penumbra – of certainty and uncertainty – in rules? Hart's empirical method entails that this can be determined only by actual social (linguistic) practices. Concepts, as has been seen earlier, are not considered to have meaning in isolation from the specific contexts in which they are used. Particular situations 'do not await us already marked off from each other, and labelled as instances of the general rule. . . nor can the rule itself step forward to claim its own instances' (1961: 123). Thus, certainty in rules is not a feature of rules themselves but of the social practices in which they are used. It follows that the distinction between core and penumbra is not an analytical distinction referring to aspects of the structure of rules; it is a representation of social practices.

The important point, then, is that it is not rules which govern and provide certainty according to this line of thinking; certainty derives from the relatively settled conventions of usage and practice which reflect a degree of social consensus. As with most aspects of Hart's legal theory, categories which are presented as analytical ultimately reveal themselves as references to presumed social facts. But there is still no concern to examine the relevant matters sociologically rather than in terms of philosophical speculation. Thus there is no real clarification of the relationship between rule and discretion, certainty and uncertainty in law. While portraying the problem as an analytical one, Hart actually sets it up as a sociological one. Yet no sociological inquiry is made into the actual conditions (relating, for example, to the organisation and character of the judiciary) under which interpretive agreement about the meaning of legal rules becomes possible or becomes problematic.

Kelsen's Conceptualism

Hart's work has had and continues to have great influence in Anglo-American legal philosophy. The same is true also of the prolific writings of Hans Kelsen. Yet they have never had the same centrality despite being among the most profound contributions to legal theory in the present century. One reason is that Kelsen's writings are informed to a considerable extent by the traditions of continental civil law thought rather than the specific experiences of Anglo-American common law. This can be only a partial explanation, however. After fleeing from Nazi Germany to Switzerland in the 1930s, Kelsen eventually settled in the United States and spent the remaining three decades of his life there (he died in 1973), holding the position of professor of political science at the University of California until his retirement in 1952. Thus, he worked for a considerable period – writing prolifically – in an Anglo-American environment. Equally, he made considerable efforts to explain and interpret his ideas in relation to Anglo-American legal and political institutions and the major tendencies of Anglo-American legal philosophy.

The main reason why Kelsen has remained an outsider is that his approach to theory is a thoroughly *conceptualist* one, in the sense explained earlier in this chapter. In this respect it runs counter to ideas rooted in the common law tradition, as well as, perhaps, counter to broader cultural tendencies in Britain and America. Whatever view we take of classical common law thought, it remains the case that the Anglo-American common law tradition emphasises piecemeal, case-by-case legal development, and what the sociologist Max Weber termed 'empirical law-finding' (cf. Weber 1978: 785–8). That is to say, concepts in common law are not imposed on the law but are assumed to be drawn from the detail of case-by-case legal experience. Legal ideas are found empirically in the practical business of deciding cases. Thus, the kind of empiricism in legal theory which has been treated as a theme of the earlier part of this chapter, actually reflects in a direct way major underlying assumptions about common law methods – even if in analytical jurisprudence it gives rise to theories which appear to supplant classical common law thought.

Yet Kelsen is a most instructive outsider. Given this book's exclusive concern with Anglo-American legal philosophy, the importance of his normative legal theory is in the contrast of methods which it offers when set against Hart's empiricism. As will appear, Kelsen's conceptualism avoids some of the dilemmas which we have seen Hart's normative legal theory led into by its empiricist outlook. In addition, some political and professional ramifications of Hart's theory can be clarified by noting parallels in Kelsen's thinking and drawing on the rich and detailed political theory which accompanies Kelsen's legal philosophy. The following sections will be concerned with these matters.

Kelsen's conceptualism reflects the influence of continental neo-Kantian philosophy. Knowledge, according to this tradition, is not simply given by experience. We only begin to understand empirical reality by imposing concepts on it which enable us to organise as meaningful what we observe. Concepts do not reflect experience; they organise it and make it intelligible. Every science, every knowledge-field, must, therefore, create its own conceptual apparatus. Because of this necessity, each science, or form of systematic knowledge, is unique and distinct from all others. Consequently, legal science must have its own unique framework of concepts which cannot be shared or integrated with those of other sciences. It follows, therefore, that Kelsen wholly rejects what he calls syncretism of methods; the 'uncritical mixture of methodically different disciplines' (Kelsen 1967: 1). The unique nature of legal science is determined by its subject-matter, law, and Kelsen, like Hart, sees one of the most important characteristics of law as its normativity. Law is a matter of 'ought-propositions' or norms. 'By "norm" we mean that something ought to be or ought to happen, especially that a human being ought to behave in a specific way' (Kelsen 1967: 4). Legal science must be a normative science.

Several consequences of these positions immediately highlight differences from Hart's approach. First, whereas, as has been seen, Hart's normative legal theory continually drifts towards sociology (yet holds back from serious sociological inquiries), Kelsen's rejection of syncretism entails that there can be no link of any kind between the legal theory he develops, as the theory of a purely legal science, and sociology. They are totally different conceptual frameworks appropriate to different subject-matter. Legal theory, as Kelsen understands it, must therefore be purified of all foreign concepts and methods. Indeed the name which Kelsen gives to his normative legal theory is *the pure theory of law*. It is unconcerned with law as it should or might be – for that would be the concern of politics or moral philosophy. Its subject-matter is positive law in general. Kelsen's conceptualism entails that the purpose of the pure theory of law is to provide a set of interpretive concepts which make it possible to organise knowledge about the law of particular legal systems. The theory does not itself provide that knowledge. The pure theory of law merely provides the concepts which normative legal science can use in describing the actual norms of a particular legal system. But this task is, in Kelsen's view, nonetheless essential. It provides the framework of ideas on which law as an intellectual discipline and professional practice is based.

Thus, there is no suggestion that the concepts of the pure theory of law are derived from or reflect empirical reality – the circumstances of actual legal systems. Empiricism, together with the syncretism of methods which tends to go with it, is firmly rejected. In other respects, however, the thrust of Kelsen's theory is similar to Hart's. Both are committed to the idea of a legal theory which provides objective, detached explanation of the character of law and both see the recognition of law's normative character (in Hart's terms, the internal aspect of rules) as essential to that theoretical explanation. Originally Kelsen wholly rejected behavioural (which he equates with sociological) explanations of law. Thus, in his early writings a sociology of law is treated as impossible and misguided since it fundamentally mistakes the nature of law, ignoring its essential normative character.

Later, however, he adopted a view more in keeping with his neo-Kantian outlook. Treating sociology as the science whose methods and concepts are created specifically to interpret causes and effects of social behaviour, he came to recognise that a sociology of law is possible and important insofar as it concerns itself with explaining 'the actual conduct of the individuals who create, apply and obey the law'; it 'must investigate the ideologies by which men are influenced in their law-creating and law-applying activities' (Kelsen 1941b: 271). Among its most important and promising tasks, in Kelsen's view, is the critical analysis of the idea of justice as an ideology. But such investigations would be *wholly distinct* from those framed by the pure theory of law. While the latter treats law as norm and constructs concepts appropriate to that subject matter, sociology of law takes behaviour in legal contexts as its concern and constructs the wholly different concepts appropriate to causal analysis of that material.

One important virtue of Kelsen's method is that by recognising explicitly that normative legal theory's task is to construct concepts to make possible the interpretation of law as a structure of norms he avoids the persistent ambiguities of many of Hart's conceptual formulations. Kelsen's work emphasises the need for conceptual rigour because it recognises straightforwardly that normative legal theory is deliberately *constructed* to provide a means of interpreting actual law. By contrast, because Hart's concepts are presented as discovered in actual linguistic practices or social situations they inherit the vagueness and indeterminacy of many of those practices and situations or are dogged by controversy whenever sociological evidence of the nature of the practices and situations is demanded.

'The Machine Now Runs By Itself'

In many respects, Kelsen's image of law, as portrayed through his pure theory, is similar to Hart's, despite the radical differences in methods adopted by the two jurists. Frequently, in his writings, Kelsen remarks on the 'most significant peculiarity' of law that it regulates its own creation[3]. That is, the creation of legal norms is authorised by other legal norms. The decision of a judge, creating a norm governing the circumstances to which the decision relates, is authorised by norms defining the court's jurisdiction. Such norms may be expressed in a statute, the enactment of which was authorised by other, more fundamental norms, defining the proper procedures for legislation. Those norms may be contained in a constitution, which was itself established on the authority of the norms contained in an earlier constitution. The process by which 'higher', more general norms authorise the creation of 'lower', more specific ones is termed, in Kelsen's theory, 'concretisation'.

There is no suggestion that the process of norm creation is governed *only* by other norms. Just as Hart recognises judicial discretion as the 'non-legal' element which necessarily supplements the legal element of rules in judicial interpretation and development of law, so Kelsen notes that 'every law-applying act is only partly determined by law and partly undetermined' (1967: 349). Law regulates its own creation but does not determine conclusively its own content: 'There is simply no method. . . by which only one of several meanings of a norm may gain the distinction of being

---

[3]   See e.g. Kelsen 1967: 71, 221; 1945: 124, 126, 132, 198, 354.

the only "correct" one' (1967: 352). Nevertheless the non-legal determinants of new law (for Hart, discretion; for Kelsen, politics) are beyond the scope of the pure theory of law. Its concern is only to know *law*, not politics or any of the miriad considerations that may shape legal change or legal interpretation.

This is a wholly uncompromising position. Like Hart's concept of law in terms of primary and secondary rules, Kelsen's view of law as a structure of norms authorising their own creation, modification and destruction provides a picture of law from which human beings have almost disappeared.

At the pinnacle of Hart's legal system of rules is the rule of recognition validating all other legal rules. The actions and attitudes of officials and citizens are taken into account in Hart's theory merely to identify the system of rules as being in existence. Hart's empiricism forces him to identify the rule of recognition as an actual legal or constitutional rule or cluster of rules found in actual legal systems. Viewed externally the rule of recognition is a social fact; the observable fact that officials are acting on the basis of uniform presuppositions about what counts as valid law. Viewed internally it is the presupposition made by 'insiders' of the legal system of the validity of legal rules.

By contrast, Kelsen's conceptualism requires no such search for some ultimate legal rule, in each actually existing legal system, providing validity for all other rules in the system. Kelsen postulates a 'basic norm' (*Grundnorm*) which gives validity to (authorises the creation of) all legal rules. But this is, as with all the concepts of the pure theory of law, deliberately created as a theoretical idea (not found in experience) for a specific theoretical purpose. The purpose of Kelsen's basic norm is to portray the unity of the legal system, the fact that all its norms trace validity from a single source and must do so if they are to be considered part of the same legal system. Thus, if the sequence of authorisation of norms is traced back from the court's decision, through the statutory norms providing jurisdiction, through the constitutional norms authorising enactment of the statute, to the original constitution, the pure theory of law deliberately postulates a further single norm 'standing behind' and giving validity to the original constitution. The basic norm is, thus, explicitly, a presupposition or hypothesis (Kelsen 1967: 204) – a theoretical necessity. In later writings Kelsen terms it a fiction.

It is not appropriate in a book devoted specifically to Anglo-American legal theory to discuss in detail the complexities surrounding Kelsen's ideas. It is enough to note some contrasts between the basic norm and the rule of recognition which illustrate the different results of Kelsen's conceptualism as compared with Hart's empiricism. The basic norm is postulated by Kelsen as *pre-legal*, like Austin's sovereign, rather than legal as with Hart's rule of recognition. For Kelsen this is obviously the case because the basic norm is nothing more than the *assumption* on the basis of which an original constitution, or whatever is the highest legal source of the particular legal system, is treated as valid. Legal norms derive their validity from other legal norms. Eventually this process of attributing validity must come to a halt. The basic norm is the necessary theoretical postulate of the validity of the norms of the original constitution.

Because it is only a conceptualisation of the pre-legal sources of validity of law its exact formulation as a theoretical matter is not very important and is likely to be purely formal: for example, 'coercion of man against man ought to be exercised in the manner and under the conditions determined by the historically first constitition' (Kelsen 1967: 50). The content of the basic norm becomes significant only when the pure theory of law is applied to analyse an actual legal system. Then, of course, it may be important to try to identify the exact content of the normative presupposition on which the ultimate validity of the legal system depends. For a legal system to exist its basic norm must be actually presupposed to be valid (1967: 208–12), that is, presupposed or acted upon in much the same way that Hart's rule of recognition is assumed to be. But the crucial point is that for Kelsen there is no necessity to identify an actual fundamental rule of the legal system which provides the system's unifying criterion of validity. Hart's attempt to ground concepts in empirical experience necessitates this identification. For Kelsen all that is necessary is to recognise that legal science must treat law as a unity, since legal practice and law as an intellectual discipline presuppose the possibility of relating in terms of legal logic all the norms of a single legal system. Because of this necessity the pure theory of law must create the concept of the basic norm to represent the unity of a legal system. To say that a basic norm is effective means only that this unity is actually being presupposed in legal thought and practice.

Beyond these methodological differences the parallels in Hart's and Kelsen's thinking are clear. Austin's idea of law as an expression of political power has been replaced in both theories with the idea of law as a relatively self-contained system of rules or norms. In Kelsen's theory the unity of the legal system, expressed in a single basic norm from which all other legal norms derive, entailed, until the last phase of his work, that no contradiction between norms within the same system was possible. If norms contradicted each other, one of them, at least, could not be valid. Equally Kelsen denies the possibility of gaps in the law (1967: 245–50). Where the norms of the legal system make no provision they can be treated as permitting what they do not proscribe. At the same time, if a matter relating to a supposed gap in the law is brought before an appropriate law-interpreting agency, such as a court, the court can determine the legal position relating to that matter. Hence the supposed gap is closed. Thus law, as portrayed by Kelsen's normative legal theory, becomes a web of normative ideas from which human agency is excluded. Neither Kelsen nor Hart deny the human, creative element in law. But in neither theory is there a place to analyse it. In Hart's case this is because it is pushed outside the model of rules and designated as discretion; in Kelsen's case it is because the pure theory of law develops concepts only for the purpose of analysing law as norms and assigns all concern with human behaviour to other disciplines (such as sociology, political science or psychology) whose concepts and methods are seen as having no possibility of influencing or interacting with those of legal science.

What has appeared to happen in this twentieth century normative legal theory is well expressed by the German jurist Carl Schmitt: 'The sovereign. . . the engineer of the great machine [of law], has been radically pushed aside. The machine now runs by itself' (Schmitt 1985: 48).

Democracy and the Rule of Law

Plainly, in any realistic view of law, the machine does *not* run by itself. There are, no less than in Austin's time, people in positions of power pulling its levers. What is the real significance, then, of this emphasis on the self-regulating character of modern law? Its purpose surely is to demonstrate law's integrity as an independent intellectual field and as a specialised field of professional practice. The ideas of unity and system in law, which were noted in Chapter 1 as having considerable importance for the conception of law as a field of professional knowledge and practice, are presented in both Hart's and Kelsen's theories in ways which make strenuous efforts to exclude political considerations or any explicit recognition that law is an expression of political power. Admittedly, neither theory is concerned to prescribe how law ought to be; both purport only to describe (in Hart's case) or provide the conceptual means of interpreting (in Kelsen's) law as it is. Thus, neither theory claims that law *should* be 'above' politics. They do not explicitly advocate the ideal of the Rule of Law – that governmental action should be controlled by known rules preventing arbitrariness – as something which should guide legal and political practice. But because both theories present a de-politicised image of law and claim that such an image is an appropriate way to view law, they implicitly suggest that law can have a unity, system and integrity independent of politics and, therefore, that the idea of the Rule of Law is in some sense built into the very notion of law.

In Kelsen's theory this is obvious. He refuses to recognise 'the state' as an entity standing above law and creating law. The state is merely *the legal order itself* viewed from a certain standpoint. State functions, offices and jurisdictions are all defined by legal norms insofar as legitimate authority attaches to them. They have no identify apart from the content of the legal norms defining them. Thus, Kelsen makes the, at first surprising, claim that every state is a *Rechtsstaat*, a state governed by law (1967: 313). To this extent the notion of the Rule of Law is reduced to a pure issue of semantics.

There is, however, much more to the matter than that. Reading both Hart's and Kelsen's work one gains the impression that the need for legal controls on arbitrary powers of government is a matter of great political concern to both of them. When Kelsen writes (1955: 77–80) of the Rule of Law as a substantive idea of effectively controlling governmental arbitrariness he has no illusions about the difficulties of doing so. A major reason why he refuses to accept the state as an entity above law is because, when it is recognised as such, appalling things can be done in its name: 'whereas the individual as such is in no way thought entitled to coerce others, to dominate or even kill them, it is nevertheless his supreme right to do all this in the name of God, the nation or the state, which for that very reason he loves, and lovingly identifies with, as "his" God, "his" nation and "his" state' (Kelsen 1973: 67).

These sentiments, expressed in an article first published at the beginning of the 1920s, suggest a firm rejection of all supra-individual forms – such as the state – insofar as these are treated as entities possessing independent significance; that is, a significance beyond that of the individual human beings who make use of these forms in one way or another. Thus, Kelsen adds that, if the masks are stripped away from actors on the political stage and we no longer see the impersonal state 'condemning and making war', what is revealed is the reality of 'men putting coercion on other men' (1973: 67). Such comments reveal something of Kelsen's commitment to political freedom and his hostility to all forms of autocracy justified by appeals to an entity – state, God, nation – transcending mere individuals and claiming dominion over them. Given such an outlook it is hardly surprising that his political theory forcefully defends the ideal of democracy as government (directly or by means of representatives) by the people as individual citizens.

This side of Kelsen's thinking, expressed eloquently in his political writings, is totally ignored in almost all Anglo-American discussions of his legal philosophy. Yet it provides an essential context for understanding the full significance of the methods underlying his pure theory of law. Kelsen's conceptualism assumes, as has been seen, that each science or intellectual discipline must create its own concepts by which to secure knowledge of its subject-matter. All 'truth' is therefore relative to the particular science concerned, because knowledge-claims can only be evaluated within the context of the particular science within which they are made. Each separate science alone provides the concepts which give meaning to, and allow evaluation of, the knowledge-claims made within it. Thus, the method of the pure theory of law denies that there is such a thing as 'absolute' truth. But it asserts that the knowledge produced within particular sciences, for their particular purposes, is no less valuable as a result. And Kelsen claims that philosophical relativism of this kind, with its denial of absolutes, correlates in many important ways with political relativism – the idea that there are no absolute political values (Kelsen 1955). Democracy is the most appropriate practical recognition of political relativism. Democracy accepts that a conflict between political values can only properly be resolved by taking the majority view for the time being. But democracy equally protects the minority's right to oppose that view because today's minority may be tomorrow's majority which will be no less entitled to insist on the 'correctness' of its views. Underlying democracy is a commitment to tolerance – an ideal to which Kelsen frequently refers. Democracy is the political embodiment of the tolerance of opposed views.

Thus, the pure theory of law portrays a legal system not as the expression of supreme political values but as a framework of norms which 'always has more or less the character of a compromise' (Kelsen 1973: 76). To the extent that law forms itself as a system of norms whose integrity as a system can be recognised by an independent legal science (founded on the concepts of the pure theory of law) it is not the mere servant of politics but a structure governed by its own logic which makes possible the compromise of individual wills. To this extent, law is the essential social technique available to harness coercion to make possible civilised co-existence of individuals within a society (Kelsen 1941a). From the point of view of the pure theory of law, therefore, the political authority of the state is a mere derivative of law. The pure theory of law dissolves away the state's legitimacy as a potential agency of intolerance. It insists that the state is properly seen as merely the effect of the structure of norms governing the relationships of individual human beings. For Kelsen the doctrine of sovereignty is harmful precisely because it asserts the existence of a supreme entity above law (1973: 71).

Equally, the pure theory of law does its best to dissolve away the *nation*, as a supreme entity, too. Kelsen argues that the logic of the pure theory leads to the recognition of international law as a single supreme legal system; one in which the norms presented as the basic norms of national or municipal legal systems now appear in a new light – as subordinate norms within the international legal order whose validity is ultimately governed by a basic norm of international law. By contrast, Austin's theory of law as the sovereign's command denied that international law should be considered law at all, but only positive morality, because only independent political societies (states) have sovereigns to command law. No sovereign of an international community exists. Kelsen's rejection of sovereignty as a concept entails not only a rejection of the claim that the state is above law but also of the claim that there can be no higher political allegiance and legal obligation than to the nation state.

As for the appeal to 'God on our side', the third source (with 'state' and 'nation') of autocracy and intolerance specifically mentioned by Kelsen in the passage quoted earlier, it is firmly excluded by the pure theory of law because, as its author never tires of insisting, the pure theory is not concerned with debates about justice. It cannot be so concerned because, in Kelsen's view, such debates do not lend themselves to scientific resolution. 'If the history of human thought proves anything, it is the futility of the attempt to establish, in the way of rational considerations, an absolutely correct standard of human behaviour, and that means a standard of behaviour as the only just one, excluding the possibility of considering the opposite standard to be just too' (Kelsen 1957: 21). Again Kelsen's message is the same: a denial of absolutes; a denial which in many circumstances enjoins tolerance as the wise and courageous response to the relativity of values. The pure theory of law tries to provide concepts for an autonomous science of law (the systematic professional knowledge of lawyers) which is not the servant of autocracy but dignifies law by insisting on its integrity as a normative system.

No comparable explicit political theory is contained in Hart's major writings. Nevertheless a commitment to liberal individualism and an aversion to authoritarianism – attitudes not dissimilar to Kelsen's – are apparent; for example, in his writings on responsibility and the functions of criminal law (Hart 1963; Hart 1968). Some of Hart's warmest praise for Bentham is with regard to Bentham's discussions of elements of the Rule of Law and the liberal constitutional state: 'One by one in Bentham's works you can identify the elements of the *Rechtsstaat*. . . Here are liberty of speech, and of press, the right of association, the need that laws should be published and made widely known before they are enforced, the need to control administrative agencies, and the importance of the principle of legality, *nulla poene sine lege*' (Hart 1958: 51). The list might be considered a summary of the standard concerns of many lawyers in mid-twentieth century Britain, at the time Hart was developing his normative legal theory, about the legal framework of the interventionist welfare state. Kelsen's pure theory purports to demonstrate the integrity of legal science – lawyers' methods of analysis of law – in opposition to the twentieth century absolutisms (for example, fascism or Stalinism) which have claimed it as merely an appendage of politics. In a parallel manner, Hart provides the reassurance of a concept of law entirely in terms of rules. He gives an implicit theoretical promise that despite the proliferation of discretionary regulation and administrative structures of the modern state it is still possible to distinguish from them the rules which constitute not only the familiar stock of lawyers' knowledge, but also the formal political guarantees of autonomous citizenship and the Rule of Law.

Conclusion

How, finally, should we assess the developments in legal philosophy which have been discussed in this chapter? In Kelsen's case it can be said that the sophistication of method which underpins his theory, the range of its reference and his single-minded devotion to explaining the possibility of an autonomous science of law, ensure that his writings address illuminatingly a host of issues which found no place in Austin's thought. The scope of Kelsen's work is simply different from that of Austin's. Yet, as has been seen, Kelsen's political theory and his particular conception of the professional and intellectual requirements of an autonomous discipline of law, may help significantly to illuminate major points at which his claims appear to conflict directly with those of Hart or Austin.

It is harder to assess Hart's advance on Austin. Most

commentators today have no doubt that his theory is better – in the sense of having more explanatory power. But the content and approach of this chapter should suggest that the question of what makes a theory 'better' is a complex one within the field of normative legal theory. Hart's progress beyond Austin has been portrayed here primarily as the construction of theory which highlights a set of political and professional concerns about law which are significantly different from those of Austin. Dicey defined the central political problem of his late-nineteenth century era (in which Austin's theory had its greatest impact) as how 'to give constitutions resting on the will of the people the stability and permanence which has hitherto been found only in monarchical or aristocratic states' (quoted in Sugarman 1983: 109). This concern to contain the potentially disruptive effects of democracy seems to explain the shape of much of Austin's theory, which puts questions of political power in central place through the concept of sovereignty, sees liberty as a by-product of rational government, and is developed in the context of a belief in the virtues of government by elites. Equally, in legal professional terms, the need Austin recognised was that of establishing a scientific foundation of legal knowledge which would replace classical common law thought and firmly relate the structure of professional legal knowledge to the reality of the political authority of the centralised modern state. The themes of liberal individualism, democracy and citizenship, and the importance of the Rule of Law as a demarcation of law from politics are not Austin's. Their reflection in Hart's (and Kelsen's) work obviously marks a significant political advance on Austin in the sense of a recognition of vitally important modern concerns.

Much of normative legal theory has 'progressed' by emphasising felt concerns of its time, rather than by providing theories that can be considered better than earlier ones in some absolute sense. Thus, if Hart and Kelsen can be interpreted as addressing lacunae in the range of Austin's concerns, the theory to be considered in the next chapter appears, correspondingly, to address important political and professional concerns beyond those reflected in their work.

5   The Appeal of Natural Law

It might seem that analytical jurisprudence has made redundant the ideas and perspectives of classical common law thought with which Chapter 2 was concerned. But this book's discussion of the development of English analytical jurisprudence in the writings of Bentham, Austin and Hart and the associated development reflected in Kelsen's work has tried to show that normative legal theory does not necessarily progress through a straightforward superseding of inadequate theory by better theory addressing the same concerns. Rather, it sometimes shows important shifts of emphasis and *altered* concerns. These, in turn, may be the result of felt political or professional necessities. Analytical jurisprudence can be understood in part as reflecting a demand for a systematic, rational legal science to underpin modern legal professionalism and to accommodate the political idea of law as a technical instrument of government in modern western states. Classical common law thought flourished in a different era with different preoccupations. Nevertheless, analytical jurisprudence has not necessarily provided a fully adequate perspective from which to view contemporary Anglo-American law. The modern so-called 'natural law' theory to be considered in this chapter can be viewed as, in part, an attempt to push the methods of analytical jurisprudence to conclusions more satisfactory in various ways than those the analytical jurists themselves typically reach. At the same time it can be seen as, in part, a means of recovering certain themes in classical common law thought which analytical jurisprudence seems to have largely relegated to the sidelines of theoretical concern.

Legal Positivism and Natural Law

One aspect of the aspiration towards a 'science' of law reflected in the work of such different writers as Bentham, Austin, Hart and Kelsen is the insistence on an analytical separation of law from morality. In no case does this imply that morality is unimportant. But it does entail the claim that clear thinking about the nature of law and its analytical structure necessitates treating it as a distinct phenomenon capable of being analysed without invoking moral judgments. Hence, as Austin explains in a famous passage: 'The existence of law is one thing; its merit or demerit is another. Whether it be or be not is one enquiry; whether it be or be not conformable to an assumed standard, is a different enquiry. A law, which actually exists, is a law, though we happen to dislike it. . . This truth, when formally announced as an abstract proposition, is so simple and glaring that it seems idle to insist upon it. But simple and glaring as it is. . . the enumeration of the instances in which it has been forgotten would fill a volume' (Austin 1832: 184).

So Austin, like Bentham before him, criticises Blackstone for continually confusing legal and moral analysis in his *Commentaries*; for treating as law what he thought *ought* to be law; for declaring that human laws are invalid if contrary to the laws of God; for asserting that all human laws derive validity only from God's superior law (cf. Blackstone 1809 I: 41). The invocation of moral precepts – whether or not linked to a supra-human authority such as the will or law of God – as part of the criteria of the validity of man-made law seemed to Bentham and Austin to be dangerous. It prevented an objective, 'scientific' analysis of the nature of law as a human creation, and a clear set of indisputably objective criteria for determining which regulations should be recognised as possessing the authority of law. It left such matters to ethical speculation. Since ethical views vary, the way is opened for anyone to claim the right to 'second guess' the authority of law and state. Danger lies also in another direction, according to Bentham. To confuse legal and moral authority allows reactionaries to claim 'this is the law; therefore it must be right'; existing law is assumed to possess not only authority as law but also moral authority. Blackstone's primary failing in Bentham's eyes was, thus, his tendency to merge legal and moral authority, which went along with a complacency implying that English law as expounded in the *Commentaries* was the best of all law for the best of all possible worlds (Bentham 1977: 498–9; Hart 1958: 53).

This chapter is concerned with the claim of the major analytical jurists that law and morality should be clearly separated for purposes of analysis, and with some important challenges to that claim. Since the term analytical jurisprudence refers only to an aspiration and effort to analyse systematically law's conceptual structures, on the basis that they are worthy of study in their own right as distinct objects of analysis, it does not *necessarily* demand this law-morality separation. So, although writers who have considered themselves or been considered to be analytical jurists have typically subscribed to the separation of law and morality, it is convenient to use a more specific term to refer to the adoption of this analytical separation. As has been seen, Austin treated positive law as the appropriate focus of legal science and distinguished it from all moral rules or principles not specifically 'set down' (posited) or legislated in some form but merely accepted, as well as from (religious) rules or principles attributed to some supra-human authority. Thus, the term now generally used to refer to insistence on the separation of law and morality is *legal positivism*. It is sometimes used imprecisely to refer also to a number of actual or supposed characteristics of analytical jurisprudence (cf. Hart 1958: 57–8). In this chapter, however, legal positivism will be taken to mean specifically the insistence by Bentham, Austin, Hart, Kelsen and many other jurists on the necessity of analytically separating normative legal theory's inquiries into the nature of law from inquiries into its moral worth.

In contrast to legal positivism stands a tradition of thought adopting an apparently diametrically opposed position – that law cannot be properly understood except in moral terms; that it is fundamentally a moral phenomenon; that questions of law's nature and existence cannot be isolated from questions about its moral worth. This tradition is usually termed *natural law theory*. Its history extends through at least 2,500 years of Western philosophy. One of its most powerful themes (though an ambiguous one, as will appear) is expressed in the declaration that *lex iniusta non est lex* – an unjust law is no law at all. It may well be that statements like this in the history of natural law theory have never meant what they seem, at face value, to mean (Finnis 1980: 363–6). Nevertheless, they do suggest the persistent claim that questions about the nature of law and the conditions of its existence as an authoritative normative order cannot be treated in isolation from questions about its moral foundations. Thus typically, in many different ways throughout its long history, natural law theory has postulated the existence of moral principles having a validity and authority independent of human enactment, and which can be thought of as a 'higher' or more fundamental law against which the worth or authority of human law can be judged. This fundamental 'natural law' is variously seen as derived from human nature, the natural conditions of existence of humanity, the natural order of the universe, or the eternal law of God. The method of discovering it is usually claimed to be human reason. Natural law thus requires no human legislator. Yet it stands in judgment on the law created by human legislators.

Natural Law and Classical Common Law Thought

Why might this dispute about the relations of law and morality bear on the question of whether any of the perspectives or concerns of classical common law thought survive their displacement by positivist analytical jurisprudence, from Bentham onwards? As was seen in Chapter 2, classical common law thought assumed various sources of law's authority. Law was seen as rooted in immemorial custom, or community life; in a transcendent reason, or the accumulation of ancient wisdom greater than that of any individual. By contrast, Bentham's and Austin's writings ground law's authority in the existence of habitual obedience to a sovereign, a purportedly objective 'test' to distinguish law from non-law and identify legal authority. Hart and Kelsen focus on the fact of social acceptance of a rule of recognition or a basic norm as the fundamental prerequisite for a determination of legal authority. Positivist theories attempt to provide criteria of the 'legal' and of law's authority in specific formal conditions which avoid vague ideas of the nature of the community or of social organisation, or of some transcendent reason. Because common law thought identified the source of legal authority, not in the state or sovereign or in rule-governed procedures of legal enactment but in reason or community, it allowed at various times, as has been seen, for the possibility that – in theory, at least – some legislation or judicial decisions could be void either as abuses of legal authority or as misstatements of the law.

Given this facet of classical common law thought it is unsurprising that at times it related closely to natural law ideas (Gough 1955: ch 3; Haines 1930: ch 2), which also claimed the possibility of evaluating law's authority before the tribunal of reason. The notion of common law as something not residing in rules but in more fundamental principles expressing a transcendent reason or ancient wisdom had close affinities with natural law doctrines asserting the existence of some higher (moral) law governing and providing ultimate authority for the ordinary rules of human (positive) law. On the other hand, natural law theory was always a two-edged sword. In English history it was used to defend the divine right of the monarch, as expressed in prerogatives, against the claims of common law (Pocock 1957: 55). Equally, it could be used to assert limits on, or a limiting interpretation of, the powers of Parliament, as in Coke's famous pronouncements in *Calvin's Case* (1608) (Gough 1955: 44–5). But appeals to natural law as a set of principles which could control the substance of human law ceased to be practically significant in England once parliamentary sovereignty was recognised. As classical common law thought had to accommodate and eventually give way to a view of law as created by political authority, so natural law thought gave way to legal positivism.

In the United States, natural law ideas proved important in the formative era of judicial interpretation of the Constitution, since the temptation to fill out the meaning of a written fundamental constitutional document by appealing to an unwritten fundamental natural law proved irresistible to the courts. Constitutional adjudication entrusted to a Supreme Court which assumed the authority to pronounce on the constitutional validity of legislation[1] raised special issues. Indeed, this may be one consideration which has made legal positivism somewhat less secure in modern American legal philosophy (as exemplified by Lon Fuller's work discussed later in this chapter, and the literature considered in Chapter 6) than it has been in England (but cf. Fuller 1940: 116–21).

Today, in the Anglo-American context, the fate of common law thought is not unconnected with that of natural law thought (although, outside the Anglo-American context, natural law's history must necessarily be understood in different terms). Common law thought has had to find a place, if at all, in an environment dominated by conceptions of law as posited by sovereign law-makers of various kinds or their delegates or agencies. Equally, natural law theory, insofar as it has survived at all in the Anglo-American legal world, has tended to locate itself in the interstices of legal positivism, accepting much in positivist analytical jurisprudence and seeking to supplement or correct, rather than dismiss out of hand, many of the ideas which have been the concern of Chapters 3 and 4.

Is Natural Law Dead?

Our concern is not with the long history of natural law theory in Western civilization but with its particular appearances in the modern Anglo-American legal context. In this perspective the decline of natural law theory can be dated conveniently from Bentham's attack on natural law ideas in Blackstone's *Commentaries*. Bentham's view that natural law was a 'formidable non-entity', and natural law reasoning a 'labyrinth of confusion' (Bentham 1977: 17, 20) based on moral prejudices, or unprovable speculations about human nature, went along with a profound

---

[1]   *Marbury v Madison* (1803) 1 Cranch 137.

political distrust of resonant phrases about the 'rights of man' enshrined in constitutional documents such as those inspired by the French Revolution of 1789. In a single line of positivist legal thinking in England, running from Bentham to A. V. Dicey's late nineteenth century work on *The Law of the Constitution*, specific positive rules of law providing clearly defined rights enforceable in the ordinary courts are contrasted favourably with 'practically worthless' (Dicey 1959: 256) broad declarations of the rights of man grounded in natural law conceptions but unenforced in practice. The rise of legal positivism is often associated with the nineteenth century prestige of 'science' in general and the aspiration to produce a specific legal science which has been noted in previous chapters. But more is at stake than that. It is not a change in attitudes to science, morality or religion which should be held primarily accountable for the decline of natural law thinking and the rise of modern legal positivism but a change in the nature of law itself and its political and professional environment.

Insofar as law became seen as an instrument of state policy – and in the utilitarian view an instrument of progress, if used with caution – it was revealed as an amoral and infinitely plastic device of government. Insofar as it regulated increasingly complex and differentiated Western societies it could be seen as, above all, a means of controlling the interplay of conflicting interests. The social theorist Max Weber, writing of nineteenth century developments, noted that: 'In consequence of both juridical rationalism and modern intellectual scepticism in general, the axioms of natural law have lost all capacity to provide the fundamental basis of a legal system. . . The disappearance of the old natural law conceptions has destroyed all possibility of providing the law with a metaphysical dignity by virtue of its immanent qualities. In the great majority of its most important provisions, it has been unmasked all too visibly, indeed, as the product or the technical means of a compromise between conflicting interests' (Weber 1978: 874–5). Such an interpretation of law as a compromise (above all, of economic interests) could be offered even for constitutions, such as that of the United States, which expressed principles purportedly grounded in ideas of 'natural rights' – truths declared to be self-evident because founded in the nature of mankind or of human society (see e.g. Levy 1987).

Classical natural law theory (broadly, that developed before the nineteenth century) sought a grounding for human law in unchanging principle, derived from 'nature' in some sense – the natural order of things, and usually held to be discoverable by reason. But two legal developments in Western societies have made it especially hard to accept any such approach to understanding the general character of law. One is legal doctrine's ever-increasing technicality and complexity. This is partly the result of law's methods of compromise between conflicting interests being extended to cover more and more sectors of social life, and being invoked in support of more, and more diverse, interests within the regulated populations. The other development is the deliberate use of law as a steering mechanism in society. This presupposes that law can change rapidly and continuously but also that it does so not as a reflection of enduring principle but as a mechanism aimed at *creating* principles of social order. These principles are, however, time-bound; pragmatic principles for the moment and the context, quite unlike timeless principles of natural law. As the social theorist Niklas Luhmann has written, 'it is increasingly questionable whether principles and ultimate perspectives [such as those of natural law] withdrawn from all variation and relativity' can 'provide an apt instrument for stabilisation and control' in modern societies (Luhmann 1982: 103).

Thus, the issue is not exactly that of being unable to agree about ultimate values; or that it is impossible any longer to accept that reason can discover universal 'truths' about human nature, or God's plan, or the hidden order of the universe or any such postulated foundation of natural law. The fact that agreement is difficult to reach does not show that principles of natural law are non-existent (cf. Finnis 1980: 24). As the political philosopher Leo Strauss remarks, 'by proving that there is no principle of justice that has not been denied somewhere or at some time, one has not yet proved that any given denial was justified or reasonable' (Strauss 1953: 9). The problem is that even if there *are* universal principles of natural law they may not offer a convincing guide or grounding for complex, highly technical and ever-changing modern law. After all, legal positivism does not deny that the substance of law can be subject to moral criticism[2]. The issue is not whether law can be morally evaluated but whether its *essential character* must be explained in moral terms. As an effort to provide such an explanation, natural law ideas are, in the view of many writers, 'devoid of any and every convincing theoretical justification' (Habermas 1974: 113).

---

[2]   Although for Kelsen, it would be not the law as such but the content of its norms which could be re-evaluated from a moral perspective: cf. Kelsen 1945: 374–5.

Natural Law and Legal Authority

None of this should necessarily lead to the conclusion that the problems which natural law theory addressed in the past have disappeared. Different kinds of classical natural law theory confronted a variety of issues. Among the most important are the following: what is the ultimate source of authority or legitimacy of human law and of human lawmakers; assuming this authority to be in essence a moral one is it limited and, if so, what are the limits and whence do they derive; by what criteria is it possible to evaluate the moral worth and authority of laws; how should one view laws created by abuse of lawmaking authority; in what circumstances, if any, do governments and laws cease to command moral authority with the result that any obligation to obey them ceases? If the word 'moral' is replaced in these questions with the word 'legal', all of them are ones which positivist analytical jurists have sought to answer in various ways. The concern which links positivist analytical jurisprudence and natural law theory is a concern with the nature of legal *authority*; with identifying its sources and its limits.

In positivist theory this concern is treated as raising technical issues. It is, above all, a matter of adequately conceptualising the highest authority of a legal system – for example, in terms of sovereignty, rule(s) of recognition, or basic norm – and determining the logical or practical relations between this authority concept and the other conceptual components of legal analysis and legal practice. For natural lawyers, however, the issues raised are moral ones. Almost inevitably, however, they turn into – or serve as cloaks for – political issues. This is because, while moral reasoning as applied to matters of private conscience may produce a coherent ethics to govern an individual's life, moral reasoning applied to such a social and public matter as legal regulation will typically produce prescriptions as to how the power of the state should be exercised or limited in controlling citizens' actions. Natural law theory, when taken seriously, becomes a force in political struggle – usually in defence of existing legal and political systems (by demonstrating their legitimacy grounded in 'reason' or 'nature'), but occasionally as a weapon of rebellion or revolution (cf. Kelsen 1945: 416–7).

As regards law's authority, therefore, the primary difference between positivist theory and natural law theory is not a polar opposition but a difference as to how far inquiries about law's ultimate authority should be taken, insofar as positivists are prepared to admit that law's authority over the individual can be evaluated in moral terms and natural lawyers are prepared to recognise political authorities (such as the state) as having general, inherent law-making authority. The medieval theologian St. Thomas Aquinas, whose writings are one of the primary sources of natural law theory, recognised the state's authority to legislate on numerous morally neutral matters about which natural law – the part of God's eternal law which can be grasped by mankind's unaided reason – would have nothing directly to say. The moral significance of this legislation would be only as part of the state's overall system of regulation which must, in Aquinas' view, serve the common good in order to conform with natural law.

Even as regards exercises of state authority which transgress dictates of natural law, issue is not necessarily clearly joined between classical natural law theory and legal positivism. Aquinas does not declare that all such laws lack validity or force. The philosopher John Finnis has argued that the 'central tradition of natural law theorising' – essentially that grounded in Aquinas' ideas and their antecedents – recognises the *legal* validity of unjust laws. That is, it recognises them as laws according to criteria (such as Hartian rules of recognition) that positivist theorists would emphasise (Finnis 1980: 364–5). Certainly, where laws represent an abuse of the authority indicated by natural law (as where they are not created for the common good but for the vain whim of the law-maker) one should, in Aquinas' view, obey God rather than the human lawmaker. But where laws are unjust merely because they do not conform to the established norms of human welfare (for example, because they impose an unjust distribution of burdens on those subject to the law) he suggests that it might be better to obey. Even if the laws do not bind in conscience one should avoid the corrupting example and civil disorder attendant on law-breaking (cf. Finnis 1980: 360).

This apparent hedging of bets on the moral obligation to obey unjust laws can be understood as an attempt to work out realistically the idea that the authority of a legal system as a whole is founded on its dedication to the 'common good'. Hence even where some laws are unjust, obligation to the system as a whole may remain insofar as it is of sufficient worth to justify its being protected against adverse effects arising from the corrupting example and disorder of law-breaking. The conflict between natural law and positivism thus tends to become a dispute as to whether the authority of a legal system as a whole can only be understood and judged in relation to some specific moral *purpose* (such as promotion of the common good) for which all legal systems exist. In general, the answer of natural lawyers is yes, and of positivists, no.

The 'Rebirth' of Natural Law

The key to the debate around natural law is thus the issue of the nature of legal authority. Natural law theory seems to become significant in debate at times when political and legal authority are under challenge. In times of stability positivist criteria of legal authority typically seem sufficient. In times of political turmoil or rapid political change they frequently seem inadequate; legal understanding seems to demand not merely technical guidance about the nature of valid law but moral or political theory. Questions as to what rules are valid as law become elements of ideological struggle; a matter of winning hearts and minds for or against established regimes. Some of the material in Chapter 4 hinted at this dimension of the determination of legal validity. Kelsen's efforts to establish a pure theory of law are, in part, an attempt to protect law from politicisation; an attempt made in full awareness of the difficulties of doing so 'when in great and important countries, under the rule of party dictatorships, some of the most prominent representatives of jurisprudence know no higher task than to serve – with their "science" – the political power of the moment' (Kelsen 1945: xvii). Indeed, Kelsen recognises that acceptance of a positivist science of law, such as his own, may be possible only 'in a period of social equilibrium' (1945: xvii).

Thus, it is tempting to suggest that the enduring appeal of natural law arises precisely from its willingness to confront directly the moral-political issues of legality which arise in times of disorder and conflict, while positivist analytical jurisprudence presupposes a political stability which it cannot, itself, explain or even consider as a subject within the concerns of legal philosophy. However, the situation is more complex than that because modern versions of natural law theory have been developed in relatively stable societies such as those of twentieth century Britain and the United States. This suggests that legal positivism is seen by natural law writers as inadequate even where political authority is not being seriously challenged. Perhaps the best way to understand the matter is to recognise that a degree of 'instability' as regards law-making authority is actually built into the structure of stable legal systems as portrayed by positivist analytical jurisprudence. This is because key questions about how law changes remain apparently impossible to address in modern positivist theory. This has been seen in Chapter 4 where it was noted that judicial law-making is, for Hart, the exercise of 'discretion', which his normative legal theory cannot really analyse, and is, for Kelsen, explicitly a matter of politics outside the compass of the pure theory of law.

Certain processes of law-making are, therefore, 'unstable' in the sense that what determines their outcome is a matter which positivist theory cannot subject to rational legal analysis. Given this state of affairs it is not surprising that natural law began to become a focus of attention again precisely at the time when modern legal positivism might be thought to have consolidated its victories. In 1911, the American jurist Roscoe Pound wrote: 'It is not an accident that something very like a resurrection of natural law is going on the world over' (Pound 1911: 162; cf. Pound 1921: 82) and Charles Grove Haines, analysing this twentieth century rebirth, saw, as an important reason for it, the felt need to elaborate principles of 'higher law' to guide the actions of judges in developing law (Haines 1930: 323–30). In the common law world where, traditionally, the role of the judge has seemed central within the legal system this matter is, no doubt, of special importance. It returns us to the link, noted earlier, between common law thought and natural law theory.

Nevertheless, part of the motivation for rethinking the relative virtues of legal positivism and natural law theory has come from twentieth century experience of tyranny and political instability, and especially from *ex post facto* reflection by jurists on the legal history of the German Third Reich (1933–45). Here issues of the ultimate authority of law are thrown into sharp relief and the theme of the Rule of Law, which was identified in Chapter 4 as an important political preoccupation informing modern analytical jurisprudence, is highlighted in a new form. In this context, the Rule of Law appears not just as a matter of protecting the autonomy of legal structures, processes and professional knowledge against politicisation by overweening state direction, but as a defence against uncontrolled terror and arbitrary violence. In the light of the Nazi experience, professional legal knowledge founded on a separation of law and morals – the positivist science of law – can be portrayed in a natural law perspective as, itself, a weapon of tyranny. This is precisely because it refuses to confront ultimate questions about the necessary *moral* criteria which state regulation must conform to in order to possess authority which a lawyer, or any other citizen, must recognise. The debate between positivists and natural lawyers, in this context, becomes a debate about the meaning of the Rule of Law. Should it be understood as the positivist aspiration to remove political and moral choices as far as possible from the determination of rights and duties; or should it be seen as the natural lawyer's insistence that morally acceptable purposes must govern the unavoidably political decisions as to what rights and duties will be held to exist?

Anglo-American Lessons From the Nazi Era

The historical legacy of the Nazi era has explicitly influenced modern Anglo-American debates between legal positivists and natural lawyers. One of the most direct confrontations, between the positivist H. L. A. Hart and the American natural lawyer Lon Fuller, centred in part on discussion of the way in which post-war German courts were apparently evaluating the legality of acts done during the Nazi period and which were claimed to be lawful on the basis of Nazi law (Hart 1958; Fuller 1958). More generally, the influence of emigré scholars, who fled from Germany during the 1930s and, in many cases, settled eventually in the United States, helped to feed into Anglo-American legal and political consciousness insights and dilemmas about the nature and authority of legal regulation which experience of Nazi practices and policies inspired (e.g. Neumann 1944; Neumann 1986; Kirchheimer 1961). In addition, reflection on the character of war crimes trials and their basis of legitimacy and on the ultimate foundation of the principles applied to judge guilt in them, undoubtedly made the issue of the nature and authority of Nazi regulation a matter of direct concern in the Anglo-American world and, at the same time, informed wider speculation about legal methods and reasoning (e.g. Shklar 1964: Part 2) and the adequacy of legal positivism (Paulson 1975).

The 1958 Hart-Fuller debate is a good starting point in considering the recent confrontation of legal positivism and modern natural law in the Anglo-American context, and especially as an introduction to Fuller's influential ideas which will be the concern of much of the remainder of this chapter. At the time of his exchange with Hart, Fuller was professor of jurisprudence at Harvard University, where he taught, with a break during the 1940s, for more than thirty years until his retirement in 1972. As his biographer notes, he is 'unquestionably the leading secular natural lawyer of the twentieth century in the English-speaking world' (Summers 1984: 151).

Hart argues that the positivists' analytical separation of law and morality is an aid to clear thinking; it avoids confusing legal and moral obligation. To say that a rule is a valid law (judged by such positivist criteria as its being the sovereign's command, authorised by a rule of recognition or imputed from a basic norm) merely asserts the existence of *legal* obligation. Whether one ought *morally* to disobey an unjust law is a matter about which positivist analytical jurisprudence can remain uncommitted, for moral issues are not within its province. For Fuller, however, such a view is both unrealistic and dangerous. It oversimplifies problems of obligation under a manifestly unjust regime and it sets up an unreal opposition – a legal obligation to obey as against a moral obligation to disobey; as if one can keep them separate. It assumes that there can be order in a legal system without any moral content in it. For Fuller, the legal obligation to obey laws does not automatically follow from their enactment by a recognised, formal procedure. It depends on the legal system's claim, and ability to command, what Fuller calls *fidelity to law*. When certain minimum moral qualities cease to exist in a legal system, it ceases to command fidelity; that is, it ceases to have a claim to citizens' obedience. The order and coherence of a legal system (its ability simply to go on functioning) depend on a minimum moral content. Without this it ceases to be a legal system at all.

It is not very clear what is involved in this last claim. It seems to relate to the question of the definition or specification of law; to what it is to be able to say that law *exists*. In terms of normative legal theory's concerns, therefore, the claim is that a general concept of law necessarily entails moral elements of some sort. If, however, the criticism is raised that – as suggested earlier in this chapter – much of modern regulation is technical and conventional (for example, a requirement that a will must be attested by two witnesses to be valid; or the rule that in England one must drive on the left hand side of the road) rather than the expression of moral values – Fuller's answer is that law's existence depends on its authority (its capacity to demand fidelity) and this authority ultimately depends on certain elements of moral worth. Again, however, a positivist critic could deny that *legal* authority requires any moral component. As Austin noted: 'The most pernicious laws, and therefore those which are most opposed to the will of God, have been and are continually enforced as laws by judicial tribunals. . . An exception, demurrer, or plea, founded on the law of God was never heard in a Court of Justice. . .' (Austin 1832: 185). Must we say, therefore, that the positivist view offers hard-headed realism about the way legal systems actually function (with no necessary direct dependence on moral principle), whereas Fuller's thesis is merely wishful thinking about values which *ought to be*, but are not necessarily, built into law?

In his 1958 paper, as in earlier writings (1940: 101, 110; 1946), Fuller distances his thinking from classical natural law theory. As has been noted, this classical theory was generally vulnerable to the positivist criticism that modern law – in Weber's terms, a technical means of compromising or managing conflicting interests – is no longer usefully analysed in terms of moral absolutes and requires a 'science' explicitly recognising its human origins and instrumental political character. Fuller's strategy is to emphasise that the necessary morality of law is a *procedural* one, relating to the way law is created, expressed, interpreted and applied, rather than to any particular substantive content of legal rules. Looked at this way, even purely technical rules, such as the one requiring two witness attestations for a valid will, have a moral dimension. Everything depends on how the rule operates, *how* it comes into being, is expressed, interpreted or enforced.

The historical example of Nazi Germany provides material to illustrate Fuller's thesis. To assume, as Hart does, that the only difference between Nazi law and English law was that the Nazis used their laws to achieve purposes odious to English people is, Fuller argues, to ignore the much more fundamental moral differences between the two legal regimes. Nazi law made frequent and pervasive use of methods which show, in terms of Anglo-American standards, a most serious perversion of procedural regularity. For example, frequent use was made of retroactive statutes to cure irregularities. A notorious example occurred after the Roehm purge of June 30th and July 1st 1934 when, on Adolf Hitler's orders, more than seventy members of the Nazi party were shot. On July 3rd, a law was passed ratifying the massacre as a series of lawful executions. Hitler apparently later declared that at the time of the purge 'the supreme court of the German people consisted of myself' (Fuller 1958: 650). Secondly, Fuller notes 'repeated rumours' of secret laws and regulations making it impossible for most people even to discover the rules upon which officials were supposed to act. More generally, however, since 'unpublished instructions to those administering the law could destroy the letter of any published law by imposing on it an outrageous interpretation, there was a sense in which the meaning of every law was "secret"' (Fuller 1958: 652). Thirdly, when legal formalities and procedures became inconvenient to the Nazi regime they could be bypassed by means of Nazi gangs taking action 'on the street' and achieving the required objective by violence. Fourthly, 'the Nazi-dominated courts were always ready to disregard any statute, even those enacted by the Nazis themselves, if this suited their convenience or if they feared that a lawyer-like interpretation might incur displeasure "above"' (Fuller 1958: 652).

Assuming this picture of Nazi law in action is correct, what should be said of a legal system like this? The first point is that it seems less like a system of legal order than of discretions in policy-implementation organised around the furtherance of political aims of the regime in power (cf. Kirchheimer 1941). Not only is it inefficient, as a functioning system of *rules*, but it lacks all procedural fairness and propriety. These latter deficiencies point to a decline in what Fuller terms the *internal morality* of law. Thus, for him, they involve not just issues of efficiency but moral issues. We should be prepared to say (irrespective of the substantive content of Nazi laws) that the way the laws were applied was not merely procedurally inefficient but manifestly unjust. Fuller argues (1958: 642) that the authority of law (its capacity to demand fidelity) derives from a moral understanding[3] between rulers and ruled, such that citizens accord moral respect to the constitution which governs them as 'necessary, right, and good'. In the 1958 paper this is inadequately analysed because there is no clear indication of the criteria to be satisfied to ensure this recognition by citizens.

The best way to support Fuller's argument about a link between the moral authority of law and its procedural proprieties would be to suggest that a gross and cynical discarding of formal and predictable procedure constitutes a kind of 'fraud' on those who must obey. There can be no moral understanding between rulers and ruled in such circumstances. The ruled have no chance to orient themselves to the dictates of the ruler's authority. Although they must obey, they are not given a reasonable chance to do so in an orderly and rational manner. This is not, however, spelled out in Fuller's 1958 paper, though related arguments appear in his later writings (cf. Fuller 1969a: 153, 159–62). Instead he claims, without any real justification, that a decline in the moral aims or purposes of law, which he calls law's 'external' morality and which determine the authority and respect attaching to the legal system, is likely to be accompanied by a decline in the (procedural) internal morality, and *vice versa* (Fuller 1958: 645).

The Ideal of Legality and the Existence of Law

However, the important point being made from the Nazi example is that the stable forms and procedures of law and the nature of its authority are linked and Fuller is specific in his claims about the consequence of disintegration of these forms and procedures in practice in Nazi Germany. He suggests that the decline in procedural propriety, in the internal morality of law, was so serious that a legal system, as such, *ceased to exist* in Germany during

---

[3]   In later writings Fuller refers to this, following the social philosopher Georg Simmel, as a 'kind of reciprocity': see Fuller 1969a: 39.

the Nazi period. Hence, post-war courts should not recognise Nazi law. Matters of legality in the Nazi period should be clarified, where necessary, by retroactive legislation. This claim about the non-existence of law in Nazi Germany is, indeed, one which other writers had already made, and on the basis of similar arguments about the effects of the procedural arbitrariness of the Nazi regime. Franz Neumann, a distinguished jurist who practiced law in Germany during the years leading to the Nazi accession to power in 1933, wrote, observing Nazi Germany from exile in America, that 'there is no realm of law in Germany, although there are thousands of technical rules that are calculable' (Neumann 1944: 468). Another eminent German scholar, Otto Kirchheimer, wrote to similar effect: 'With the access to power of National Socialism the common legal bond of a generally applicable civil law disappeared more and more. . .' (Kirchheimer 1941: 89).

Obviously a specific definition of the word 'law' is involved here and Nazi regulation is being tested against it. But, in Fuller's 1958 essay, no such definition is made explicit. In Kirchheimer's and especially Neumann's writings, however, the concept of law employed is elaborated. Indeed Neumann used it in major writings of the 1930s and 1940s as the criterion for assessing general changes in the character of twentieth century regulation and as the organising concept for the most detailed historical analysis available in English of the notion of the Rule of Law (Neumann 1986).

Neumann writes bluntly: 'the National Socialist legal system is nothing but a technique of mass manipulation by terror' (1944: 458). If law is merely the sovereign's command such a system must be recognised as legal. But if law 'must be rational either in form or in content' Nazi regulation definitely does not deserve the name of law. For Neumann, law is both *voluntas* (the expression of sovereign power) and *ratio* (the expression of reason, or rational principle grounded in general ethical postulates) and the legal history of Western civilization is a history of the attempt to reconcile these typically incompatible yet essential components of legality (Neumann 1986: 45–6; 1944: 451–2). The component of *ratio* insists that law be a matter of general rules, not special individualised commands. It requires also that these general rules be clear and predictable in application, not vague general norms providing broad authority for virtually free official discretion. Hence, although Nazi regulation made considerable use of technical rules, it lacked the character of law.

Kirchheimer elaborates similar arguments. He sees Nazi regulation as guided wholly by policy demands. These necessitated technically rational norms of a purely provisional character which could be changed quickly to meet the needs of the moment, without notice and, if necessary, retrospectively. Such requirements precluded the existence of a stable body of general laws which could only hamper governmental freedom to shape, adjust and implement policy. The aim of adjudication and rule application in such a regime is not to maximise legal stability but to execute given commands 'so as to have the maximum effect in the shortest possible time' (Kirchheimer 1941: 99). Thus, the legal regime of contract is largely replaced by a system of private command and administrative order; that of family law becomes a regime of policy regarding population development and social organisation. Even the idea of the state, as the abstract source or structure of regulation, is discarded in favour of the ultimate 'total and all-embracing' personal authority of the leader (Krausnik et al. 1968: 128; Neumann 1944: 467–70)

For Fuller, the point of referring to evidence from a grossly pathological regulatory system is to try to show that legality is a more complex notion than legal positivism understands it to be. For rules to be 'legal' it is not enough that they conform to the legal criteria expressed in a rule of recognition, or can be imputed from some basic norm of the legal system. Legality is a matter also of the way rules operate, of how they are drafted, promulgated, applied, interpreted and enforced. Neumann and Kirchheimer had already offered a broadly similar message. Neumann, however, rejects natural law theory in his writings as a mystification usually adopted to justify the *status quo*. He is concerned only to confront positivist analytical jurisprudence with political and social realities and to demonstrate its descriptive inadequacy in failing to take account of them. Fuller, by contrast, eventually chooses the terrain of natural law on which to fight (cf. Fuller 1969a: 96–7). The message of Nazi experience for him is that legal positivism cannot appreciate the moral conditions under which legality is possible. Legal order must be 'good order' so as to create conditions for fidelity to law. Good order demands conformity, at least a minimum extent, with the internal morality of law. Legality, for Fuller, is thus a special kind of morality.

Before considering Fuller's ideas expressed in other writings it is appropriate to take stock, in a preliminary way, of this critique of legal positivism, since it remains substantially unchanged in his later work[4]. A familiar positivist reaction to Fuller is to express approval of all the procedural proprieties upon which he insists while denying their moral character, and denying also that Fuller's

[4]   And see generally the extensive criticisms of positivism in Fuller 1940.

conception of legality in any way invalidates positivist analyses of law. The positivist claim is that the theoretical relationships between legal rules (in Hart's concept of law) and legal norms (in Kelsen's theory) are not invalidated by procedural impropriety. They exist even if denied in practice. Indeed, as has been seen, part of Kelsen's objective is to defend a rational legal science (as professional legal reasoning) in the face of political manipulation of law. The proper framing, application and interpretation of law are thus not moral matters for Kelsen and Hart, but consequences of adherence to a coherent positivist view of a legal system and of the necessary relationships between its doctrinal elements.

Fuller's claims are symptomatic of an impatience with legal positivism's *silences* – with what it refuses to say about law – rather than with its explicit tenets. In Chapter 4 it was noted that modern analytical jurisprudence contributes to lawyers' professional concerns by attempting to establish a coherent concept (Hart) or science (Kelsen) of law which adequately reflects the normative view of rules or norms held by legal 'insiders'; in other words, above all, by lawyers. At the same time, a political dimension to these theories was noted. They suggest an image of the Rule of Law as somehow inbuilt in the very concept of law or legal system, because of their portrayal of law as a self-regulating system. But Fuller's procedural natural law theory seeks to show the inadequacy of this formal Rule of Law conception. Legality is typically reduced in the implicit positivist conception to a professional understanding of the doctrinal consequences of a logically integrated system of rules. The actual operation of rules is ignored and, indeed, is largely irrelevant to this conception. Fuller, however, passionate about the evils of Nazism (Summers 1984: 7, 152), insists on the inadequacy of any such abstract and formal view of legality and the Rule of Law and emphasises the need to examine the practical conditions of the making and application of rules.

Nevertheless, if the legal professional concern for a coherent portrayal of doctrine in its logical relationships is the concern which analytical jurisprudence as a type of normative legal theory is attempting to meet, its failure to address wider political and ethical dimensions of law in action is not necessarily inimical to the achievement of its objectives. Its silences on the moral issues of Nazi law do not, in themselves, invalidate its theses or render them incoherent. On this view, Fuller's natural law approach merely strains at the limits of normative legal theory as a rationalisation of legal professional knowledge; it asserts a need to infuse a more profound political awareness into normative legal theory. As will appear later, even legal positivists have realised that this might be desirable.

A Purposive View of Law

Fuller's other writings make it clear, however, that his main concerns about law's morality are not with such questions of legal pathology as whether Nazi law was too evil to be law, but with constructive issues as to how to infuse the highest legal virtues into systems, such as those of Anglo-American law, which he would regard as far from pathological. The principles of internal morality of law – the procedural criteria by which Nazi legal tyranny is measured in the 1958 essay – are discussed in Fuller's most influential book, *The Morality of Law*, first published in 1964, as criteria also of possible legal excellence.

In *The Morality of Law* Fuller distinguishes between two kinds of morality or moral judgment. The morality of duty refers to the basic moral demands of order without which mere existence (whether of a society or of a legal system) becomes impossible. The morality of aspiration, by contrast, refers not to a moral minimum, but a maximum. 'It is the morality of the Good Life, of excellence, of the fullest realisation of human powers' (1969a: 5). Duty and aspiration constitute the ends of a moral scale rising from the bare moral necessities for any human achievement, through to the highest moral ideals. Moral demands can be pitched at various points on this scale. For example, a judgment about the morality of gambling could stress that extensive gambling directly harms society, the individual and the individual's family in economic, psychological and other ways. These 'duty' considerations might suggest that gambling should be legally prohibited. On the other hand, gambling on a small scale and for low stakes might not seem harmful in these basic ways but only a matter for regret that the individual can find no better use of time and energy. The aspiration that people should live 'good lives' is not something to which they should be compelled. We assume that law should require the moral minimum, not try to force citizens to become saints.

This idea of a moral scale enables Fuller to pose, as a fundamental problem of all legal regulation, that of deciding where the pressures of duty stop and the excellences of aspiration begin. Law's impositions must be sufficient to sustain duty but they become tyrannous if they seek to impose excellence. Hence one of the most important arts of law-making is that of judging for each issue, each law and each activity or situation, what level of moral demands law should operate with. But the demand for legality is itself a moral demand. Therefore, it is necessary to decide how far it relates to the morality of duty and how far to that of aspiration. Where on the moral scale is the internal morality of law to be located? In *The Morality of Law* law's internal morality is first presented negatively as 'eight ways to fail to make law'. These are (i) a failure to achieve rules at all, so that every issue must be decided on an *ad hoc* basis; (ii) a failure to publicise the rules to be observed; (iii) the abuse of retroactive legislation 'which not only cannot itself guide action, but undercuts the integrity of rules prospective in effect, since it puts them under the threat of retrospective change'; (iv) a failure to make rules understandable; (v) enactment of contradictory rules or (vi) rules requiring conduct beyond the powers of the affected party; (vii) introducing such frequent changes in the rules that those addressed cannot orient their conduct by them; and (viii) a failure of congruence between the rules and their actual administration (Fuller 1969a: 39). Total failure in any one of these directions, or a pervasive general failure in them (as with Nazi regulation) would, for Fuller, result in the non-existence of a legal system (1969a: 39). At this basic level, therefore, the internal morality of law provides a minimum morality of duty without which the existence of a legal system is impossible.

Beyond such rare pathological cases, however, the internal morality of law is primarily a morality of aspiration; the aspiration to maximise legality, to make legal order as good an order as can be. The internal morality can then be expressed as eight excellences which are the reverse of the 'eight ways to fail to make law': government always by rules, which are always publicised, prospective, understandable, non-contradictory, etc. Yet Fuller stresses that it would be counterproductive to try to realise fully all eight excellences in a working legal system. No system of rules could function on such a basis but would collapse in chaos or paralysis. For example, retroactive laws are sometimes inevitable, not all legal disputes can be solved by existing rules, and rules cannot achieve perfect clarity in advance of all applications of them. Thus, the achievement of legality is not merely the acceptance of a set of moral principles. It is a matter of judging the point on the moral scale between duty and aspiration where each component of legality, as related to each concrete problem of legal regulation in the particular legal system concerned, should be set. And the point on the scale will vary with circumstance and time. The achievement of legality is, thus, a task requiring all the skills of legislator and jurist. It is the heart of 'the enterprise of subjecting human conduct to the governance of rules' (1969a: 91, 96).

The use of this last mentioned phrase is the closest Fuller comes to defining law (cf. 1969a: 106), but the definition, such as it is, is instructive. It emphasises that law is a purposive activity (not merely rules or norms which are the product of the activity). Equally Fuller's definition reflects his view (readily acceptable to many legal sociologists but sometimes less so to lawyers and legal philosophers) that the term 'law' need not be limited to refer only to rules enforced by state agencies. Fuller's purposive concept of law allows it to be applied to rule structures governing numerous social institutions – such as schools, hospitals or business corporations – and social groups. The internal morality of law provides criteria of legality by which rule systems of many kinds can be judged. Indeed, this concept of legality has been used in sociological studies in such fields as industrial relations (Selznick 1969) and policing (Skolnick 1975).

There is much of value in these ideas. Nevertheless, it is clear that we have moved on to different terrain from that of positivist analytical jurisprudence. What is now offered by Fuller no longer appears as a direct critique of legal positivism but as a different enterprise concerned with the examination of law in purposive terms. Although Fuller presents his ideas as an attack on legal positivism, they cannot be defended as a critique of the logic of positivist analytical jurisprudence but only of the inappropriateness, narrowness or political and social irrelevance of its projects. His claims are strong ones. But they amount to saying: you should have devoted your researches to this rather than that. And the positivist can still reply: maybe so, but your arguments are no criticism of what I *have* done in seeking to rationalise the legal knowledge which is important to lawyers.

Fuller and the Common Law Tradition

One further line of attack on legal positivism presents itself in Fuller's work and, though it is usually the least discussed, it is the strongest attack mounted in his writings. In an important 1946 article Fuller attacks positivist analytical jurisprudence at what has already been identified in this and earlier chapters as one of its weakest points – its understanding of the judicial process and the practice of judicial development of case law. Using a dichotomy very similar to Neumann's contrast between *ratio* and *voluntas*, he argues that judicial development of law necessarily involves both reason and fiat or 'order discovered and order imposed' and 'to attempt to eliminate either of these aspects of the law is to denature and falsify it' (Fuller 1946: 382). Classical natural law theory cannot convince us that law can actually be pure reason; it cannot supplant the need 'for authority, for a deciding power' (1946: 388)[5]. But, equally importantly, positivism cannot convincingly portray law as pure fiat (that is, a formal structure of authority) because the legal outcomes of judicial decisions cannot be understood except in the light of reasons for the decisions. In case law, reason and fiat are inseparably intertwined. The judicial decision is an exercise of authority but is also a search for, and attempt to construct, reason in legal doctrine. The common law method entails an appreciation of both fiat and reason in case law. At its best, it keeps these aspects of law in balance.

Thus, Fuller suggests that an extreme positivism, which sees law only as fiat, is 'essentially alien to the American spirit' (1946: 394). It cannot adequately represent the common law method of legal development. Hence the emphasis on 'reason', which in Fuller's later writings develops into the procedural version of natural law represented by the internal morality of law, connects with a defence of common law methods.

There is, however, more to this defence than a device for attacking legal positivism. In Chapter 2 the image in classical common law thought of law's deep roots in community life was discussed. Fuller, also, asserts in his writings that the case law of the common law tradition projects its roots 'more deeply and intimately' into the actual patterns of human interaction than does statute law (Fuller 1969b: 26). His concern over the years to understand these social patterns and their relationships with legal procedures and institutions gradually led him to deeper study of sociology, anthropology and social psychology. What resulted was a body of writing examining the social roots and consequences of particular forms of law and of particular kinds of legal procedures and institutions.

The most interesting aspect of all this for the concerns of this book is the way in which Fuller's researches led him to a kind of restatement of elements of classical common law theory, but in a sophisticated form which replaces the mystical images of

[5] No doubt it is this point which, several years later, makes Fuller in *The Morality of Law* – now explicitly accepting the label natural law for his own theory – address that theory primarily only to the procedural forms by which the deciding power expresses and implements its decisions, and not directly to the substance of the decisions (as classical natural lawyers typically have done).

community encountered earlier in Chapter 2 with specific sociological claims about law in society. For Fuller, the necessity of human interaction is what gives purpose to law, and the principle of reciprocity is a major foundation of social interaction and social institutions (1969a: 20–1, 61). His writings portray social life as a kind of collective endeavour; a matter of co-operation (for example, in maintaining legality: 1969a: 91); ideally, the collaborative working out of a reasoned view of human affairs. The overriding task of law is, thus, to keep open lines of communication between members of society (1969a: 185–6), by means of which disputes can be resolved, projects planned, and individual and group objectives achieved. Fuller's image of social life is one in which a network of free individual initiatives sorts most matters out. Governmentally imposed solutions to social problems may often be of limited use. Thus, for Fuller, negotiation, arbitration and mediation are specially important means of resolving social difficulties. He served for twenty years as an industrial relations arbitrator of grievances under collective bargaining agreements and devoted much energy to this role (Summers 1984: 7).

Such a view of social life and its ordering does not, therefore, lead to the simplistic conclusion, so often associated with classical common law thought, that the wise judge as repository and distiller of communal knowledge and custom is always the ideal regulator. Fuller plainly considers this *often* to be the case (Fuller 1940: 131–8). But courts cannot, for example, deal well with polycentric problems – those where the interconnections of the problem posed with other problems of practical social ordering are sufficiently complex to make attempted solutions counterproductive unless their ramifications in a variety of contexts are systematically considered (Fuller 1978). Beyond this, the criteria of legality – the internal morality of law – are not necessarily appropriate to all kinds of government action, for example in economic planning and allocation (Fuller 1969a: 171), or to private rule making by negotiation between the parties. Different kinds of social order and organisation require different kinds of regulation and regulatory mechanisms and procedures. Much of Fuller's later work is concerned with exploring the relationships between the inherent character of various means of regulation (for example, custom, contract, adjudication, legislation, managerial direction, and democratic collective decision-making) and the types of social order for which they are appropriate (cf. Summers 1984: ch 6).

Nevertheless, Fuller's later writings attach special significance to a kind of social order which seems close to that suggested by the idea of the community in classical common law thought. Fuller terms it the relationship of 'friendly strangers' (1969b: 27). It is neither the relationship of intimacy which is the ideal of family life, nor that of antagonism as between hostile nations. It seems to be the social order in which individuals pursue their own objectives in a spirit of co-operation through social relationships of reciprocity. In discussing the ideal legal framework for such a social order, Fuller distinguishes between three types of law. Customary law derives directly from patterned interaction between individuals and it changes as the patterns of interaction change. What Fuller calls 'enacted law' is any officially imposed law. Between these two categories stands contractual ordering or the 'law of the contract'. This refers to the rules which interacting parties make as between themselves and for themselves by negotiation; the rules of private ordering which lawyers would call terms of the contract. Contractual ordering is ill-suited to the ordering of intimate or hostile relations but ideally suited to 'the habitat of friendly strangers, between whom interactional expectancies remain largely open and unpatterned' (Fuller 1969b: 27, 29). Customary law can operate across the whole spectrum of social contexts from intimacy to hostility, but enacted law (the kind of regulation which must demonstrate legality in the sense of Fuller's internal morality of law) is, like contractual ordering, most appropriate within the social order of friendly strangers. Its task is, indeed, for Fuller, above all that of facilitating contractual ordering of relationships.

Striking similarities with the orientation of classical common law thought can be seen in these ideas. First, there is the somewhat unclear legitimacy of enacted law which, as in classical common law thought, is seen as in partnership with and even subordinate to other regulatory structures which emerge in the conditions of everyday social life (contractual negotiation, custom). For Fuller, even enacted law must find its roots in the conditions of human interaction. The internal morality of law – legality – helps to ensure this since it expresses the moral relationship of reciprocity between rulers and ruled (1969b: 24). Secondly, customary law, which Austin did not even recognise as law (Austin 1832: 31) and which plays little role in positivist legal thinking, re-emerges in Fuller's later writings with all the centrality which classical common law theory gave it. Customary law, for Fuller, consists of the established patterns of social interaction which provide the stable structure of expectations within which people can co-operate, negotiate, plan and act. Social science shows how important these stable structures are – often much more important than those provided by enacted law. Finally, Fuller's writings emphasise the autonomous, spontaneous processes by which regulation (especially contractual ordering and custom) develops. They challenge the positivist emphasis on creation of law by fiat. Again this is strongly reminiscent of the evolutionary picture of law offered in classical common law thought. Thus, a sociological perspective on regulation allows Fuller to demystify some old themes of classical common law thought. In the modern dress of social science they confront the legal science of positivist analytical jurisprudence.

Politics and Professional Responsibility

In earlier chapters, an attempt has been made to show why positivist analytical jurisprudence has been potentially significant as the basis of a science or a concept of law demonstrating the intellectual autonomy and unity of professional legal knowledge. Fuller's theories seem to have none of the qualities which would make them professionally useful in this respect: they deny any sharp demarcation between law and non-law and claim instead that the existence of law (as measured by the criteria of legality) can be a matter of degree (Fuller 1969a: 122). Equally, Fuller refuses to see 'lawyers' law' as uniquely distinctive and is happy to apply the term 'law' to the rule systems and processes of social groups and social institutions of many kinds. None of this seems very promising as support for the thesis that influential varieties of legal theory have been relevant for the clarification of problems of legal professionalisation. Yet a colleague of Fuller wrote that he 'reached more American law students and stimulated more speculative thought about the law than any other American law teacher' (quoted in Summers 1984: 15).

In fact, it is not necessary to read far into Fuller's work to see that his concerns are very strongly organised around the dilemmas and responsibilities of legal professional practice[6]. This is, for example, obviously the case with his attack on legal positivism in relation to the Nazi regime. One of the failures of positivism, as seen by Fuller, is that of not making clear the moral responsibilities of legal practice. The lawyer is *not*, because of his or her professional allegiance to the legal system as a part of the state apparatus, absolved from moral responsibilities to other

[6]   For Fuller, 'the task of the legal philosopher is to decide how he and his fellow lawyers may best spend their professional lives': Fuller 1940: 2. And see generally Fuller 1940: 2–4, 12–5.

individuals; or from a political responsibility to defend the liberty of others, which is the price to be paid for the privilege of living in a democracy. Yet German legal positivism, in Fuller's view, encouraged lawyers to accept as law anything that called itself by that name, was printed at government expense, and seemed to come from higher authority (Fuller 1958: 659).

Fuller has no doubt that such passive views of legality helped the rise of Nazi tyranny. 'The first attacks on the established order were on ramparts which, if they were manned by anyone, were manned by lawyers and judges. These ramparts fell almost without a struggle' (1958: 659). Thus, legal forms and structures were instruments in establishing the legitimacy of Nazi tyranny (Bracher 1971: 350–1). The notion that legal positivism blinds lawyers and others to the moral issues that may surround governmental action when that action is dressed in the garb of 'law' is a common theme in discussion of the Nazi period and the years preceding it. The Protestant theologian Emil Brunner wrote: 'The totalitarian state is simply and solely legal positivism in political practice. . . the inevitable result of the slow disintegration of the idea of justice'. And he adds: 'If there is no justice transcending the state, then the state can declare anything it likes to be law; there is no limit set to its arbitrariness save its actual power to give force to its will' (Brunner 1945: 15–6). To similar effect, Neumann (1944: 47) writes of Kelsen's theory that 'it is virginal in its innocence. . . it paves the way for decisionism, for the acceptance of political decisions no matter where they originate or what their content, so long as sufficient power stands behind them'.

The issue seems to come down to whether the separation of law and morality necessarily, in practice, leads to a neglect of the moral aspects of regulation. It has been seen earlier that, *in theory*, there is no reason why it should and, further, that the fusion of legal and moral issues has been asserted by legal positivists to be a potential weapon of reactionaries or authoritarians (claiming 'this is the law; therefore, it must be right'). Nazi writers did, indeed, claim that a fusion of law and morality had finally been achieved in Germany by National Socialism (Kirchheimer 1941: 88). And Kelsen affirms that the totalitarian state is founded on the assertion of 'absolute' values inseparable from its law (Kelsen 1955: 42). By contrast, legal positivism can co-exist (as in Kelsen's own work) with a relativistic approach to values which requires the individual to face the dilemmas of conscience without moral solutions 'legislated' by moral authorities (whether those of the state, the nation or the churches) considered to be absolute and infallible. Equally, it can co-exist with a belief in moral absolutes as long as legal analysis is seen as in no way dependent on these absolutes. Either way, positivism today is defended as a means of keeping 'the final sovereignty of conscience' separate from claims of legal validity (MacCormick 1985: 10).

Thus, there is nothing in positivist analytical jurisprudence as such that guarantees moral myopia. But there is a sense that positivism does not actively *encourage* a concern with the moral responsibilities of legal practice. Fuller's belief in a humanistic and broad approach to legal scholarship and legal education is part of his reaction against professional narrowness of moral vision. He wrote extensively on questions of legal education, supported broad curricula, loathed mechanical rule manipulation by the 'black-letter mind', and emphasised that basic problems of law and government can be solved by 'reason' (Summers 1984: ch 11). Thus, reason – the lodestar of classical natural law – remains an object of faith. The lawyer should refuse to accept fiat without reason.

Fuller's dissatisfaction with positivist analytical jurisprudence may, thus, be inseparable from a dissatisfaction with the limited technocratic image of legal professionalism which it seems to support. Excluding moral issues from the professional sphere of legal knowledge is unsatisfactory, from a standpoint such as Fuller's, if it seems to make these issues of *less* concern to the lawyer than to other citizens. Further, treating law as wholly distinct from non-law is unsatisfactory if it disguises the fact that lawyers are in the job of *creating* legality, of building law from non-law and preventing legality declining or slipping away into arbitrariness. Finally, criteria of legal validity provided by definitions of the sovereign's command, by rules of recognition or a basic norm, are inadequate if they make lawyers think that the practice of law does not involve them in a *political* responsibility when they recognise the formal authority claimed for laws and regulations. Fuller's image of the requirements of legal professionalism in modern conditions does not, therefore, deny the image which legal positivism sets up or implies. As in all his confrontations with legal positivism, Fuller's position is, in essence, that positivism is not enough, and that twentieth century history should have warned us clearly of its inadequacy.

Natural Law Tamed?

No other natural law theory in the Anglo-American context in modern times has been widely seen as posing a stronger challenge to modern positivism than has Fuller's. And this despite the fact that his claims constitute only a modest and cautious version of natural law theory – essentially related to the procedural proprieties of law and not the substance of its rules which concerns most classical natural law theories. Has, therefore, natural law really become obsolete, as Weber seemed to suggest at the beginning of this century?

Certainly, in recent times, natural lawyers' demonstrations of legal positivism's inadequacies when a broader understanding of law is required in modern political and ethical conditions have been influential. Even such an eminent positivist legal philosopher as Neil MacCormick has seen a convergence between natural law and legal positivism once it is recognised that 'those who exercise power and discretion *within* a legal system must always at least purport to be acting on the basis of seriously held and seriously considered values' (MacCormick 1981b: 144; cf. MacCormick 1981a: 161-2). Even Hart (1961: 194) has accepted a 'core of good sense' in the doctrine of natural law, in that the very conditions of all human existence necessitate certain kinds of social rules in any society if it is assumed that its members have a common aim of survival. Five features of the human condition – vulnerability, approximate equality of physical power, limited altruism, limited resources and limited understanding and strength of will – are such that society would be impossible without *some* rules protecting persons, property, promises and exchanges, and providing for sanctions to ensure compliance (Hart 1961: 189-95). This minimum content of natural law, as Hart calls it, is far from the natural law which has has been discussed in most of this chapter. It provides no significant criteria for criticism or justification of the substance or procedure of positive law (since survival may be achieved 'even at the cost of hideous misery': Hart 1961: 188), but only a set of truisms which indicate broad areas in which some kind of regulation must, as a matter of natural necessity, exist.

Tendencies among legal positivists towards rapprochement with natural law typically amount to a recognition that principles to guide or structure legal development are necessary but are not to be found through positivist analysis of legal doctrine alone. Indeed, the increasing technicality of modern law and its apparent character as a mere compromise of interests may make the identification of guiding principles seem more relevant and important, not less. Thus, Hart has treated the Oxford philosopher John Finnis' recent natural law philosophy (Finnis 1980) as 'in many respects complementary to rather than a rival of positivist legal theory' (Hart 1983: 10). This seems fair. Finnis' theory rejects any claim to judge the legal validity of rules and so avoids any confrontation with legal positivism. It essentially offers a moral philosophy to provide guidance as to what law's substance and purposes *should be*, rather than a normative legal theory seeking to explain the actual doctrinal components or characteristics of particular legal systems. Thus, it cannot be central to the concerns of this book. But some features of Finnis's theory are important here as illustrating the role which natural law theory seems to be coming to play as an adjunct to positivist analytical jurisprudence.

Finnis is concerned with what he understands, following Aristotle, as a 'focal' conception or the 'central case' of law. This focal conception is an ideal or pure form, of which actually existing forms are mere derivatives or imperfect examples. Hence Finnis is less interested in the law present in actual legal systems than in the law (in a focal sense) which can be philosophically deduced as necessary and appropriate from certain moral postulates revealed by speculative analysis. It is this method of analysis which is Finnis' most important contribution to modern natural law theory. As noted earlier, most earlier natural law theory sought to reason out philosophical consequences from observed characteristics of the human condition, or to deduce moral principles from rational argument, or from imagined states of nature existing before societies or governments came into being. These approaches have usually been considered vulnerable to the criticism that an unacceptable sleight of hand is involved in seeking to deduce what morally *ought* to be from speculation about what *is* (for example, what the state of nature or the human condition actually is). Indeed, as has been seen, even in Fuller's procedural version of natural law theory the procedural criteria which *ought* to govern a system of legal rules are derived from speculation on what a working (efficient) system of rules *actually* involves.

Finnis' approach appears to bypass these traditional difficulties by grounding natural law not in reason but in intuition; in what is 'self-evident', requiring no rational justification. In this, his method follows and develops that of Aquinas. Thus, For Finnis, seven objects of human striving are self-evidently good. These basic human goods are life (every aspect of vitality which makes possible human self-determination), knowledge (for its own sake and not merely as a means to an end), play (activity with no purpose beyond the activity itself), aesthetic experience (the appreciation of beauty), sociability or friendship (acting for the sake of friends and their wellbeing), practical reasonableness (being able to bring one's intelligence and judgment to bear in choosing how to live one's life) and religion (understanding something of what life is for). It is not necessary here to assess Finnis' claim that these are indeed self-evident and that all other goods can be understood as combinations or derivatives of them. But his attempt to avoid the derivation of 'ought' from 'is' marks a methodological advance over many other expositions of natural law. The basic human goods are not derived from rational speculation on what *is* the case in nature. As intuitively recognised goods they are already normative in effect: because they are self-evidently 'good' it is equally self-evident that they should be pursued and promoted. Practical reasoning (itself one of the basic goods) provides, in Finnis' view, general prescriptions of reason ('basic methodological requirements') which should guide the pursuit of these goods. Further, since they cañ only be sought in communal life, in interaction with other people, a legal system to secure them is necessary.

From Finnis' detailed filling out of this analytical framework, three matters, related directly to the themes of this chapter, can be mentioned. They are the discussions of 'community', 'authority' and the Rule of Law. A link between the idea of community implicit in classical common law thought and the purposive view of law reflected in natural law theory has been noted earlier – as has the appeal to reason which characterises them both. Indeed, modern literature on the basis of moral authority often strongly emphasises the concept of community (cf. Weinreb 1987: 249-59). So it is not surprising that Finnis, like Fuller, attaches much importance to analysing the nature of the moral community (in Fuller's case the collectivity of 'friendly strangers') to which law relates most directly. Finnis notes that part of the unity of community is physical and biological (for example, in family ties), part in intelligence and shared modes of understanding, part in common technology and cultural unity, and part in common action or interaction. While the last of these is most relevant to the analysis of practical reasoning in human communities, it presupposes the other elements.

Finnis acutely notes the different character of business, play and friendship relationships and that political communities combine elements of all of these (1980: 149). This complex variety of relationships is typical of 'complete' communities – the ones to which law in its focal sense relates. A complete community is thus 'an all-round association' in which are co-ordinated 'the initiatives and activities of individuals, of families, and of the vast network of intermediate associations'. Its point is 'to secure the whole ensemble of material and other conditions, including forms of collaboration, that tend to favour, facilitate, and foster the realisation by each individual of his or her personal development' (Finnis 1980: 147). This is obviously, for Finnis, a philosophical ideal. But like any group, a community in this sense has definite conditions of existence. It can be said to exist 'wherever there is, over an appreciable span of time, a co-ordination of activity by a number of persons, in the form of interactions, and with a view to a shared objective' (1980: 153). It is enough to note here that, like the exponents of classical common law thought, Finnis sees the moral and rational strength of law as grounded in its purposive contribution to the continuance and fulfilment of a complete community. Unlike the classical common lawyers, however he also sees the need to make some effort to elaborate rigorously what this concept entails.

Finnis' ideas about authority and the Rule of Law can be considered together. Influenced here, as elsewhere, by Max Weber, he sees the basis of the authority of rulers not, for example, in the consent of the governed nor in a notional social contract such as Hobbes or John Locke described, but merely in the likelihood of compliance by those over whom authority is claimed (1980: 249). The existence of constitutional structures and the issue of whether the ruler has the consent of the governed are relevant in asking whether someone guided by practical reason ought to obey the claimed authority; but this does not derogate from Finnis's surprisingly Austinian position that authority depends on the 'sheer fact' of likely obedience (1980: 250).

On the other hand, a Fullerian view of the Rule of Law and its demands is built on to this positivist conception of political authority. Acknowledging Fuller's influence, Finnis stresses reciprocity between rulers and ruled as the foundation of the moral demands of legality (1980: 274). Elaborating the main features of legal order, Finnis produces a general picture strikingly like Fuller's. Thus, law is a coercive structure but, more fundamentally, a system of rules. It brings clarity and predictability to human interactions, regulates its own creation and modification, allows individuals to adjust their circumstances rationally within a rule governed environment, provides reasons for future actions, and postulates a gapless framework of regulation. Finnis' descriptive emphasis on these characteristics seems to reflect a recognition of the importance of technical imperatives in the application of legal rules which no modern legal positivist could quarrel with. The Rule of Law, then, as in Fuller's characterisation of legality, is the requirement to make these elements of rule-governed reliability and predictability as pervasive as possible in a legal order. And, like Fuller, Finnis emphasises the reciprocal relationship between ruler and ruled (together with the virtue of maximising the dignity of individuals as free, responsible agents) as the foundation of the

Rule of Law and the conditions which make it a component of political virtue.

At the point at which Finnis' natural law theory meets legal positivism's direct concern with working systems of legal rules, it restricts itself, like Fuller's theory, to elaborating and lauding the virtues of the Rule of Law. But, whereas Fuller attacks positivism at this point, Finnis seems to offer no challenge to positivism on its own ground. Natural law has, it seems, become an ally and supplement to legal positivism. In times of social and political stability it does not seem to displace the reassuring picture of orderly legal knowledge and uncontroversial, professionally understood structures of authority in legal systems, which positivist analytical jurisprudence offers. If Western political arrangements become significantly less stable, however, natural law theory may well become powerful again, enlisted for or against the *status quo*.

Only in one area of analysis does the natural law theory considered in this chapter seem to have found a general and major analytical weakness in the theories it opposes. The judicial function still remains problematic within the tradition of modern analytical jurisprudence. In the common law world, lawyers and non-lawyers alike are reluctant to accept that the judge is merely the delegate of an Austinian sovereign and that judge-made law is merely what Fuller terms fiat. But post-Austinian legal positivism, as represented by Hart's and Kelsen's theories, offers little or no analysis of how judges reach decisions in controversial cases and what the nature of their authority as legal innovators is. Fuller's work, echoing older common law conceptions, at least reopens this question, while Finnis' re-examination of community points towards sources of legal authority independent of political structure. But different approaches, free of the controversies of natural law and firmly focussed on felt professional concerns of lawyers, have seemed necessary to take these inquiries further. They will be considered in the following two chapters.

6 The Problem of the Creative Judge: Pound and Dworkin

Looked at in relation to legal environments beyond that of England, legal positivism as embodied in analytical jurisprudence has sometimes seemed ridiculous. How can law be understood in isolation from politics and social values when so much of it is a matter of judicial interpretation (of constitutional and legislative provisions, and of earlier judge-made law) and of interpretation of what judges say? Throughout the Anglo-American legal world this question is significant but in the United States it has seemed especially pressing (cf. Hart 1958: 49–50). The American legal environment (which has inspired much of the theory to be considered in this chapter and the next) is framed by a written constitution explicitly recognised as the repository of fundamental political values, and by a heritage of common law which, it is assumed, 'must continually reflect currently held social attitudes'; in this context a recognised role of judges is 'to integrate constitutional principles with changing social attitudes and values' as manifested in common law and other legal doctrine (White 1976a: 18). Law seems hardly recognisable by applying litmus-like tests but is rather argued over, or teased out of judicial pronouncements by creative interpretation. Classical common law thought, however, seems no more able than positivist analytical jurisprudence to take account of this reality of creative legal development. Seeing law as reason, classical common law thought ignored the 'fiat' side of the equation (to use Fuller's terms). Denying that judges make law, it portrayed legal processes not as purposive, innovative and creative, but as passive, responsive and evolutionary. Whether or not judges legislate, they are clearly significant actors in managing the processes of legal development. Neither positivist analytical jurisprudence nor classical common law thought seems capable of explaining the nature of this activity and the principles governing it.

The problem of developing a normative legal theory explicitly recognising, as a principled enterprise, the activity of judges and other officials in developing law is the focus of this chapter. Although this is a task of normative legal theory in relation to any legal system, it should be a special concern in the context of Anglo-American law where the tradition of common law thinking elevates the judge to a central position in the legal system. In England, however, positivist analytical jurisprudence, as has been seen, met legal professional needs for rationalisation of legal knowledge while reflecting the political realities of a centralised state, and a concentration of law-making power subsuming special jurisdictions (cf. Arthurs 1985). Perhaps the only fully explicit political theory of the judge's role offered by English positivist analytical jurisprudence is Austin's explanation of the judge as the sovereign's delegate, an official theoretically much like any other charged with governmental decision-making. This, however inadequate, does at least purport to explain the character of the activity in which a judge is involved in creating new law and the authority (that of the sovereign) which justifies this law-making. Hart's theory, by contrast, explains (in terms of secondary rules) the legal powers and constraints within which the judge operates, but treats the exercise of judicial discretions (the activity itself) as beyond the concern of legal theory. Both Hart and Kelsen explain what makes a judge's decision binding as law; but not where the judge obtains authority specifically to develop law. To stress, as Kelsen and – by implication – Hart do, that law regulates its own creation does not solve the problem since while law regulates this process it does not control it. Human agencies are at work reaching beyond the presently stated rules of law. What directs and impels them?

Two American writers, whose work is rarely compared, are the most important twentieth century contributors to the attempt to solve this problem within the scope of Anglo-American normative legal theory. Despite major differences in methods and approaches to theory construction, the writings of Roscoe Pound and Ronald Dworkin show similar practical concerns and a fundamentally similar restructuring of common law thought in defence against positivist analytical jurisprudence. Yet very little attention has so far been paid in jurisprudential literature to the parallels between them (cf. Burnet 1985).

A partial explanation lies in the fact that, despite an important closeness in the broad theoretical aims of their writings, the form in which the substance is presented differs considerably between them. Pound, who was dean of Harvard Law School from 1916 to 1936 and whose immensely prolific writings span almost the entire period from the first years of the twentieth century until his death in 1964, directed his criticisms broadly against a wide range of competing approaches to legal thought in the twentieth century Anglo-American context. Constructively, his writings seek to develop a self-proclaimed 'sociological' jurisprudence presented as an amalgam of largely continental European influences and indigenous American tendencies in philosophy. Pound's theories thus appear as syntheses marshalling the strengths of a diversity of pre-existing legal philosophies. This apparent catholicism and openness carries the risk of producing a hotchpot of ideas lacking unity and rigour (what Kelsen castigates as syncretism of methods). Indeed the criticism that Pound failed to integrate and systematise the diverse trends of his thought has often been levelled against his contributions to legal theory. By contrast, Dworkin elaborated his original theory by systematically developing a sustained attack on positivist orthodoxy as represented in Hart's work, but with little direct reference to other major theoretical predecessors. Dworkin's present institutional position is, indeed, that which Hart previously held. He replaced Hart as professor of jurisprudence at Oxford University after the latter's resignation in 1968 and continues to hold that post together with other academic responsibilities in the United States.

Interestingly, while Dworkin is now one of the most influential and widely discussed contemporary legal philosophers, Pound's intellectual reputation, once unassailable as that of the unquestioned doyen of American legal scholarship (cf. Wigdor 1974: ix), has fallen considerably so that his ideas no longer play a significant role in the mainstream of debate in normative legal theory. In this chapter it will be necessary to account for this dramatic change in evaluation of Pound's significance, as well as for the immense disparity between the present statuses of Pound's and Dworkin's theories. The situation is only partly explicable in terms of the unquestionably greater rigour and philosophical sophistication of Dworkin's work. This chapter will argue that the explanation lies, in part, in a widespread misunderstanding of the nature of Pound's enterprise, which obscures both his achievement and the true nature of the problems of his theory. This, in turn, raises the possibility that Dworkin is actually retracing by very different means some of the ground which Pound travelled and that a somewhat similar ultimate assessment of the broad import of both theorists' work will emerge with time. But Dworkin's work is still developing so that any general assessment of it can only be provisional.

Pound's Rejection of the Model of Rules

It is customary to approach discussion of Pound's writings by taking seriously the label which he himself gave to his theoretical outlook.

Pound called it sociological jurisprudence and it is true that – especially in the first decade of the century, when he taught in Chicago at Northwestern University and the University of Chicago – he was significantly influenced by social scientists working in the city, and by the sociologist Edward Ross who had been a colleague at the University of Nebraska (Wigdor 1974: 111–3, 141–6; cf. Reuschlein 1951: 127–8). Ross and others offered ideas about the organic nature of social development and about the nature of social control (of which law could be considered one aspect) which aided Pound's efforts to escape the constraints of both positivist analytical jurisprudence and traditional common law thinking. But, if the main themes of Pound's normative legal theory – those which make him a significant figure in the progression of legal ideas with which this book is concerned – are to be understood, it is necessary to discount heavily any suggestion that his major theoretical work is sociologically informed to a significantly greater degree than that of other writers so far discussed in these pages.

In essence, for Pound, the label 'sociological' was a banner to symbolise and rally serious efforts to view law in a broader, more dynamic perspective than that which positivist analytical jurisprudence offered, and in a more realistic, practically oriented and reformist perspective than that which much other legal philosophy (such as classical natural law theory) provided[1]. A prerequisite for establishing a dynamic view of law – one which could recognise law as something developed and interpreted and in continuous flux – would be to discard the idea that it could be understood merely as rules or norms. For Pound, the concept of law must include not only the 'static' elements of law expressed as rules, but also those elements which direct and propel legal development. He writes: 'Law, as distinguished from laws, is the system of authoritative materials for grounding or guiding judicial and administrative action recognized or established in a politically organized society' (Pound 1959 II: 106). Law, in this broad view, is not merely a model of rules but a doctrinal system in movement. Thus, even if we consider only legal doctrine in a strict sense (what Pound terms 'precepts' of law) this is not exhausted by rules ('precepts attaching a definite detailed legal consequence to a definite

---

[1] Holmes J in *Lochner v New York* (1905) 198 US 45 refused to follow the mechanistic reasoning of the majority of the United States Supreme Court in striking down as unconstitutional a statute limiting employees' working hours. Pound hailed Holmes' dissent as 'the best exposition of . . . sociological jurisprudence' extant in America. Cf. White 1972: 100.

detailed state of facts or situation of fact'). Precepts also include *principles* ('authoritative starting points for legal reasoning'), *conceptions* ('authoritatively defined categories', such as trust, sale, bailment), and *standards* ('defined measures of conduct, to be applied according to the circumstances of each case', such as the standard of due care, or of fiduciary responsibility). Beyond this, however, law in Pound's broad sense includes also 'an authoritative technique of developing and applying the precepts, and a body of received ideals as to the end or purpose of the legal order, and hence to what legal precepts ought to be and how they ought to be applied' (Pound 1941: 256–7).

It might seem that this includes not only what positivist analytical jurisprudence typically treats as legal, but also much of what natural lawyers would wish to include in an understanding of law. But Pound's writings show little sympathy for classical natural law. They emphasise that law is an affair of values, and of techniques for elaborating and applying values to the solution of particular problems. The values themselves are, however, never timeless and universal as classical natural law sought to prove, but only values for the time and place, related specifically to the conditions of a particular legal system and to the kinds of claims and expectations brought to it for recognition and satisfaction. Pound was sometimes prepared to see an affinity between natural law ideas and his emphasis on values underlying law, but the latter would be a 'practical natural law'. Insofar as he approved of the revival of natural law thought in the twentieth century this was because it brought a renewed emphasis, like his own, on values in law, and only to the extent that it denied (as a natural law with a 'changing or a growing content') that any *absolute* values underlie law (Pound 1923: 149). On this matter – unlike much else – Pound's views seem to have remained fairly constant throughout his career.[2]

What inspires Pound's very different approach to normative legal theory as compared with that of positivist analytical jurisprudence? His early writings show an obvious impatience to reform archaic legal procedure and extend professionalisation of law. The impatience is strangely like Austin's, half a century earlier in England – the irritation of a highly able and imaginative, if conservatively minded lawyer at the unsystematic and irrational practices of his own profession. Like Austin's, Pound's reform impulses were limited, largely focussed on making existing legal institutions work better, and tended to evaporate with the passing years.

[2]   But cf. Wigdor 1974: 167, 274, 276.

Both men saw their legal theory as an aid in developing and providing direction for a modernising legal profession. When Pound was a boy of ten in Nebraska in 1880 the American legal profession was relatively unorganised. During the nineteenth century the public image and status of the legal profession had fluctuated considerably. Wigdor claims that '[t]hroughout the country, no legitimate profession had a more tarnished reputation' and in Nebraska, when Pound entered practice in 1890, 'almost anyone willing to read law for a few weeks could become a lawyer' (Wigdor 1974: 81; cf. Stevens 1983: 25). Elsewhere, legal professionalism had strongly reasserted itself but had not yet put behind it a nineteenth century history of decline and disorder. There was an urgent need for a strong rational foundation of legal education and scholarship to aid this professional consolidation (Stevens 1983: chs 1 and 2). Parallels with Austin end here, however, for Pound saw Austin's kind of legal science as a wholly inadequate theoretical basis for professional development and institutional reform in the legal system. As will appear, Pound's odyssey in legal theory is, in essence, an effort to secure, purify and develop in the twentieth century context, the tradition of common law which Bentham and Austin had so impatiently brushed aside.

In a country just emerged from pioneer times when Pound's ideas were being first formulated, it plainly made sense to treat courts (dispersed widely through states and territories) as the focus of legal authority, rather than to think in terms of lines of delegated authority derived from some centralised Austinian sovereign. Even much later, however, – and Pound continued through to one of his last, posthumously published, articles in 1967 (Pound 1967) to praise common law methods and defend them – his most illuminating legal theory is primarily a vehicle for exploring ways of revitalising common law techniques of legal development in the face of challenges to them presented by the immense legislative and administrative power exercised by a modern twentieth century state. By the same token it is a context for defending and developing the common law conception of reason in law in the light of modern forms of systematic knowledge (especially social science) which have become increasingly important in the forming of legislative and judicial policy (cf. Rosen 1972). Pound's sociological jurisprudence, viewed in this perspective as a serious attempt to refurbish common law thought in twentieth century terms, is an important contribution to the themes of this book, however misleading the label 'sociological' which he gave it (cf. Hunt 1978: ch 2; Cotterrell 1984: 76–8).

The Outlook of Sociological Jurisprudence

An attempt to explain the basis on which judges develop law could move in one of two directions – emphasising either instrumental or organic aspects of the judicial role. David Wigdor has demonstrated clearly Pound's original ambivalence between these directions of analysis and explanation (Wigdor 1974: ch 9). An *instrumentalist* approach would argue that the determinants of judicial creativity derive from outside law or legal doctrine as such – in a variety of policy considerations, social pressures, political factors or economic imperatives. Pound's use of the adjective 'sociological' to describe his jurisprudence in contrast to analytical jurisprudence (which he tended to associate with mechanical, blindly deductive legal reasoning), and his frequent advocacy of social science as an aid in developing the law, suggest an instrumentalist outlook. So does his reiterated view that law's task is 'social engineering'. But when a closer look is taken at what is being suggested in his writings, and especially when his ideas are viewed in the light of their evolution over the decades, it becomes clear either that – as Wigdor argues – Pound eventually deserted the instrumentalist ideas of his early career, or (the reading I prefer) that instrumentalism was never for Pound more than a minor supplement to, or perhaps just a useful form of rhetoric in aid of, a clearly *organicist* view of law. This organicist view can be expressed in the following ideas: that (i) law contains within itself the doctrinal resources for its own development in the form of values and principles capable of giving content and shape to evolving law (rather than relying inevitably on inputs of change from 'outside' through deliberate political action resulting in legislation or administrative rule-making); (ii) law has a natural momentum for change, an inbuilt tendency to develop (it is inherently dynamic rather than static); (iii) legal development is a matter of orderly adjustment within the legal system to the changing patterns of human demands being registered within it (a process of adjustment to be managed primarily, if not exclusively, by lawyers and judges in the context of established legal techniques and principles); and (iv) the task of the jurist is to keep these orderly processes of legal development working freely.

To think of the lawyer's task as one of social engineering did not mean, for Pound, the engineering of reform (Wigdor 1974: 230) except insofar as the fourth of the above principles required it. Certainly in his early writings Pound is much concerned with the failure of lawyers and others to keep the orderly processes of legal development working. These are seen by him as natural processes much like those assumed by classical common law thought. Hence procedural reforms in the legal system are urgently advocated. Pound made his name, ironically, as a radical critic of the legal profession with a famous address to the American Bar Association in 1906 at St. Paul, Minnesota, on 'The Causes of Popular Dissatisfaction with the Administration of Justice'. The central concern of Pound's paper is, indeed, with practical defects of procedure and organisation in the administration of justice. It carefully notes, however, that in *all* legal systems, causes for popular dissatisfaction exist. They include the mechanical operation of legal rules; the inevitable divergences of law and public opinion; the popular assumption that the administration of justice is an easy task which does not require high professional skills; and popular impatience with legal restraints. Equally, the Anglo-American common law system (quite apart from particular procedural and organisational problems) is not blameless. Its individualist spirit 'agrees ill with a collectivist age'; it arouses impatience and resentment by turning great social or economic issues into private legal disputes; it lacks general ideas or legal philosophy and so encourages 'petty tinkering where comprehensive reform is needed'; the adversary system 'turns litigation into a game'; and 'defects of form' arise from 'the circumstance that the bulk of our legal system is still case law' (Pound 1906: 185).

These remarks caused a storm in the American legal profession at a time when blunt, even if carefully modulated, criticism of law's inadequacies was unusual. And they show that Pound's original defence of common law, and his critique of the conception of law as fiat which positivist analytical jurisprudence suggested, is not an attempt to turn the clock back. Some of his early writings strongly defend legislation against mindlessly destructive interpretations by the courts, castigate the sterility of case law, and argue that only legislation can provide a new starting-point for legal development (Pound 1908: 614, 621). Analytical jurisprudence in its Austinian form is criticised not because it seems to make legislation central to its conception of law but because it considers only the formal authority by which law is made and not the purposes for which that authority should be exercised.

On the other hand, Pound's defence of legislation has *some* Savignian overtones. Legislation is implied to be the handmaid of spontaneous legal development through the courts – clarifying doctrine where it has become confused, consolidating it, and suggesting lines of development where none clearly emerges from current case law. Legislation is necessary to provide a restatement of law 'from which judicial decision shall start afresh' (Pound 1908:

622). But this involves 'new rules, then new premises, and finally a systematic body of principles as a fresh start for juristic development' (1908: 612), so there is no suggestion that legislation is restricted merely to consolidation. For Pound its role is dynamic, not passive; to move law forward in the light of modern social needs when other forces of legal development are failing. Reading Pound's early essays one is made to see legislative action as a kind of shock treatment to get the heart of common law beating regularly again. It follows that, given this importance of legislation, lawyers must become knowledgeable in its techniques and effective professional advocates in debates about its content. Hence, in the twentieth century, according to Pound, such a role demands lawyers' attention to social science which provides important material in these debates.

It is also clear from these essays that, for Pound, the reason why legal doctrine as developed by the courts has reached an impasse is that the essence of common law method has not been followed. Courts have adopted blindly deductive reasoning – 'mechanical jurisprudence' – antithetical to the common law concern with precepts in relation to their 'conditions of application' (1908: 611–2). The time-honoured methods of common law require in modern conditions that lawyers make use of the sources of knowledge of community values and needs which modern social science can provide.

The St. Paul address, although atypical of Pound's work in its sharp criticism of professional practices, usefully highlights some of his early, central, practical reformist concerns which help to explain the direction which his normative legal theory takes. The address notes criticism of common law methods for their individualist emphasis in a society which attaches increasing attention to broad social interests. It seems to follow, then, that a theory in defence of common law methods in contemporary conditions should direct attention systematically to these social interests and show how they are and should be taken into account in the adjudicative and lawmaking processes. Equally, if a cause of dissatisfaction is the distortion of broad social issues into matters of private dispute, it is surely necessary to show how individual and social concerns can be kept analytically distinct, considered on their own separate planes: individual against individual, social against social; with disputes of broad consequences being considered primarily in terms of the social issues raised, rather than confused with private or individual concerns. Again, if litigation seems too much like a game, perhaps what is needed is a theory of the adjudicative process emphasising its objective character: as a balancing process in which opposing interests are systematically identified, weighed and compared. Finally, if the common law system is a bewildering mass of case law, what is surely required is a theoretical scheme by which its contents can be systematically ordered – not just in terms of the chaotic doctrine thrown up by the mechanical jurisprudence of modern courts[3], but in terms of the general interests, demands and claims of individuals, groups and society generally, reflected in case law and recognised and protected by law. If common law lacks appropriate theory such theory must presumably be true to the ideal character of common law as a legal expression of the life of the community. Hence it must be a theory of law's substance – of the elements of community life expressed in legal claims and conflicts, not (as with positivist analytical jurisprudence) a formal theory of law's structure.

Whether or not there is a direct link between the complaints registered in the St. Paul address and the central tenets of Pound's sociological jurisprudence as it gradually took shape, it is easy to see the theoretical positions sketched above – all of which are, as will appear, directly expressed in Pound's legal theory – as a natural outcome of the list of practical dissatisfactions which caused such a sensation in the American legal profession in 1906.

A Theory of Interests

Pound's programme for sociological jurisprudence, reiterated many times in his writings (e.g. Pound 1941: 261), involves a set of juristic tasks which clearly ally jurist, judge and practising lawyer in the same enterprise of making the legal system work with – to use one of Pound's favourite phrases – the minimum of friction and waste. The first task is to list and classify all interests (claims, demands or expectations which people individually or collectively seek to satisfy) pressing for recognition by law, so that in the task of deciding which should be protected, and to what extent, none will be ignored. At first sight this appears to entail a definite sociological basis for Pound's project. Surely the identification of interests in society is a task for the social scientist. But here, as in all other aspects of Pound's theoretical outlook, social science is firmly subordinated to the lawyer's professional skills. Pound

---

[3] Though Pound also ardently supported the project of the American Law Institute to produce Restatements of the law in the form of codifications of principles distilled from systematic analysis of case law: see Stevens 1983: 136.

sees social scientific surveying of interests as impractical, at least for the foreseeable future. Interests are to be identified by noting the claims actually brought before courts and so reflected to some extent in case law, or those lobbied before legislatures. Legal and legislative records thus reveal the presence of interests, whatever the extent of legal protection of these interests. In Pound's outlook, therefore, pressures for change in law arising from changing social needs become relevant to the legal system, its theorists and practitioners only when the pressures are registered in legislative or judicial processes. The picture offered is one of a legal system waiting for change to be brought to it, not used as an engine to promote or direct social change.

It was suggested in the previous section that an emphasis on interests as the units of legal theory reflects the need to keep central the common law idea of law's intimate relationship with social life or community needs and problems. It is important to notice that for Pound the base units of legal theory are only *potentially* legal in a strict sense. When interests are legally protected they become legal *rights*. As claims pressed upon the legal system for recognition they are the raw material of law. They express patterns of social interaction and structures of social relationships, and changes in the interests pressing for legal recognition reflect changes in the patterns of social interaction and relationships. Thus, it can be argued that interests are the practical components of the idea of community identified in earlier chapters of this book as at the heart of classical common law thought.

Pound's writings contain exhaustive classifications and taxonomies of interests. Three kinds (social, individual and public) are identified. Social interests are those generalised as claims of society as a whole, treated as a collectivity. They include interests in the moral health of society, in general security and the security of social institutions, the conservation of social and natural resources, and in economic, political and cultural progress. Public interests are those asserted by the state as the legal embodiment of politically organised society. Individual interests include all interests in private security of the person, of transactions, of property, family relations, privacy, reputation and belief. Since there is, according to Pound, a social interest in the maximisation of individual wellbeing it follows that the general promotion to the greatest possible extent of individual interests is a social interest too – perhaps the most important social interest of all.

Pound seemed to delight in elaborating this scheme of interests, classifying and sub-classifying, and documenting the categories with a mass of illustration from Anglo-American case law. But what is it really for? The objective is, it seems, to demonstrate order and unity in law (an objective seen in earlier chapters to be a major theme running through the modern development of normative legal theory) in a way compatible with the common law outlook. Such an approach requires, as Austin suggested, a 'map of the law', but not – as he understood this – a map of its formal structures demonstrating the top-down patterns of authority conveyed by the idea of sovereignty[4]. The map should presumably rather be of law's content in relation to actual community needs – the interests reflected in and constituting social life.

Once such an overall view of legal concerns is in place the rest of the programme of sociological jurisprudence can be attempted. Pound sets this out explicitly as (i) selecting the interests law should recognise, (ii) fixing the limits of the protection of those interests which law should provide, (iii) deciding how and to what extent law can effectively provide that protection and (iv) formulating principles of valuation by which the three previously stated tasks are to be accomplished (Pound 1941: 261). All these tasks are clearly very different from the descriptive objectives of analytical jurisprudence. They are prescriptive – specifying how legal development is to take place. At the same time they can be understood as an explication (description) of the prescriptive guidelines actually adopted in a working common law system. In that sense the enterprise is also descriptive. Hence an ambiguity is written into Pound's project. Prescription and description of legal processes and adjudicative practices go together; it becomes difficult to distinguish one from the other. What is becomes inseparable from what ought to be. Again, this position is closely compatible with that of classical common law thought (custom being simultaneously what is and what ought to be), although wholly opposed to the outlook of positivist analytical jurisprudence.

Interests are to be balanced 'on the same plane' (Pound 1943: 2); that is, individual against individual, and social against social (public interests eventually seem to disappear from Pound's major concerns). Individual interests are never to be balanced directly against social interests, and, where possible, interests are to be compared in 'their most generalised form'; that is, as social interests (Pound 1943: 3). It can be inferred that what really lies behind Pound's insistence on this point is his wish to enable the adjudicative processes of common law to deal effectively with the clashes of social interests which seem so fundamental to twentieth century life, and so avoid the criticism of common law as excessively

---

[4]   Cf. Chapter 3, above, p. 80.

individualistic. At the same time, since Pound sees protection of the individual life and its aspirations as perhaps the pre-eminent social interest, the new theoretical elevation of social interests does not destroy the traditional particularistic focus of common law case development but affirms its social importance within the larger field of social conflicts and the balancing of social interests.

The Search for a Measure of Values

Viewed in this way, Pound's sociological jurisprudence – in its overall shape and emphasis – is a not-unsophisticated refurbishment of the common law outlook in the light of modern conditions. Looked at in detail, however, as a practical (prescriptive) guide for legal development or as an explanatory (descriptive) theory of the way Anglo-American law evolves, it reveals serious problems which go to the heart of the project being attempted in this kind of normative legal theory.

Pound's theory is a kind of 'bootstraps' theory of law, by which I mean that to explain the character of law it relies on concepts which are themselves constructed from what is to be explained. This is true of the concept of interests itself. What counts as a distinct interest for the purposes of the theory is far from clear (Llewellyn 1930a: 14) and depends on possibly controversial interpretations of the body of existing legal doctrine (which is what the theory is meant to illuminate). The identification of the 'measure of values' which the theory demands to provide guidance in the balancing of interests (that is, deciding how far interests should be recognised, and how far legally protected in each particular case, when they conflict with others) is equally problematic. Like classical common law thought, Pound sees this measure of values as somehow implicit in law itself – secreted in the developing patterns of legal doctrine.

A great deal of Pound's writing is devoted to the search for this elusive evaluative measure which can provide guidance for future legal development. In Chapter 2 it was noted that classical common law thought avoided the difficulty by assuming legal change to be merely an aspect of cultural change – expressed in the idea of custom as evolving spontaneously without direction by any explicit guiding principle. But this position remains wholly unsatisfactory as a basis for legal theory appropriate to common law since it suggests no legal basis for change and removes the evolutionary development of law (central to the common law concept of law) entirely from the ambit of legal explanation. Pound's theory tries to replace this mystical core of classical common law thought with an explicit set of evaluative principles.

Following the German writer Josef Kohler, he terms them the *jural postulates* of the time and place. They are 'ideas of right to be made effective by legal institutions and legal precepts' (Pound 1923: 148). They are in no sense absolute values, but merely those recognised or implied in a particular society at a particular time. Kohler wrote of the postulates as underlying values of civilisation. Pound asserts: 'There is no eternal law. But there is an eternal goal – the development of the powers of humanity to their highest point. We must strive to make the law of the time and place a means towards that goal in the time and place, and we do that by formulating the presuppositions of civilisation as we know it. Given such jural postulates, the legislator may alter old rules and make new ones to conform to them, the judges may interpret, that is, develop by analogy and apply, codes and traditional materials in the light of them, and jurists may organise and criticise the work of legislatures and courts thereby' (Pound 1923: 148).

But where are the jural postulates to be discovered? The answer for Pound is in law itself. Legal doctrine reveals its immanent values. Again, although the postulates are theoretical devices to enable us to understand law better, we rely on study of law itself in order to understand its postulates. This is less absurd than it appears. Pound seems to see the jural postulates as merely the most abstract and generalised normative components of a particular legal system at a particular time. As such they provide its fundamental internal structure of values, reflected in numerous detailed decisions made within the system. For example, Pound's original identification of the postulates of Anglo-American law early in the twentieth century presented them as a general affirmation of the wrongfulness of intentional aggressions, of the importance of good faith in a wide variety of contexts, of the sanctity of private property, of the importance of due care to avoid injury to others, and of the obligation to prevent potentially dangerous things which one owns from getting out of hand (cf. Pound 1942: ch 4).

In many ways the list of postulates which Pound elaborates is an odd one; a strangely cramped and myopic view of the scope of civilised values, seen through the prism of professional legal practice. That, however, is less important than the point that the postulates have little explanatory or prescriptive power. They provide broad generalisations from the doctrine of a legal system at a certain time. Yet, as Pound recognised, they need continual revision as law and civilisation evolve and change their character (Pound 1959 III: 11–4; 1940: 83); and this revision can only be in the light of legal change which is already complete and not of that which is to come. Because of this, the postulates cannot guide or explain the future development of law in reliable ways because no theoretical explanation is offered as to how they themselves alter or are developed. And in an age of change it may be impossible to discover what existing postulates are (Pound 1942: 133–4; 1959 III: 14–5).

In defence of Pound it can be said that there is no suggestion that the jural postulates are the key to understanding all present and future legal development. The vague aim of avoiding friction and waste in human affairs is offered as the primary key (Pound 1942: 133–4). 'No matter what theories of the end [i.e. purpose] of law have prevailed, this is what the legal order has been doing, and as we look back we see has been doing remarkably well' (1940: 76). The postulates represent merely an effort to identify the most abstract and intractable components of law as understood in terms of the broad, multifacetted conception of it which Pound counterposes to the restricted positivist conception of law as rules or norms. And they can be seen as the product of a serious effort to make explicit those components of the inherently dynamic character of common law which are located within legal doctrine itself. That the product is so limited might suggest, however, that the attempt to explain any of law's processes of development in terms of the character of legal ideas themselves (that is, as something internal to law, rather than imposed upon it by external forces, as an instrumentalist might argue) could, itself, be misguided.

The Wider Context of Pound's Jurisprudence

Pound's continual reference to the avoidance of friction and waste as a basic aim of legal ordering suggests an enduring instrumentalist tinge to his thinking, despite the dominance of the organic common law conception of law. But his failure to devote any attention to serious theoretical elaboration of what might count as friction and waste and what would actually be entailed in their avoidance confirms that this strand in his thought, for all its prominence, is essentially a rhetorical supplement to a fundamentally organicist view of legal development.

Wigdor is no doubt correct to argue that in Pound's early career his outlook appeared, to himself and to others, as fully compatible with various political positions and reform movements sympathetic to instrumentalist views of law (Wigdor 1974: chs 8 and 9). Pound supported the Progressive movement in American politics early in the twentieth century. This advocated rational and deliberate government action for social reform within the framework of and in support of what were considered fundamental established values of American life. If the Progressive movement had had an explicit legal theory it 'almost certainly would have been instrumentalist and pragmatic' (Summers 1982: 29). Pragmatism, as a philosophical movement, undoubtedly appealed to Pound and some of his early writings express unequivocal support for it as a basis for modern legal thought. This too, has been apt to mislead some commentators on Pound's jurisprudence into overemphasising its instrumentalist aspects and the compatibility between Pound's ideas and those of younger American scholars who wholeheartedly adopted instrumentalist approaches to law (cf. Summers 1982; Rumble 1968: 13–20; and see Chapter 7, below). Pragmatism implied a distrust of fundamental values and a belief that values (including the value of truth) are realised only in practice, as the successful means of achieving deliberately chosen ends. But, for Pound, the word 'pragmatism' is, it seems, no more nor less useful than the word 'sociological'. Both are labels for approaches which emphasise law's purposes rather than its abstract logic. 'The sociological movement in jurisprudence is a movement for pragmatism as a philosophy of law; for the adjustment of principles and doctrines to the human conditions they are to govern rather than to assumed first principles; for putting the human factor in the central place and relegating logic to its true position as an instrument' (Pound 1908: 609–610). For Pound, that instrument is to be used not, as jurists unequivocally inspired by pragmatism would later insist, for planning and social reform by means of government and law, but for realising the destiny of common law as a continuous expression of the changing patterns of community life. Indeed, the clearest proof of Pound's outlook is in the fact that as soon as it became clear to him that pragmatism was being taken seriously as a basis for thoroughly instrumentalist views of law, he opposed this tendency with a fervour reserved for few other objects of his criticism (Pound 1931: cf. Twining 1973: ch 5).

Through the nine decades of Pound's life his view of the destiny of common law methods seems to have changed very significantly. In his early writings at the beginning of the century the problem is seen as one of freeing these methods from the stagnation which mechanical jurisprudence – formalistic, abstract legal logic – produced. Legislation and administrative action are seen as aids in solving the problem and Pound's writings have an open, progressive tone in their advocacy of modern methods of legal development and the use of a wide range of resources from the social sciences to set legal development on an appropriate course to meet twentieth century challenges. In his later work the tone is quite different. Administrative rule-making, in particular, is seen as a fundamental threat; part of the broader threat of political 'absolutism' – uncontrollable governmental power (Pound 1940: ch 1) which eventually, for Pound, comes to include most governmental programmes of social reform (Pound 1950: ch 3). Common law is now portrayed as embattled; threatened from all sides by governmental legislative and administrative action inimical to the natural processes of common law development. Judges appear no longer in Pound's writing as objects of criticism but as the heroic defenders of legal reason (e.g. Pound 1963). It is frequently implied by his actions (for example, in opposing the appointment of social scientists to law faculties: cf. Wigdor 1974: 223–4, ch 10) and in his writings that the legal profession must close ranks against threats to the professional world of law, which has the judiciary at its centre and is defined by its custody of the immanent reason of common law. On such a gloomy note, Pound's modern reworking of common law thought evaporates, with the conservatism of age and perhaps under the sheer weight of the positive law and administrative regulation created by the modern state, into a narrow defence of old professional prerogatives.

Dworkin and Pound

Dworkin's writings hardly refer to Pound[5], yet have many similar concerns. However, they adopt methods which hold out the possibility of avoiding many of the thickets into which Pound's sociological jurisprudence falls. Much of Dworkin's early writing, which began to become influential in the late 1960s, a few years after Pound's death, is concerned to attack the positivist model of rules in a much more rigorous and systematic manner than Pound adopted. While Pound merely asserted that law should be understood in the broad sense of precepts (including rules, principles, conceptions and standards), techniques and ideals, Dworkin tries to show exactly why the model of rules is inadequate. Ultimately, however, the demonstration comes down to an assertion of much the same truths about law as those which Pound sought

[5]   There is a brief discussion in Dworkin 1967. Of Dworkin's three major books only the first (Dworkin 1977) contains index references to Pound. These identify two brief and peripheral comments early in the text, one of which (p. 4) seems to indicate that Dworkin thinks of Pound primarily as an instrumentalist.

to emphasise. Analysis in terms of rules alone, Dworkin insists, cannot explain the full range of legal materials which a judge uses in deciding a 'hard' case; that is, one for which an answer is not given merely by logical application of existing rules.

On the other hand, Dworkin's worries about the model of rules seem significantly different from Pound's. Dworkin's focus is not on interests – the elements which for Pound are the key to understanding those roots of law in community ignored by positivist analytical jurisprudence – but on rights. This emphasis signals Dworkin's preoccupation with positivism's inability to give a clear legitimacy to judicial decision-making. According to positivist analytical jurists, judges in hard cases cannot apply law to reach their decisions but necessarily exercise discretion. Since the authority for this exercise of discretion cannot easily be explained in legal terms, the judge as 'legislator' is a highly problematic figure unless seen in Austinian terms as the delegate of a sovereign electorate. Such a judge must, in a democracy, defer always to the democratic will as expressed in legislation. Consequently, the judge's tendency will always be to favour the majority will so expressed. He will lack the authority to protect minorities through the exercise of creative discretion *against* the majority (cf. Dworkin 1971: 158–9). Yet rights are precisely those legal entitlements which should be enforceable against anyone – even an opposed majority. Must it be said that in hard cases there are no rights to be relied on?

Looked at in this way, Dworkin's concern to escape the limitations of positivism is part of a strategy to affirm law's capacity to defend broad liberal values of individual freedom and autonomy, if necessary against majority wishes reflected in government policies. Like many earlier writers he sees a central task of law as to prevent, not aid, the 'tyranny of the majority' (cf. e.g. Mill 1859: ch 1). Pound's preoccupations are, as has been seen, with the professional autonomy of the common lawyer faced with the threat of imposition of law by political authorities; a threat especially great because in the twentieth century Anglo-American environment these authorities possess the unquestionable (and, therefore, absolute) legitimacy of democracy (or 'King Demos' as Pound sometimes refers to it: cf. Wigdor 1974: 227, 230). Dworkin does not share Pound's general suspicion of democracy although he is obviously concerned at its tyrannous possibilities. Nor does he share Pound's belief in government by (legal) experts (cf. Wigdor 1974: 199). Equally, Dworkin's position is not so explicitly framed as a defence of common law thought. His emphasis is on the protection of rights and on the moral autonomy of the citizen. Pound seemed to recognise the former, if at all, only in terms of a general defence of common law methods and the latter in terms of the professional autonomy of the lawyer.

Rights, for Dworkin, are thus antecedent to and give meaning to legal rules. His rejection of the model of rules is not expressed, like Pound's, as a claim that law contains more than rules. It is a claim that law is *more fundamental* than rules and that rules are incomplete and problematic expressions of the content of law. This position is very close indeed to that of classical common law thought. As noted in Chapter 2, the classical common law conception recognises the essence of law in principles expressing the reason of law, not in rules.

Dworkin's ideas on the place of principles in law will be elaborated below. For the moment it is important to note that once the task of the judge has been defined as that of enforcing 'rights and obligations whose present power is independent of the majority will' (Dworkin 1971: 159) judges are for Dworkin – and contrary to the positivist analytical jurists' view – in no sense legislators. They do not derive authority, like a democratic legislature, from their representing the will of the majority. Nor is the judge's task one of implementing that will, however it is to be understood. Judicial authority, for Dworkin, must derive from a different source and support a different role from that of a legislature. Like Pound, he sees the judge as deriving both the authority to develop law and the resources to do so from *within* law itself, not from some external source such as an Austinian sovereign whose policies define this authority and the resources available to the judge in the task of interpreting hard cases. As will appear, however, Dworkin's explanation of what it is, internal to law, which provides resources and authority for the judge's interpretive activities is significantly different from, and richer than, Pound's discussion in terms of precepts, techniques (left vague in his discussions) and a measure of values centred on the jural postulates of the time and place.

Principles and Policies

In the rare general comments which Dworkin offers on Pound's work, he praises the earlier writer's recognition of the legal significance of principles but criticises Pound for having stopped short of an effective critique of legal positivism since he fails to show that principles are a part of law 'in the *sense* that particular rules are, that they in fact control and regulate officials' (Dworkin 1967: 217). Without this demonstration, positivist analytical jurists could agree that principles and other general ideas associated with law are significant for the interpretation of rules but deny that the model of rules needs amendment to accept these elements as essential components of law. In effect, much of what Pound treats as precepts other than legal rules could be seen by positivist analytical jurists as merely a segment of the discretionary (non-legal) considerations which judges or other officials take into account in making decisions in hard cases. The positivist image of law would remain inviolate. The judge's creative role would remain legally inexplicable and legally unjustifiable.

Dworkin's strategy is, therefore, to show that principles, which cannot be reduced to legal rules, are treated in practice by courts as legal authorities which cannot be ignored; that they are essential (not optional or discretionary) elements in reaching decisions in hard cases. Indeed, Dworkin seeks to argue that in all cases a structure of legal principles stands behind and informs the applicable rules. The only difference, then, between a hard and simple case is that in the latter the relationship between applicable principles and relevant rules is seen by the deciding court and by interpreters of the court's decision as clear and unproblematic.

A favourite illustration, in Dworkin's writings, of legal principles is the American case of *Riggs v Palmer*[6] in which the New York State Court of Appeals refused to allow Elmer Palmer to inherit property as a beneficiary under the will of his grandfather, whom he had murdered by poisoning. The applicable legal rule appears to be that legacies contained in legally valid testamentary dispositions are to be guaranteed by law in accordance with the wishes of the testator. Yet the court in *Riggs v Palmer* consciously decides not to apply the rule and does so by relying on a general principle that a wrongdoer should not be allowed to profit from his own wrong. It is not judicial discretion which operates to defeat the ordinary rule as to legacies but an interpretation of the rule in the light of a governing principle. And the principle here is legal since it is not taken out of the air as a purely discretionary invention of the court but is one which has its own legal history as something developed, applied and interpreted in earlier cases and in relation to different legal rules and circumstances.

This is not to say that because law contains principles as well as rules, the former are to be equated with the latter. While legal rules may be identifiable by using some positivist test expressed in terms of rules of recognition, basic norm or sovereign command, legal principles cannot be so identified. They emerge, flourish and decline gradually through their recognition, elaboration and perhaps

---

[6] (1889) 115 NY 506. See Dworkin 1977: 23; 1986: 15–20.

eventual discarding over time in the ongoing history of the legal system concerned. As such, they reflect and express the legal system's underlying values or traditions – in a sense, its underlying political philosophy. Constitutional principles, and principles underpinning the basic structures of private law (for example, expressing the basic values of the enforceability of agreements or good faith), show these characteristics. Because they defy positivist tests which neatly distinguish law from non-law they cast doubt on the whole structure of positivist explanation. And this is fundamental because, as *Riggs v Palmer* shows, principles *control* the applicability of rules – those elements of the legal system which, according to positivist analytical jurisprudence, lend themselves to definite tests of legal validity.

The direction of Dworkin's argument at this point might seem to suggest the conclusion that the internal-external dichotomy dividing law from non-law, or – in another aspect – legal insiders from legal outsiders, is to be discarded. But this is far from his position[7]. The recognition that principles governing cases can be *legal* principles merely enlarges law's scope but does not, in Dworkin's view, render the idea of law as a distinct phenomenon incoherent. Equally, as will be seen later, he maintains a sharp distinction between legal insiders and outsiders. Insiders are those participating in the interpretation of legal rules and principles and so involved in determining creatively (rather than mechanically through the application of positivist tests) what is and is not law, while outsiders are those uninterested in or unable to play the interpretive game.

Principles differ from rules in other fundamental ways. They do not apply in an all-or-nothing fashion, as rules do (Dworkin 1977: 24). Rules are either applicable or not; principles have what Dworkin calls a dimension of weight. Legal rules cannot logically conflict – if they seem to do so one rule must be an exception to the other and can be written into it. Otherwise one of the rules must be invalid (1977: 25). But there may be conflicting principles applicable in the same case. The task of legal interpretation, then, involves a weighing of the principles against each other as they relate to the case in hand. The parallel with Pound's balancing of interests in the specific case is obvious. One might consider equitable principles as examples. The maxims 'equity regards as done that which ought to be done', 'equity will not perfect an imperfect gift' and 'equity will not allow a statute to be used as

---

[7]   Cf. Dworkin's critique as 'illogical' of Fuller's idea that the existence of law can be a matter of degree: Dworkin 1965: 677–8.

an instrument of fraud' may suggest different results when applied to the same case. The judge's task would be to assess their relative weight in the particular circumstances, so as to reach a conclusion by applying them.

Why should we not say, as a positivist would, that a judge merely exercises discretion or adopts a certain policy in making such a judgment? Dworkin does not deny the need for 'weak' discretion – by which he means merely creative judgment in the application of legal doctrine, whether rules or principles. But he denies the existence of 'strong' (that is, legally uncontrolled) judicial discretion in essentially the same way that classical common law thought would deny it. Judges do not *make* law because all the resources for their proper decisions are provided by the existing law as correctly understood. A judge does not decide a case in a legal vacuum but on the basis of existing rules which express, and, at the same time, are informed by, underlying legal principles. The task of the judge faced with a hard case is, therefore, to understand what decision is required by the whole doctrinal structure of existing law. Even if rules, understood in positivistic fashion, seem to give the judge no guidance, a broader understanding of the patterns of values which have gradually developed in the legal system and are expressed in the combination of rules and principles, does offer that guidance. The task of the judge is to understand the content of the legal system in this broad sense and give effect to it in his judgments to the best of his ability. His task is undoubtedly a creative one. Yet it is not a legislative one. Properly understood, the judicial role is not the dynamic one of making law like a legislator, nor is it the purely passive one of 'finding' law. The judge must make the law the best that it can be through his *creative* interpretation of existing legal resources. But he uses, according to Dworkin, no non-legal materials in doing this. Thus, Dworkin is able to make the claim, which has long puzzled many of his critics, that existing law provides an answer for every hard case (although judges and lawyers may argue interminably as to what that answer is). There is simply no room for the exercise of strong judicial discretion (Dworkin 1985: ch 5).

While the application of principle is fundamental to the judicial function, this is, for Dworkin (1977: 22; 1986: 221–4), to be distinguished clearly from the invocation of *policies* – standards setting out economic, political or social goals to be reached. The latter are normally not a matter for judges, but for legislatures. While the law which the Dworkinian judge is required creatively to apply will have been influenced by policy matters, policy should not shape his legal judgments in the way that principles – the expression of the community's moral and political values reflected in law – must (Dworkin 1986: 244).

Many critics have doubted that principle and policy can be clearly distinguished in the manner Dworkin seems to require, but the distinction is fundamental to his thinking. The reason for this can best be understood by referring back to the controversy surrounding the organicist and instrumentalist dimensions of Pound's thought. While ultimately, as has been seen, Pound's conception of law is thoroughly organicist, his failure to distinguish principle from policy leaves ambiguities which have misled some commentators. In Dworkin's writings there is no such ambiguity. He never expresses the matter in terms of the organicist-instrumentalist opposition; nevertheless, by making principle central to adjudication Dworkin affirms implicitly that judges must operate with an organicist conception of law, developing it from within. Through its own resources, creatively interpreted, law can 'work itself pure', according to the strange phrase of classical common law thought[8].

Policy, by contrast, is a matter for instrumentalists. It relates to pressures from outside the legal system directing law towards specific goals. Dworkin's position is here considerably clearer and less conservative than Pound's, for there is no suggestion that law must essentially develop itself by its own 'internal' resources of common law reason, with legislation (reflecting policy) no more than a handmaid. Dworkin has no doubt of the necessity for instrumentalist approaches to law providing essential policy input (as a liberal he favours considerable government intervention to protect, extend and realise in practice the promise of equality of citizen's rights: see e.g. Dworkin 1985: ch 14). His position, however, asserts a quite clear division of labour between a policy-driven legislature and a principle-driven judiciary. For Dworkin, in effect, Pound's common law image of twentieth century law holds good for courts and their responsibilities. But it does not hamper wide-ranging legislative activity to promote social change.

The Closed World of Legal Interpretation

Such a neat reconciliation of organicist and instrumentalist conceptions of law is, unfortunately, ultimately unstable and illusory, because Dworkin, like Pound, must decide between two

---

[8]　*Omychund v Barker* (1744) 1 Atk 21 at p. 33 (argument of Solicitor-General Murray, later Lord Mansfield). Cf. Dworkin 1982: 187; 1986: 400.

opposite views. Can law control its own destiny from its own resources – is it morally and politically autonomous in that sense; or is it essentially an instrument of political power, subject to control and direction from beyond its own doctrinal resources?

In Dworkin's recent writings it is made clear that the organicist conception triumphs. In other words, for Dworkin, as for Pound, the common law judge should still dominate the legal system. One might be forgiven for thinking that as long as rules can be distinguished from principles and understood in positivist fashion, they import into the arena of judicial interpretation normative material which the judge cannot but give effect to; the material controls him. Thus, insofar as law consists of policy-shaped legislative rules, the judge can only be an instrument of policy without independent creativity. Yet, as has been seen, for Dworkin, principles control the interpretation of rules. Hence, the rule-principle distinction has lost much significance in his recent writings. Principles are expressed through rules; rules derive their meaning from principles. Law is entirely a matter of interpretation. In this specific sense, no law is *imposed* on the judge. All law which comes out of the judge's decisions is the result of his creative interpretation, whether of legislation, prior case law or ultimate constitutional provisions (such as in the written United States Constitution).

It follows that, in a sense, principle trumps policy because the interpretation of law derived from policy considerations must be conducted in accordance with the judge's obligation to fulfil the elements of principle in law. There is no law other than that which results from creative interpretation of existing legal materials guided by the attempt of the interpreter to make the law the best it can be.

Law as Interpretation

In recent writings Dworkin has used analogies with literary interpretation to explain the judge's obligation in creative legal interpretation (e.g. 1982: 166–8; 1985: ch 6; 1986: 228–38). A judge is like a writer trying to continue a story started by earlier writers. The writer must make the story as good as it can be. This necessitates that what he adds must be consistent with what went before (the requirement of 'fit'), and must make the best of that existing material by interpreting it in the most plausible and attractive way and then adding a contribution which will further enhance it. Since the task of the writer is to continue the story, he cannot simply go off on his own literary frolic but must create his own contribution in a way that is consistent with the best interpretation of the meaning of what went before. Of course, the writer must supply that interpretation. What will determine whether it is the best possible? Ultimately this will be a matter of whether it shows the previous contributions plus his own as an integrated whole, consistent and rich in meaning and clear in development. Similarly, a judge must tell the best story – construct the best legal meaning – from the work of previous contributors to legal doctrine. In adding his own contribution (the new decision in the case before him) he is constrained by the need for 'fit' with existing legal materials. Some interpretations which he might as a matter of personal preference like to adopt and act on are ruled out because they would not be consistent with the need to portray law as an integrated, principled whole.

Thus, Dworkin claims that his theory does not give judges the freedom of legislators, as the positivist idea of judicial discretion seems to do. They are constrained by the entire structure of values which the legal system represents. They are required to decide cases in ways that will further those values and portray legal doctrine as a whole, as an integrated and consistent expression of them. The need for consistency requires that a judge will put a high value on precedent and on the need to give effect to clearly expressed legislative provisions, quite apart from the fact that the legal system he serves may well have principles of *stare decisis* and of deference to the will of democratic legislatures as part of the fundamental structure of legal values which the judge must recognise (Dworkin 1986: 401).

At the same time, as in classical common law thought[9], Dworkin's theory allows a judge to assess critically the work of his predecessors even to the extent of declaring, and refusing to follow their 'mistakes'. Similarly, legislative provisions are to be considered in relation to the whole environment of relevant legislative history. In some instances this approach could lead a judge to conclusions about legislation which would be very much more than a straightforward application of statutory words (Dworkin 1986: 343–50).

The overall shape of Dworkin's theory is, therefore, remarkably like that of classical common law thought, as described in Chapter 2. Pound's sociological jurisprudence can be seen as prescriptive but also presents itself as an attempt to describe the common law system in objective terms as a set of balancing operations and procedures informed by a measure of values. As has been seen, the attempt at description runs into serious difficulties when the

---

[9]   See Chapter 2, above, pp. 25–6.

measure of values has to be objectively identified, and, perhaps, even when the initial task of identifying, listing and classifying interests is attempted. Classical common law thought was, however, never a descriptive theory of law but always a set of prescriptions and expectations as to how judges should go about their job. From this standpoint Dworkin's theory is more in harmony with classical common law thought than is Pound's because Dworkin effectively discards any claim to be offering objective description of law from some detached observer's standpoint. Once it is recognised that law is entirely a matter of interpretation it follows that all who are involved in discussing it must be engaged in the same interpretive exercise. Otherwise they cannot communicate information about law amongst themselves. The judge, the lawyer and the legal philosopher thus become, for Dworkin, participants in the same 'game' of interpretation. They are all involved in debates about what law is (whether for the purposes of arguing a particular case, or of understanding a line of precedents, or developing a theory of a specific legal field or of the legal system as a whole). But what law is depends on how the values understood as informing a legal order are to be interpreted. Thus, all participants in legal interpretation, according to Dworkin, are concerned also with what law ought to be. They cannot be *describers* of some objectively existing datum of law. They must be full participants in the discourse of legal argument of the particular legal system with which they are concerned.

One great advantage of this approach over Pound's is that the problem of objectively identifying a measure of values in the legal system disappears. Instead it is recognised that this measure is continually being constructed and reconstructed by participants in the system and makes sense only from a participant perspective. It is to be understood as the ongoing interpretive project of participants in the legal order and not as a set of postulates to be described from some external theoretical standpoint.

Law's Community

But there is a price to be paid for this apparent theoretical advance. What happens, for example, to the relationship between law and community which has been identified in this book as central to classical common law thought? It becomes, for Dworkin, what it is for classical common law thought: something which cannot be examined empirically but only taken for granted. This is because the theory offers no external or detached standpoint from which law's relationship with community can be analysed. Here is an illustration of the inherent and admitted limitations of Dworkin's theory arising from its wholly internal, insiders' perspective on law. All of the other major theorists so far considered in this book have sought to hold open the possibility of an external, uncommitted view of law, even if (as with Hart's concept of law) the quest for objective description of a legal system is combined with a proper insistence that an understanding of the internal, insiders' viewpoint on law is essential to any such objective description.

Dworkin writes extensively about community as the basis of law and about how it can be conceptualised (1986: 195–215), yet he can never offer any analysis of the actual social conditions under which a community can exist, of what the concept means when related to actual patterns of social life, or of the specific political and social circumstances in which it is useful to think of law as an expression of community values. Since previous chapters in this book have sought to suggest that these are important questions and that more sociologically sensitive theorists such as Fuller (pp. 139–42, above) have made valuable efforts to address them, Dworkin's silence about the empirical significance of a concept which is inevitably important to his theory is frustrating, even if understandable.

Equally, if we consider only the possibility of a philosophical analysis of the concept of community, Dworkin sees it as a moral-political structure of human interaction in which the collective development and fulfilment of values of justice, fairness and integrity are sought. But this is merely a projection of his image of what it is to participate in a legal system. Just as the classical common lawyers glimpsed community as an extension or projection of what they understood law to be, so for Dworkin the image of community is seen through a legal prism, as something implicit in the outlook of legal insiders participating in legal interpretation. For Dworkin, participants in legal interpretation within a legal system *are*, by virtue of their participation, the community.

This can be contrasted with Finnis' consideration of community which, although equally lacking empirical grounding in a study of actual social conditions, does proceed philosophically from first principles (pp. 147–8, above). The contrast here between Finnis and Dworkin is easily understood. Like Hart, but unlike Dworkin, Finnis asserts the possibility of a descriptive, rather than prescriptive or committed, legal theory (Finnis 1980: ch 1), even though it must accept the inevitability of moral evaluations and be founded on assumed universal moral intuitions. Hence Finnis' starting point is not Dworkin's wholly internal legal perspective but one in which both law and morals can be viewed from a standpoint which is not just that of participants in practical legal interpretation. Community is, therefore, something which can and should, for Finnis, be analysed for its moral significance as such. It does not appear merely as a projection of the outlook of legal 'insiders' on their law.

For Dworkin, therefore, the attempt to explain judicial creativity, in terms of law itself, leads to the conclusion that this can be done only by becoming a participant – adopting the standpoint of a lawyer or judge – in interpretation of law in the particular legal system concerned. But it will be seen in the final section of this chapter that ultimately Dworkin's approach leads to serious problems for normative legal theory as an explanation of judicial decision-making and processes of doctrinal development.

Politics, Professionalism and Interpretive Communities

Throughout this book normative legal theory has been consistently interpreted as, in part, a response to specific problems of legal professionalisation. There is little difficulty in interpreting Pound's defence of common law methods and the role of legal experts in these terms. But Dworkin seems to make some determined efforts to avoid his theory becoming a defence of professional prerogatives or of the intellectual or moral autonomy of professional legal knowledge. Thus he insists that the community of participants in legal interpretation is not just a community of lawyers. Anyone living within a society and actively committed to the values – the moral and political foundation – of its legal system is properly seen as a participant in the task of interpretation of that society's law. It follows that a citizen can quite properly disagree with the interpretation of the law offered by the highest court of the legal system. 'A citizen's allegiance is to the law, not to any particular person's view of what the law is, and he does not behave unfairly so long as he proceeds on his own considered and reasonable view of what the law requires' (Dworkin 1977: 214). What is reasonable is a matter of interpretive debate, like everything else entailed in deciding what the law is. But lawyers and judges have no necessary monopoly of such judgments. Thus, Dworkin provides a justification for civil disobedience; not one justifying *breach* of law, but one which justifies following a reasonably held interpretation of law which happens to differ from that made by official legal authorities. For Dworkin, this is not a licence to disobey but an assertion that there can be cases where the meaning of law – judged not just as rules, but as the whole structure of legal doctrine including the particular moral and political values crystallized in the doctrinal and institutional history of the legal system – is a matter of legitimate dispute. In such cases the view of citizen dissenters should be respected and their acts, based on such a view, should be judged with official tolerance. Dworkin has consistently maintained this view (see 1985: ch 4). Yet it seems profoundly unrealistic to ask for official toleration of acts which will be seen, by those who control the coercive power of a legal system, as law-breaking, not as alternative legal interpretation. It is also profoundly unrealistic to consider non-lawyer citizens, on the one hand, and lawyers or judges, on the other, as part of the same community of legal interpreters. For example, are we somehow to imagine the views expressed in scholarly law review articles on the meaning of current legislation as part of a debate with the opinions of poor people in decaying inner city neighbourhoods as to whether the fundamental values and principles of the legal system are accurately expressed in recent judicial pronouncements? This image of community is hardly convincing. If law is to be understood as interpretation, it is important to recognise clearly in legal theory that lawyers almost entirely monopolise that interpretation. Any other view seems either naïvely idealistic or a wilful refusal to recognise evidence from social experience. And it is tempting to suggest that Dworkin's strange lack of realism here derives from what was noted in the previous section – the impossibility of seriously examining the actual conditions of existence of a community within the terms of a theory expressing only the perspective of participants in that community. Since the participant perspective is inevitably that of the lawyer within a community of legal interpreters it becomes hard to see realistically, in terms of such a theory, the position of other social groups in their relationship with the professional group of lawyers.

Despite Dworkin's wish to defend a basis of citizen participation, his major writings in normative legal theory are almost entirely concerned with judicial interpretation of law. They consistently assume the judge to be the central figure in the interpretive community. Interpretation of legal meaning is treated as a matter for professionals. Hence we can consider what Dworkin's theory tells us about this *professional* interpretive community and the way it works. Here surely are to be found the answers to questions about the principles which guide legal development and judicial creativity?

But the theory cannot provide these answers. If law is entirely a matter of interpretation, as Dworkin now insists, the meaning of legal provisions cannot be controlled by any objective historical documents, conditions or events. This uncompromising position allows Dworkin to deny that any objectively existing legal or social conventions (such as Hart's rule of recognition or any other positivist criterion of law) determine what is valid as law. Equally it avoids Pound's problem of needing to identify jural postulates as objectively existing components of a legal system. But, of course, *something* must control legal interpretation. One radical answer as to what that might be is given by the literary theorist Stanley Fish in a law review debate with Dworkin. Fish agrees with Dworkin that law – like any literary text – is a matter of interpretation. He goes on to argue, however, that what is interpreted (a literary text or historical legal materials) cannot be distinguished from the interpretation itself – that the interpretation *constitutes* what is interpreted (Fish 1982; 1983). On Fish's view the controls that operate to limit possible interpretations are in no way given by the item interpreted itself (the statute or the precedent case, for example, does not, 'by its nature', rule out certain interpretations). The actual controls on interpretation arise from the conventions, expectations, shared understandings and structure of the interpreting community (for example, a legal profession, or a judiciary) and the skill in argument of the interpreters. Thus, it would seem to follow that in order to understand law-as-interpretation we must understand the social structure of the interpretive community and the pressures, constraints, modes of consensus formation, and conditions of conflict which actually exist within it and determine how the business of interpretation of law actually goes on. In other words, what seems to be required is a sociological view of the interpretive community of legal professionals and of their practices.

Although Fish's view preserves the idea of law as interpretation it appears to entail that constraints on interpretation can only be understood sociologically. But this denies the utility of what Dworkin advocates – a normative legal theory developed entirely from a legal insider's perspective. A sociological view of lawyers patently refuses to be restricted to such a perspective. Thus, Dworkin (1985: 176) rejects as 'extravagant' Fish's view that interpretation constitutes what is interpreted. In some way the historical legal record must be the foundation of legal interpretation, not the other way around. Therefore, he relies on the requirement of 'fit'. Legal interpretations must fit the historical materials of the legal system – the body of existing constitutional provisions, statutes, judicial precedents, etc. But this begins to look like legal positivism. What can determine the legal significance of these materials except some objective positivist criteria of law? Finally, therefore, to escape this positivist conclusion Dworkin is forced to the position that what constrain judicial interpretations are not historical legal materials in some objective sense but the judges' *convictions* about fit – again a matter of interpretation.

In what sense do these convictions constrain? Dworkin cannot rely, like Fish, on claims about the *collective* constraints exercised on judges (and lawyers) by their membership within the professional community. To understand why and how those constraints are collective (that is, arise within the professional group) it would be necessary, again, to understand the sociology of the interpretive community[10]. Thus, Dworkin's position is that the constraint on judges arises from their *personal* need as individuals to integrate their convictions about fit with their convictions about whether the interpretation they plan to adopt will show the interpreted legal practices or doctrine in the best light. The constraint is 'a structural constraint of different kinds of principle within a system of principle' (1986: 257).

But is this a constraint at all? Dworkin does, at least, recognise the obvious question: will a judge's convictions as to which interpretation shows legal practices and doctrine in the best light shape that judge's convictions about fit so that no constraining tensions between these two sets of convictions arise? (cf. Dworkin 1986: 236–7). But he gives no answer except to suggest that this depends on the complexity and structure of the individual judge's pertinent opinions as a whole. We are thus pushed into a realm of speculation about judges' personal philosophies in which realistic examination (for legal participants no less than for sociological observers) of the nature and effects of general constraints on judicial interpretation becomes impossible. The reason lies in Dworkin's refusal to abandon his vision of a self-contained arena of legal philosophical discourse which preserves intact a watertight separation of 'internal' (legal insiders') and 'external' (sociological) perspectives.

The lesson to be learned from this is surely that the search for legal principles governing judicial creativity can lead to at least three distinct projects. The most modest is Pound's – a rather unsystematic attempt to observe and describe the value elements and other considerations which, according to settled legal practice, the judge should take into account in deciding a hard case. Much more ambitious is Dworkin's singleminded attempt to see law and

---

[10] Cf. Karl Llewellyn's discussion of 'steadying factors' in judicial interpretation arising out of judges' professional and institutional environment: Llewellyn 1960, and see Chapter 7, below.

rationalise its components exclusively from the perspective of the conscientious judge and lawyer. Once it appears, however, that such an exclusively 'inside' perspective reduces to purely personal judicial convictions, only one possibility seems to remain open. This is to examine sociologically the structure and environment of the interpretive community which may determine how collective professional interpretations of law are possible. It is this remaining possibility which will be the central focus of the next chapter.

7   Varieties of Scepticism

Previous chapters have related developments in Anglo-American normative legal theory to a search for theoretical unity and system in law, as a body of knowledge and as a professional practice. In that perspective a kind of progression appears. We have observed classical common law theory struggling to come to terms with the emergence of the modern sovereign state and its centralised law-making authorities (Chapter 2). Historical jurisprudence was seen as offering some kind of support to the common law outlook in the nineteenth century through its attempts to specify theoretical links between law and culture. But this hardly seemed to solve the difficulties and positivist analytical jurisprudence appeared as a more realistic framework for confronting the relationship between law and political power. Later, as the utilitarian faith in rational government waned or assumed more complex forms, legal philosophy was pressed into service to explain law, not as the consequence of political power, but as its master or controlling normative framework. The assumed theoretical problems of sovereignty and, more fundamentally, the need to portray law in terms fitting for democratic government, in which regulatees are to be citizens rather than subjects, could be seen to inspire, at least in part, the transformations of analytical jurisprudence noted in Chapter 4. But the problem of the role of the judge remained in this theory and its inadequacy encouraged efforts – exemplified in different ways by main themes in Fuller's, Pound's and Dworkin's writings – to find a justification and explanation of judicial creativity (and legal interpretation more generally) in values inherent in Anglo-American law.

In one sense the wheel turns full circle because the virtues of classical common law thought – its insistence on the inseparability of law from an idea of community or communal values of some kind, its concern with underlying principle as much as with technical rule, its image of law as continuously and steadily developing – are now apparently what the writers considered in the previous two chapters are especially concerned to recapture. It seems as though the positivist revolution in legal thought in the nineteenth century failed; that it did not *replace* classical common law thought but merely confirmed the inadequacy of the common law outlook. At the same time, what might be called neo-classical common law thought, of which Dworkin's legal philosophy is the best example, raises difficulties of its own, explained in Chapter 6. Above all, it seems forced to give up any prospect of a science of law – in the sense of a search for something more systematic and objective than the participant perspective of a practical legal interpreter. Yet it was precisely that search for systematic theoretical explanation of the nature of law as a body of professional knowledge and as a distinctive professional practice which, as has been seen, first inspired and gave original legitimacy to modern Anglo-American legal philosophy in Bentham's and Austin's work.

Is there a way out of this impasse? Suppose we were to retrace our steps and go back to Austin's original starting point for legal science: the idea that a law is the result of a distinctive *action* (in his theory the act of commanding), and is to be understood in terms of those who perform the action (for Austin, the sovereign or sovereign body) and the means available to make the action effective (sanctions). Suppose that, without becoming embroiled again in arguments about sovereignty or the specific form of law, we were to treat these *behavioural* dimensions of law as the focus of scientific inquiry in legal theory. And suppose further, finally, that in order to avoid the problems encountered in Chapter 6 about guiding values and traditions inherent in a legal system and determining appropriate judicial innovations in doctrine, it were to be assumed as a starting point for analysis that innovations in legal doctrine are nothing more nor less than expressions of the wishes, policies, or preferences of the decision-makers (for example, judges) who create law. What would follow from such positions?

At least initially, taken without qualification or elaboration, these points of departure suggest a profound scepticism about normative analysis of law. They suggest that doctrine is less important than those who create it; that what judges do is more important than the reasoning with which they justify their decisions; that values are relevant to legal analysis only insofar as they represent the particular preferences of influential decision-makers; that legal outcomes reflect configurations of political power, not overarching social or political values. But this approach might also be called realistic, and seen as adopting the only starting points which make it possible to do full justice to the original motivating assumption of the analytical jurists – that law is a human creation, to be understood as it is and not as it might or should be. On this view, then, law is a matter of people doing the jobs of governing, resolving or containing disputes, allocating benefits or detriments and channelling state power to achieve specific purposes. It is not 'a brooding omnipresence in the sky' (Howe, ed, 1953 II: 822).

In such a 'realist' perspective it is possible to recognise that political authorities such as legislatures and administrative agencies are primary producers of legal rules and doctrine. At the same time the full extent of judicial power to develop law through creative interpretation can also be recognised, as a practical matter. Indeed, judges and courts – viewed merely as decision-makers determining disputes – might not look very different in character from administrative regulators or legislative rule-makers (cf. Llewellyn 1930a: 29–31). It will be recalled that Austin, too, was not convinced that the distinction between courts and other political agencies concerned with legal interpretation, adjudication and application of doctrine should be as sharply drawn as many lawyers and others would claim[1].

Anglo-American legal scholarship in the twentieth century has produced a broad current of writing which adopts such sceptical or realist premises as those suggested. This chapter will be concerned with the relevance of this literature, and its 'post-realist' legacy, for normative legal theory. But in discussing 'legal realism' it becomes necessary, for the first time in this book, to recognise a development in Anglo-American legal philosophy occurring on one side of the Atlantic which has had virtually no parallel on the other. In the literature of Anglo-American legal thought legal realism is almost exclusively *American* legal realism, and is known by that name. Although, in Britain, attention has been paid, alongside discussion of American developments, to the writings of some Scandinavian jurists who developed ideas comparable in some respects with those of the American realists, no similar realist movement in legal thought emerged in Britain as a significant indigenous development. Indeed, it has often proved difficult for British legal scholars to understand the immense significance of the realist movement in the United States. What, in America, became for a time (especially during the 1930s and 1940s) a set of presuppositions pervading legal scholarship and a tradition of thought which still informs much of the intellectual context of legal debate in the United States, has appeared to many legal philosophers in Britain as an almost incomprehensible naivety in thinking and writing about law; something thoroughly alien and to be accounted

---

[1]   See Chapter 3, above, pp 75–7.

for only by unique features of American law and legal history, of little relevance for legal philosophy in Britain.

Pragmatism and Realism

This situation needs explanation and there is no shortage of analyses of the social, economic and political conditions which provided the context for the loosely identifiable, broad and diverse American realist movement to flourish. Unlike much of the theory considered earlier in this book, legal realism actually encourages a contextual interpretation of itself and has been developed with *explicit* reference to its political and professional context. The reasons for this are clear. An attempt to explain law in behavioural terms entails examining its causes or origins in the decisions or directives of human actors, and its effects in terms of social consequences of those decisions or directives. Law is to be viewed *instrumentally*, not as doctrine deriving worth from its integrity or normative unity as a system of abstract ideas but as a means to practical ends, an instrument for appropriate governmental purposes (Llewellyn 1930a: 25–7). If law is understood in such terms, it should follow that legal scholarship and legal theory are also, in a realist conception, means to the ends of explaining and improving law as an efficient technology of regulation in its time and place. Hence a realist view of legal theory is likely to view developments in legal philosophy in terms of their functional relevance, or lack of relevance, to the legal needs of the time and place.

A particular philosophy, usually called pragmatism, underpins this outlook. In an orthodox pragmatist conception knowledge is 'true' to the extent that it is useful – that is, validated in experience. Indeed, there may perhaps be no better criterion of truth, in a pragmatist perspective, than the practical success of ideas in action; in this sense, knowledge *is* successful practice. Early in the twentieth century, such American philosophers as William James and John Dewey developed pragmatist philosophy in forms which seemed immediately relevant to legal issues (cf. Dewey 1924). Consider, for example, the problem of the nature of corporate personality raised earlier in Chapter 4. As noted there, H. L. A. Hart, in his Oxford inaugural lecture, takes this issue as an illustration of the sterility of much conceptual analysis in legal philosophy. His solution, as has been seen, is to consider legal statements in their specific linguistic contexts. Hence the legal meaning of 'corporation' can be understood only by considering linguistic contexts in which the concept is invoked. There is no 'thing' which can be identified with what law treats as a corporation or as corporate personality. Instead there are usages of legal language which lawyers can examine and (usually) make sense of in practical legal discourse.

From a realist-pragmatist perspective this is not sufficient. Legal discourse is not to be treated as self-validating. What determines legal usage? What is really meant when a court declares that a corporation has 'moved' its location from one city or state to another? What, in terms of actual practices, must have happened for the statement to be correct or meaningful? What is actually taking place when a corporation (not individual human beings such as its directors or employees, but the abstract entity itself) is held liable for a tort, crime or breach of contract? For lawyers none of these ideas or situations is necessarily odd or difficult, but if one seeks to consider law in terms of behaviour, as ideas which gain their validity as successful *practice* – that is, instrumentally – the particular forms of legal language may be intelligible (if at all) only as peculiarly complex and oblique ways of organising and expressing certain policies in regulatory form.

In one of the classic essays of legal realism, Felix Cohen reconsiders issues of corporate personality in just this way (Cohen 1935). Cohen's main point is that although legal language obtains significance and meaning only as a means to practical ends, much of it is expressed in forms which almost wholly obscure this instrumentality. Hence, instead of asking how particular social or economic goals are best to be served through a certain regulatory decision – for example, whether a trade union should be subject to liability in tort for the actions of its members – courts in Britain and the United States considered whether a trade union is a 'person' in law[2], an issue which, when phrased in abstract terms, is akin to the apocryphal scholastic dispute as to how many angels can stand on the point of a needle (Cohen 1935: 35, 38). The abstract question of personality is apparently treated as determining whether or not there can be liability. Frequently other concepts fill what Cohen sees as similar roles. They include the notion of 'property right' (serving as a kind of red light against interference with a private benefit or the *status quo*); 'fair value', 'due process', 'title', 'contract', 'conspiracy', 'malice' (all suggesting objective conditions rather than policy evaluations) 'and all the rest of the magic "solving words" of traditional jurisprudence' (Cohen 1935: 45).

What is in issue here? Can it not be said that what Cohen castigates

---

[2]   *Taff Vale Railway Co v Amalgamated Society of Railway Servants* [1901] AC 426; *United Mine Workers of America v Coronado Coal Co* (1922) 259 US 344.

in his 1935 paper as 'transcendental nonsense' is merely the special discourse of law, which is not that of politics or policy? Is it not absurdly naive to assert, as Cohen does, that all concepts 'that cannot be defined in terms of the elements of actual experience are meaningless' and to demand as an ultimatum of modern jurisprudence that any word 'that cannot pay up in the currency of fact, upon demand, is to be declared bankrupt, and we are to have no further dealings with it' (Cohen 1935: 48, 52)? Critics of realism among analytical jurists lost patience long ago with any such reductionist view of concepts and have usually treated statements such as Cohen's as textbook illustrations of legal realism's naive inability to appreciate the specific character of law's normative language. Why should legal ideas somehow be defined in terms of actual experience? And what is 'actual experience' for this purpose? A strict behaviouralist view ignores the reality of ideas; the possibility that legal reasoning should, in itself, be treated as part of social reality.

Although these criticisms are powerful they do not address the central questions raised. *Why* should the distinctiveness or autonomy of legal reasoning and language be accepted as appropriate or natural? Why should any line of demarcation between legal reasoning, on the one hand, and policy argument, on the other, be treated as self-evidently realistic or justifiable? Suppose we were to accept, with Cohen and other realists, that a judge is a type of policy-maker or policy-implementer; suppose we were to refuse to treat as self-evident that judges are *not* merely gowned politicians or administrators; suppose we remain unconvinced that when a judge decides a 'hard case' the decision is anything other than a legislative act (and not, as in Dworkin's view, something specially judicial and non-legislative in character); and suppose, finally, that we see the judge not as a delegate (as Austin suggested) of any identifiable sovereign, but rather (especially, perhaps, in the United States) as a functionary exercising power as part of a complex political system – a system characterised less by centralisation and delegation than by a network of law-making and law-applying jurisdictions offering considerable leeway to many judicial decision-makers. On the basis of such suppositions it makes sense to ask *why* legal language is expressed in forms which often obscure policy choices and present them as technical issues in the elaboration of legal logic. Requiring legal words to 'pay up in the currency of fact' then means requiring legal doctrine to reveal its politics on its face. And the dramatic, if philosophically clumsy, way in which the demand is made is perhaps a reflection of how urgent it seemed to many leading American lawyers in the early and mid-1930s that courts, as political agencies, should be seen to act as *responsible* political agencies, providing reasoned, intelligible policy-grounds for decisions with significant policy-impact on American society.

At another level, what is in issue is a matter much stressed by members of the recent Critical Legal Studies movement – one of the modern descendants of realism to be considered later in this chapter. Cohen's discussion highlights the aspect of language and thought (especially legal language and thought) which critical legal scholars term *reification* (see e.g. Gabel 1980). Legal ideas seem to take on a life of their own. They appear reified – 'thing-like', and are treated as having a reality distinct from the social, political or other functions which first gave them life and meaning. Hence legal reasoning becomes a kind of mystification. It becomes possible to theorise about the meaning of 'corporate personality', 'title' or 'contract' without considering as a central matter the policy, functions or settled practices which these concepts reflect, or, at least, once reflected in their origins.

Realism and Normative Legal Theory

Beyond a certain point, quickly reached, it becomes counterproductive to generalise about American legal realism. One of its most prominent figures, Karl Llewellyn, then a professor at Columbia University, declared in 1931: 'There is no school of realists. There is no likelihood that there will be such a school. There is no group with an official or accepted, or even with an emerging creed. . . There is, however, a *movement* in thought and work about law' (Llewellyn 1931a: 53, 54). Llewellyn himself claimed to have introduced the term 'realistic jurisprudence' into the modern legal literature in 1930 (Llewellyn 1930a; 1960: 512), and asserted three decades later that realism had always been merely a method or technology, not a legal philosophy. It embraced diverse work linked only by the vague injunctions 'see it fresh', 'see it as it works' (Llewellyn 1960: 509–10).

Llewellyn's 1931 defence of realism against Roscoe Pound (cf. Pound 1931) and other critics summarised the realists' 'common points of departure' as (i) a conception of law in flux, and of judicial creation of law; (ii) a conception of law as a means to an end, and not an end in itself; (iii) a conception of society in flux and of the need to re-examine law to keep it up to date with social need; (iv) temporary separation of study of law as it is from speculation as to what it should (ethically) be; (v) 'distrust of traditional legal rules and concepts insofar as they purport to *describe* what either courts or people are actually doing'; (vi) distrust of the idea that rules as expressed in the form of legal doctrine 'are *the* heavily operative factor in producing court decisions'; (vii) 'belief in the worthwhileness of grouping cases and legal situations into narrower categories than has been the practice in the past'; (viii) insistence on evaluating law in terms of its effects and on the importance of trying to discover these effects; and (ix) insistence on 'sustained and programmatic attack' on legal problems in these various ways (Llewellyn 1931a: 55–7).

Despite the vagueness of several components of this list, it is useful as indicating not only important preoccupations of Llewellyn himself, to which special attention will be devoted in the following pages, but as suggesting the divergent paths realist scholarship could take and the resulting possibility that different realist approaches could have differing relationships with normative legal theory, the concern of this book. If normative legal theory is theory attempting to explain the nature of law as a structure of legal ideas or legal doctrine – that is, in terms of the unity, autonomy, rationality, moral justification or systematic character of legal ideas or doctrine – it might appear that legal realism would necessarily deny the whole project of normative legal theory. In some of realism's most radical forms this would seem to be the case: law is to be considered in terms of behaviour *and not* doctrine. Item (viii) on Llewellyn's list indicates the realist concern with law's effects. Indeed, some legal realists concerned to examine seriously the social and economic effects of particular laws and legal institutions (for example Charles Clark on civil and criminal procedure; William Douglas on business failures and bankruptcy; and especially Underhill Moore on banking law and practice) did take very seriously a social science model of legal scholarship in which doctrinal analysis sometimes appeared relatively insignificant beside 'fact research' on the behaviour of lawyers and laymen.

Nevertheless, as J. H. Schlegel has shown, this serious activity of legal realists in conducting empirical research on law as a cluster of governmental activities and social and economic practices was a relatively shortlived matter and very much a minority concern (Schlegel 1979; 1980). For those realists most sympathetic to social science, research on legal institutions and practices came to be seen (with Moore perhaps remaining the only significant exception: see Schlegel 1980) as an aid to realistic policy analysis, to provide guidance and rational justification for legal doctrine. It would not displace lawyers' practical concerns with systematic doctrinal analysis and the rational development of legal thought but would bring those concerns into appropriate relationship with policy debate and pressing social need. This entailed a recognition that policy as an essential component of law imported social, economic and political concerns into any realistic analysis. But it did not necessarily lead to a commitment to what was called in Chapter 1 empirical legal theory – theory concerned to provide systematic explanation of the character of legal doctrine and institutions in general in terms of historical and social conditions. Policy-oriented realism suggested the inadequacy, for any realistic understanding of law, of all orthodox forms of normative legal theory, but not necessarily their replacement with any other coherent theoretical view of law.

At the same time, items (v) and (vi) on Llewellyn's list, representing what among British legal scholars, at least, are often seen as the core propositions of realist thought, suggest either a radical challenge to the whole enterprise of normative legal theory or, at least, a significant attack on the approaches to it which have been the concern of most previous chapters of this book. They suggest a greatly reduced significance of legal doctrine and its analysis as a basis for any serious understanding of the nature of law. Item (v) foreshadows Cohen's concern with the 'unreality' of legal concepts and implies that doctrine may provide little help in a realist enterprise concerned with explaining or describing law as socially significant practices. Item (vi) suggests legal doctrine's limited relevance for the prediction of behaviour – especially in predicting how judges will decide cases, not just in recognised 'hard cases' but even when they purport to be following or bound by established legal rules or precedents.

These elements of the realist outlook suggest not merely the need to supplement normative, doctrinal inquiries about law with reliable data about law's effects, but the apparently limited relevance of doctrine for an understanding of judicial practice or of social order. Thus, elsewhere, Llewellyn (1930a) contrasts 'paper' rules (such as those expressed in judicial opinions, statutes and law books) with 'real' rules (the actual patterns of decision by courts; what judges do as a matter of regular practice, as opposed to the doctrinal rationalisation of their decisions). 'One seeks the real practice on the subject, by study of how the cases do in fact eventuate. One seeks to determine how far the paper rule is real, how far *merely* paper' (1930a: 24). Llewellyn claims that, looking at the matter in realistic, behavioural terms, judges can be seen to have numerous opportunities, at least in the higher levels of judicial systems in appeal courts, to narrow or extend, apply or distinguish, restate or rephrase precedent and apparently established rules. The significance of legal doctrine and its analysis as a basis for understanding law is thus seriously put in issue.

An explicit, central concern with *predictability* of judicial decisions, which is a pervasive theme in much of Llewellyn' work and in many other realist writings, is not generally found in the theoretical writings considered earlier in this book. The theme is often traced to an 1897 speech in Boston by Oliver Wendell Holmes, later an Associate Justice of the United States Supreme Court and, in Llewellyn's (1931b: 103) words, the man 'from whom we [realists] all derive'. Holmes polemically declared: 'The prophecies of what the courts will do in fact, and nothing more pretentious, are what I mean by the law' (Holmes 1897: 461) and explained this as the realistic standpoint of a 'bad man' who cares nothing for ethical rules but merely wants to know what, if any, consequences will follow from law for him.

Holmes' 'bad man' standpoint was a useful one for deflating legal rhetoric and focussing on practical outcomes of law but it should not mislead a student of legal realism into thinking that the focus of concern is with lay rather than professional views of law, or that ultimately the focus on predictability suggests concerns any different from those which have been seen in earlier chapters as underpinning the development of normative legal theory. The predictability of judicial decisions sought by Holmes' realist followers is generally that required by professional lawyers: first, in order to be able to interpret – and so, to a reasonable extent, control – judicial development of law; and, secondly, so as to be able to claim convincingly to possess a body of systematic legal professional knowledge capable of providing reliable, practical guidance on the legal consequences of specific situations and transactions. The concern here as with other theory discussed in this book is the problem of convincingly maintaining a claim to a secure corpus of distinct professional knowledge in a situation in which law threatens to dissolve away into no more than the exercise of governmental discretions.

Llewellyn's concept of paper rules emphasises that analysis of legal doctrine could not produce knowledge of law without corresponding analysis of judicial behaviour. At no point, however, does Llewellyn deny that rules or other elements of legal doctrine are important matters for analysis. The essay in which paper rules are put in their place also contains the statement 'that I feel strongly the unwisdom, when turning the spotlight on behaviour, of throwing overboard emphasis on rules, concepts, ideology, and ideological stereotypes or patterns. . . a jurisprudence which was practically workable could not have been built in terms of them if they had not contained a goodly core of truth and sense' (Llewellyn 1930a: 37). This statement alone should invalidate the still common caricature of Llewellyn as a behaviouralist denying the importance of legal doctrine. But the threat here posed to normative legal theory is the equally forceful assertion that no reliable knowledge of law can come from examination of doctrine alone – as if it constituted or reflected the reality of law as practical activity.

Some realists, however, notably Jerome Frank, appeared virtually to abandon concern with legal doctrine in some of their theoretical writings. While Llewellyn's early writings emphasised behavioural factors which produced uncertainty and unpredictability in the way appeal courts applied rules and precedents, Frank found a more fundamental source of uncertainty in trial courts' fact-finding processes. Declaring himself a 'fact sceptic' in contrast to the 'rule sceptics' such as Llewellyn (Frank 1930: x–xi), he asserted that the rule sceptics' focus on appeal courts' interpretations of legal doctrine blinded them to the more basic uncertainties arising in trial courts' ascertainment of facts. The fallibility of witnesses, the prejudices or preconceptions of judges or jurors, the relative persuasiveness of counsel, and numerous other aspects of the courtroom environment made the process of fact-finding unscientific and unpredictable, with the result that unpredictability affected the establishment of material facts even before the trial court came to apply rules of law to them. In such circumstances appeal courts could generally do little to correct this fundamental source of unpredictability (Frank 1949: ch 3).

Frank's frequent claims that certainty was impossible to achieve in the judicial process were accompanied by the assertion that the childish quest for certainty should be replaced with an explicit concern for a clearly articulated justice of outcomes (e.g. Frank: 1930: xi). Yet Frank's legal philosophy seems to suppose that such justice can exist in isolation from certainty, and to ignore the possibility that the former might be no less elusive than the latter. Given these views it seems somewhat amazing that he became in 1941, after a series of significant governmental positions during the New Deal era of the 1930s, a judge of the United States Second Circuit. The appointment was likened in some quarters to the appointment of a heretic to serve as a bishop in the Roman Catholic Church (White 1976b: 275).

Thus, at least the following contrasting types of realist thought in relation to normative legal theory can be identified. The first, which could be labelled *policy-science realism*, emphasises 'fact research' (Nussbaum 1940) – empirical social scientific or behavioural studies – to inform and supplement doctrinal analysis and puts a related stress on the need to guide doctrinal development with a more sophisticated understanding of policy matters. Such an approach does not necessarily deny the utility of normative legal analysis or of normative legal theory as long as policy can be treated as something objectively recognisable or discoverable and incorporated into legal doctrine as a set of ideas susceptible (like rules) to rational interpretation and elaboration. A second type of realist orientation (which can be termed *radical scepticism*) is profoundly dubious about the value of orthodox doctrinal analysis and suggests that this kind of analysis offers no more than rationalisations or mystifications of legal reality as embodied in the actual practices of officials such as judges and other participants in legal processes. In this view judicial decisions or other legal outcomes may appear fundamentally unpredictable because grounded in unfathomable, or at least unfathomed, personality characteristics or preferences of the decision-maker; or they may appear intelligible only by treating them as political decisions uncontrolled by normative structures of legal doctrine or institutional or procedural constraints. Thirdly, a 'moderate' position, which might be called *constructive doctrinal realism*, does not deny the significance of analysis of legal doctrine in gaining an understanding of the nature of legal reality. But it asserts the hopeless inadequacy of any such understanding which does not take account of the behavioural factors which determine how and to what extent legal doctrine is significant in the production of judicial and other official decisions.

The crucial variable by which I distinguish these three realist orientations here is their attitude to normative legal analysis; that is, to the rational interpretation of legal doctrine. Policy-science realist writing could adopt any of a variety of positions: for example, that legal doctrine is socially insignificant or merely uninteresting, or indeterminate in its effects and therefore of unknown instrumental significance, or significant but harmful in its effects, or significant but created and applied in ignorance of its specific social consequences. On the basis of any of these positions the importance of social scientific 'fact research' on law could be asserted. By contrast, radical sceptical realism is directly concerned with doctrine but in a negative, sceptical way, denying explicitly the traditional claims made for doctrinal rationality and its significance. Its concern is to demystify or debunk legal doctrine and traditional forms of legal reasoning. Law in this radical view is, in essence, not doctrine but policy, politics, personal preferences of powerful decision-makers – or (ideally) justice.

Finally, from what I characterise as a constructive doctrinal realist position, doctrine is viewed as important and (at least potentially) socially valuable yet its character is asserted to be greatly misunderstood by orthodox doctrinal analyses and normative legal theory. New ways should be found to make normative analysis of law realistic by examining the institutional settings and social, economic and political contexts in which legal doctrine operates and is developed and by reorganising or reinterpreting doctrine in the light of these inquiries. It should be noted, also, that policy-science realism is compatible with either of the other two realist orientations, but, as noted earlier, serious social scientific policy research was always very much a minority pursuit among realist legal scholars. On the other hand, radical sceptical realism and constructive doctrinal realism are plainly mutually incompatible, although some realists might be considered to have wavered between the two; and some may have matured (or, from another viewpoint, weakened) from a radical to a constructive outlook over time.

In the remaining sections of this chapter aspects of the development of these three positions in realist and post-realist American legal thought will be traced. In important respects the third (constructive doctrinal) position (especially represented by the evolution of Llewellyn's jurisprudence) offers the most direct and sustained engagement with orthodox forms of normative theory (neither polemically dismissing it in favour of purely behavioural inquiries as Frank's fact scepticism sometimes seemed to advocate, nor merely supplementing or elaborating it through policy analysis of the actual or potential content of legal doctrine). Consequently, while the policy-science and radical sceptic approaches are, as will appear, the foundation of important modern attempts in legal scholarship to come to terms with the legacy of realist thought, constructive doctrinal realism, exemplified in Llewellyn's work, has generally been treated, by serious scholars of realism concerned with legal theory, as the variety of realist thought offering the most direct and productive confrontation with orthodox forms of normative legal theory.

Llewellyn's Constructive Doctrinal Realism

Hart (1961: 133) refers to 'rule scepticism' as 'the claim that talk of rules is a myth, cloaking the truth that law consists simply of the decisions of courts and the prediction of them'. If, as seems likely, this is intended to refer to Llewellyn's theories (cf. Hart 1961: 232, 250; Twining 1968: 6), it is a serious distortion, yet typical of the misunderstandings of realism often found, at least until recently, among analytical jurists in Britain. Llewellyn expressed regret that a single sentence ('What these officials do about disputes is, to my mind, the law itself') in one of his early works, taken out of context, 'was enough to characterise a whole man and his whole position' for many critics of realism[3]. As noted earlier, Llewellyn's belittling of paper rules in 1930 was accompanied by a firm insistence in the same essay (Llewellyn 1930a) that an emphasis on legal behaviour certainly did not make the study of legal doctrine unimportant. In Llewellyn's view, however, a sensitivity to what courts are doing (decisions and their practical consequences), as well as to the way judges rationalise their actions through legal rules and principles, ought to make legal scholars view doctrine much more cautiously and critically.

Llewellyn's writing does not usually show the kind of cynicism about orthodox conceptual thought in law which is suggested by Felix Cohen's essay on the 'transcendental nonsense' of legal ideas, or Thurman Arnold's analogies between legal reasoning and theological debate (Arnold 1935: 59–67), or Frank's deliberately provocative talk of 'modern legal magic' (Frank 1949: chs 4 and 5). Instead, Llewellyn consistently emphasises the need to narrow the scope of legal concepts, using more specific, particularised categories in doctrinal classification which reflect actual distinctions patterned in judicial practice but not necessarily recognised in paper rules and text-book concepts (Llewellyn 1930a: 27–8; 1931a: 56–7).

Thus, Llewellyn's influential *Cases and Materials on the Law of Sales*, first published in 1930, breaks down the concept of 'title' by reference to doctrinal categories reflecting specific stages at which distinct sales issues arise. And he makes explicit the way behavioural study should be integrated with study of the paper rules: 'study of the actual use of the title concept by the courts in contracts for future sale results in the conclusion that the allocation of title is in fact determined repeatedly by features of the contract which serve equally well to solve the problem without recourse to the title concept itself' (Llewellyn 1930b: xiv; cf. Wiseman 1987: 476–7). This does not mean that the 'paper' legal concept is to be discarded in a behavioural view but that 'the student can come to see title for what it really is: a concept historically conditioning the etiquette of sales discussion; a wholly unnecessary major premise introduced as a matter of inertia or of etiquette in perhaps half the cases; in other cases, a convenient bridge for moving from

---

[3] See Llewellyn 1951: 8–10, 12; 1960: 511; Twining 1973: 148–50; cf. Hart 1977: 124.

one aspect of the contract to some other in regard to which the contract is not equally explicit; lastly, a concept so hallowed by tradition that it must be reckoned with as sometimes obscuring a sensible solution of the case in hand. To get along without the title concept, to get along without learning to use it, reason with it, argue from it is impossible' but to treat it in isolation from its actual practical use (or non-use) 'is to lose perspective on modern developments' (Llewellyn 1930b: xiv-xv). This goes beyond Hart's insistence that concepts are to be understood in their legal linguistic context. Llewellyn requires that concepts be interpreted not just as elements in specific statements made by judges or lawyers. They are to be understood in relation to the outcomes which they may aid, or obstruct. Doctrine may constitute a practical problem, no less than a solution, in official decision-making.

The general issue of the relationship between judging as a problem of efficient administrative behaviour and legal doctrine as an ideal structure of rational guidance for conduct is the central focus of much of Llewellyn's most important work both as a legal theorist and as an eminent American commercial lawyer, who was primarily responsible for determining the original shape and structure of the United States Uniform Commercial Code which now provides the general framework for much American commercial law[4]. Llewellyn's method 'is to take accepted doctrine, and check its words against its results. . . If a doctrine [legal rule, principle, concept] does not, in and by itself do all that it purports to do, then *what else* is at work helping the doctrine out' (1940: 135). Thus, by 1940, at least, Llewellyn's consistent emphasis is not (as was Frank's) on the factors promoting uncertainty and unpredictability in law, but on those producing a remarkable predictability of legal outcomes, *despite* the 'leeways of precedent', the indeterminacy of doctrine or its inability to remove the human and subjective character of judging (cf. Frank 1949: 31; Llewellyn 1960: 4, 45). Equally, by this time, Llewellyn has the germ of an answer as to what else is at work helping doctrine out. 'There is the tradition of the judge's craft, stabilising the work of our judges, and guiding it; and there are the ideals of that craft, which also stabilise and guide' (1940: 135). Llewellyn's behavioural perspective on law becomes a perspective on courts and judiciaries (and other components of the legal world) as *institutions* (Llewellyn 1941; cf. Twining 1973: 176-7) – stable patterns and structures of behaviour operating within a set of normative expectations about, for example, the right way to do the job of judging, the right way

---

[4]   See generally Wiseman 1987, and literature cited therein.

to organise a court and a hearing, the right way to read precedent cases, the right way to reach and justify decisions.

In the writings of the last two decades of Llewellyn's career, and especially in his richly imaginative book *The Common Law Tradition* published just over a year before his death in 1962, this institutional view of judging is elaborated in depth. Llewellyn gained very important insights into the social and institutional conditions under which judicial craftsmanship could be developed through his collaboration in the 1930s and 1940s with the anthropologist E. A. Hoebel in studying social control and dispute resolution processes in several native American tribes. Of these studies the most important in its general influence on Llewellyn's theoretical ideas about legal institutions was that of the Cheyenne Indians (Llewellyn and Hoebel 1941; Twining 1973: ch 8). Though most of the fieldwork was done by Hoebel, Llewellyn developed a very strong sympathy with the communally based judicial wisdom which he saw reflected in the case histories of problem solving in traditional Cheyenne life collected by the researchers. The study of a small scale society in its past glory[5] was of profound concern to Llewellyn, otherwise devoting much of his time as an American commercial lawyer to intricate problems of regulation in one of the world's most complex and advanced societies.

In what he and Hoebel portrayed as well-ordered traditional Cheyenne society, Llewellyn thought he saw the simple essence of juristic method – not as the rational organisation and application of legal doctrine but as performance of a social task of good government: 'the search for serviceable forms and devices. . . the quest for their skilful use. . . the seeking to keep vital and vigorous under any form, any formula, any "rule", its living reason, its principle' (Llewellyn and Hoebel 1941: 307). For Llewellyn, doctrine is the product of a certain way of working. As such it reflects a particular behavioural style pervasive within the legal institutions of the time and place. 'Juristic method is not dissimilar in nature from style in art – an extremely complex and subtle set of somethings which affect in varying degree a whole range of craftsmen at once, yet allow huge divergencies. . .' (Llewellyn and Hoebel 1941: 308). And because the style of working and its social context is more fundamental than the doctrine to which it gives rise, legal doctrine alone does not express the whole of legal life or even its most fundamental elements.

---

[5]   Much of the case material consisted of informants' recollections of events and practices from at least half a century earlier.

Period-Style

In *The Common Law Tradition*, published nearly two decades after
the Cheyenne study, Llewellyn develops in detail, and specifically
in relation to American appellate courts, the idea of a behavioural
style of judging pervasive among judiciaries in a certain time and
place. 'It is the general and pervasive manner, over the country
at large, at any given time, of going about the job, the general
outlook, the ways of professional knowhow, the kind of thing the
men of law are sensitive to and strive for, the tone and flavour
of the working and of the results. It is well described as a "period-
style"' (Llewellyn 1960: 36; and see Llewellyn 1942). The importance
of this idea in relation to the critique of orthodox forms of normative
legal theory is that it makes possible for Llewellyn (and justifies
as absolutely essential) a fusion of behavioural analysis of judicial
work and normative analysis of legal doctrine (Llewellyn 1941).
Doctrine is the expression and reflection of a style of working –
not the cause of it but the consequence; it makes no sense to try
to understand law as a structure of ideas without recognising and
analysing the institutional settings and wider social and professional
environments which, in determining the general period-style of the
judiciary, shape the form and content of those ideas. At the same
time, period-style is revealed most clearly in the judicial reasoning
preserved in law reports. Indeed, *The Common Law Tradition* relies
on the examination of vast numbers of cases from many American
state jurisdictions to plot changes in period-style over time.

Llewellyn identifies two contrasting period-styles. Grand Style
judging (or the Style of Reason) treats precedents as welcome and
very persuasive but tests them against (i) the reputation of the
opinion-writing judge, (ii) principle, which is understood as 'no
mere verbal tool for bringing large-scale order into the rules' but
'a broad generalisation which must yield patent sense as well as
order', and (iii) policy 'in terms of prospective consequences of
the rule under consideration' (1960: 36). Grand Style allows 'ongoing renovation of doctrine' but (at its best) with no hint of
revolution in the law or even of campaigning reform. It involves
a constant quest for the best law for the future but the 'best law
is to be built on and out of what the past can offer; the quest
consists in a constant re-examination and reworking of a heritage'
(1960: 36). Parallels with Dworkin's description of appropriate
judicial methods (see Chapter 6) are clear, and it is unsurprising
that Llewellyn explicitly associates Grand Style with what he sees
as the ideal tradition of common law judging. But, unlike Dworkin,
Llewellyn does not characterise this judicial approach as something

inbuilt in the value system and doctrinal traditions of Anglo-American law (as something internal to law as a system of ideas) but portrays it as a style which waxes and wanes in American legal history as a result of complex historical causes. These operate as institutional pressures on behaviour which (presumably) demand sociological explanation.

In contrast to Grand Style stands Formal (or Authoritarian) Style, which Llewellyn describes as 'the orthodox ideology' in the American context since the late nineteenth century (1960: 38), though displaced to some extent by a renaissance of Grand Style from the early decades of the twentieth century. In Formal Style 'the rules of law are to decide the cases; policy is for the legislature, not for the courts, and so is change even in pure common law. Opinions run in deductive form with an air or expression of single-line inevitability. "Principle" [here meaning something quite different from what it means in Grand Style judging] is a generalisation producing order which can and should be used to prune away those "anomalous" cases or rules which do not fit, such cases or rules having no function except, in places where the supposed "principle" does not work well, to accomplish sense – but sense is no official concern of a formal-style court' (1960: 38).

Much of *The Common Law Tradition* is concerned with plotting the historical movement in actual judicial practice in a variety of American state jurisdictions between these two styles. Later writers have challenged Llewellyn's periodisation and offered more sophisticated accounts of the processes of transition between broad styles of legal thought (e.g. Horwitz 1977). What is important here, however, in examining the progress of debates in normative legal theory in the Anglo-American context is that Llewellyn's writings not only express realism's behavioural critique of 'pure' doctrinal analysis in law (and of normative legal theory presupposing the possibility of explaining law as a system of ideas) but suggest means of viewing law behaviourally (or institutionally) in such a way as to clarify and enhance analysis of doctrine. Just as Stanley Fish's critique of Dworkin[6] suggests the need to examine sociologically the nature of the actual community of legal interpreters (primarily judges) and the forces at work promoting or disrupting conformity and consensus within it, Llewellyn's identification of the historical importance of specific period-styles among particular judiciaries points towards the need for empirical inquiry into social, economic,

---

[6]   See Chapter 6, above, pp 179–80.

political and professional conditions which give rise to the dominance of particular, pervasive judicial styles[7].

The institutional orientation of Llewellyn's study is further reinforced by his identification elsewhere in *The Common Law Tradition* of a range of 'steadying factors' which, together with the period-style of the time and place, promote consistency and predictability in appeal court decision-making. These include the common training and experience of judges in a professional legal environment, the constraints of group decision-making and of the professional environment as a whole, shared judicial values, the public character of the judicial office, and a range of procedural factors limiting the variables to be considered in the decision-making process. Thus, doctrine is to be understood, and can only be understood, in its institutional setting. Normative legal theory, insofar as it denies the need for systematic behavioural analysis, misrepresents the character of doctrine and prevents realistic understanding of the nature of law. In the light of all this, some analytical jurists' caricature of legal realism as uniformly denying the fundamental significance of rules and other elements of legal doctrine appears as no more than a smokescreen obscuring the need to confront constructive doctrinal realism.

The Recapture of Grand Style

Llewellyn sought to make his version of realism a practical contribution to better, more predictable judicial practice. In his writings, Grand Style judging is advocated as far more conducive to certainty and predictability in law than Formal Style because, unlike the latter, it reveals the instrumental purposes of doctrine within judicial reasoning itself. The Grand Style invocation of principle and policy makes explicit what a particular newly formulated element of legal doctrine *is for*. By contrast, the air of 'single-line inevitability' conveyed by Formal Style deductive reasoning is likely to obscure reasons for doctrinal developments with the result that the real motivations behind judicial decisions remain hidden or ambiguous and so likely paths of judicial development of doctrine are harder to predict. Grand Style is more likely to produce 'rules which make sense on their face, and which

---

[7]   Llewellyn describes (1960: 24–5), for example, the 'single right answer' outlook (now strongly associated with Dworkin's legal philosophy: see above, p. 171) as one such matter of judicial style to be considered sociologically.

can be understood and reasonably well applied even by mediocre men' (Llewellyn 1960: 38).

There is much room for debate about the claimed virtues of Grand Style. Behind these positions, however, lies Llewellyn's conviction that doctrine cannot, and should not attempt to *control* judges, but should be framed to *guide* them (cf. 1931b: 110). A creative and conscientious judge constrained by Formal Style expectations may well seek to escape the limitations of deductive logic by ingenious manipulation of the precedents, fine distinctions and covert reinterpretations of established rules. Judges hamstrung by rules which give no leeway to do justice are likely to behave unpredictably (Llewellyn 1940: 144). The vital point is that the effectively operating pressures for conformity in judging are not produced primarily by rules but by the whole institutional environment in which the job of judging is done. Doctrine, for Llewellyn, should guide judges in appropriate directions while giving them creative freedom within the constraints inherent in their role as part of the judiciary as an institution.

Thus, Llewellyn's drafts in the 1940s for what became the American Uniform Commercial Code assumed that the Code would provide a framework of concepts and principles by means of which commercial law within the Code's scope would be standardised. But its provisions should be 'purposive statements of principles based on facts of commercial transactions and designed to guide flexible decisionmaking' (Wiseman 1987: 497). The aim would be to provide doctrinal guidance easily intelligible in terms of the purposes it was intended to serve (Twining 1973: 305). Courts would be encouraged to develop the rules of the Code in the light of these purposes. Lengthy 'Official Comments' in the Code would elaborate its underlying reasons, purposes and policies as an aid to judicial interpretation and application. Judges could not be forced to reason in Grand Style but the means of doing so could be made available to them in statutory form (Wiseman 1987: 498–502; Twining 1973: 321–30). At the same time, the Code, in Llewellyn's view, had to embody the realist insistence that doctrinal concepts and categories be made more functional by breaking them down into less abstract and generalised ideas more representative of the variety and complexities of practical conditions. Hence the Code would incorporate 'merchant rules' expressing the better standards and practices, understandings and needs of merchants (trade usage could, for example, be assumed to provide the shared factual and normative assumptions underlying a merchant transaction). Equally, the Code would distinguish merchant from non-merchant contexts; and it would provide for issues of mercantile fact arising under the merchant provisions to be tried by a merchant tribunal possessing expert knowledge of the field (Wiseman 1987: 503–4, 505). While important parts of Llewellyn's scheme did not survive the lengthy period of development of the Uniform Commercial Code, his proposals are a clear example of the effort to make constructive doctrinal realism serve practical professional needs for a rational system of legal doctrine.

The Political Context of American Legal Realism

Why has realism in this and other forms had little impact on normative legal theory in Britain, while it received, and still receives, much attention in the United States? It is important to note, first, that the idea of realism's limited impact in Britain needs to be qualified by recognition that post-realist developments in legal theory, to be mentioned in the remaining sections of this chapter, are having an increasingly powerful influence on legal thought on both sides of the Atlantic. Is it merely a matter of a long delayed reception of realist ideas in Britain, rather than dismissal of them?

Orthodox contextual explanations of American legal realism encourage an image of it as a product of distinctive historical and political conditions in the United States. It is seen as a consequence of the extraordinary historical role of courts in American government (Hart 1977: 124), and especially of a constitutional framework allowing judicial review of the validity of legislation. This emphasis on courts reflects a more general view of political power as appropriately decentralised and dispersed; institutionally through the federal system and the doctrine of separation of powers, and geographically and culturally through the sheer practical impossibility of imposing uniform solutions to all governmental problems in a nation of such size and diversity.

More detailed analyses along the same lines seek to explain why the realist movement arose in the early decades of the twentieth century. It was a response to a crisis of 'overload' in legal doctrine and the resultant inability of courts to operate a system of judicial precedent on the traditional common law model. 'Toward the end of the nineteenth century the rate of acceleration in printed case reports became nightmarish. Digests of all reported cases decided from the institution of courts in the American colonies until 1896 – a period of over two hundred years – take up three shelves in the Law Library. Digests of cases decided since 1896 [and up to 1960] fill more than thirty shelves' (Gilmore 1961: 1041). As Grant Gilmore explains, not only were many more cases being decided from the late nineteenth century as both the population and the number of courts and state jurisdictions grew, but a higher proportion of cases was being reported, especially as a result of the establishment of the West National Reporter system in the 1870s. When the number of reported cases 'becomes like the number of grains of sand on the beach' a precedent system cannot work (Gilmore 1961: 1041). And the problem in the American context was exacerbated by the fact that most private law problems were left to the individual states, and were left by the states to courts.

This now familiar explanation of the crisis which produced the origins of American realism is usually supplemented, at least in modern American histories, with a more specific political explanation. Justice Oliver Wendell Holmes' famous dissenting opinions in the United States Supreme Court[8] are typically seen as a protest against the mindlessly mechanical legal logic of the majority of the court at a time when (at the turn of the century) American government was faced with immense problems of adapting to social and economic change. What Pound saw as 'mechanical jurisprudence' (see Chapter 6) to be remedied by legislative inspiration and a renewal of the traditional evolutionary practice of common law judging, Holmes saw as judicial frustration of the popular will for legal change by judges who imported their own prejudices into their decisions under cover of legal logic. But Holmes' view was not realist in the sense of those legal realists who adopted him as their mentor. While he claimed[9] that courts could operate objectively and leave the expression of policy convictions to democratically elected legislators, the legal realists tended to see courts as inevitably involved in policy decision. The issue became what policies they promoted and how open they were in admitting value preferences.

Thus, the orthodox story of legal realism sees its flowering as a dominant legal theory in the 1930s as an almost inevitable expression in legal thought of the political demands which gave rise to Franklin Roosevelt's 'New Deal' government in the same period. These demands were for clear policy uniting all government agencies to attack the fundamental social and economic crises of the Depression era beginning with the Wall Street stock market crash of 1929. Thus, for some writers, legal realism is essentially the jurisprudential analogue of the New Deal (White 1972; Murphy 1972: ch 4). There is, undoubtedly, much truth in this. The urgent need for new approaches to legal scholarship which would provide

---

[8] Especially *Lochner v New York* (1905) 198 US 45, 75–6.
[9] As shown clearly in his *Lochner* dissent.

guidance for 'social planning and perspective' to lift America from 'the social and economic debacle' was the theme of the 1932 presidential address to the Association of American Law Schools (Harno 1932). Equally, the shrill political criticisms which realism as a whole attracted from some extreme critics were exactly those applied to the Roosevelt New Deal; it was held to exhibit totalitarian or fascist tendencies and a contempt for the Rule of Law (cf. Purcell 1973: ch 9). Many leading realists were fervent supporters of, and in several cases active partipants in, the governmental activities of the New Deal (see e.g. Twining 1973: 58). In this regard, as so often, the most arresting statement is Jerome Frank's. In 1934 he described himself and other 'experimental jurisprudes' as 'humble servants to that master experimentalist, Franklin Roosevelt' (quoted in White 1976b: 275). Thus, the problem of justice as the aim of judicial (and administrative) practice was solved for some realists by a belief in the inherent correctness of certain policies or of particular means of reaching them.

Two major conclusions follow if these kinds of explanations of American realism are treated as comprehensive. First, realism is essentially a parochial concern of American law and lawyers. Hence it has little, if any, wider jurisprudential significance. Secondly, realism was a response to legal and political crises which have now passed. Gilmore (1961), for example, argues that various developments helped to defuse the American legal crisis of precedent 'overload'. Especially significant were the American Law Institute's systematic Restatements of common law doctrine, which were widely relied upon by courts, certain changes in approaches to precedent, to judicial interpretation of legislation and to legislative drafting, the use of codification in important areas of American law, and the federalisation of private law.

These orthodox explanations of realism are not wrong. But they may not tell the whole story. First, the explanation in terms of the special role of courts in American government makes it hard to see why forms of legal realism developed independently in other countries having very different judicial systems. As mentioned earlier in this chapter, a form of legal realism developed in the Scandinavian countries in the first half of the twentieth century. At the turn of the century in Germany a movement known as the 'Free Law' (*Freirechtslehre*) school, uniting legal practitioners such as Ernst Fuchs and jurists such as Hermann Kantorowicz, similarly stressed the indeterminacy of legal rules – taken alone – as predictions of judicial decisions, the inevitably creative role of the judge, and the importance of explicitly recognising and responsibly developing this role – with its relative freedom from doctrinal restraint – to meet the needs of the time. A major impetus behind the Free Law movement seems to have been the perceived excessive abstraction and formalism of the German Civil Code which came into force in 1900 and which was seen as hampering judicial resolution of pressing problems arising from rapid social and economic change (see e.g. Nussbaum 1940: 187–8). In Scandinavia, also, legal realism seems to have been popularised in reaction to abstractions in legal reasoning and doctrine which appeared socially irrelevant or failed to address policy demands directly (Castberg 1955: 389–90).

Secondly, although there is much plausibility in Gilmore's tracing of American realism to the problem of precedent overload, it is doubtful whether the problem has been largely solved, as he seems to suggest, or that it can be regarded as uniquely American. It seems more likely that the undoubtedly acute form of this problem in the United States at a certain time (together with the major political and social crises of the Depression era) highlighted in a specially dramatic way a difficulty endemic to common law systems in the twentieth century. This is the difficulty of interpreting and justifying judicial decision-making in a context of increasing governmental steering of social and economic life; a context in which courts' attitudes to problems of policy-making and policy-implementation appear increasingly crucial.

Finally, to describe American legal realism as the jurisprudential analogue of the New Deal ignores the fact that arguably its most important theorist, Karl Llewellyn, was not a New Deal supporter (Twining 1973: 125) and regarded the events and issues of the New Deal as largely irrelevant to realism's primary contributions to legal analysis. The New Deal era was an 'accident' which 'threw the whole emerging line of inquiry off-centre' and, if anything, hampered its development (Llewellyn 1960: 14). For Llewellyn, at least, realism was a response to dilemmas which long antedated the New Deal and in no way disappeared with the passing of the Roosevelt era.

What all of this suggests is that, while American legal realism did become a major movement at a certain time as a response to distinctively American legal, political and social circumstances, it can also be seen as a particularly explicit, unrestrained expression of much more general problems in the development of Western law, which have remained unsolved in the forms of Anglo-American normative legal theory discussed earlier in this book. At the heart of those problems is the one which all attempts to portray law as an integrated system of ideas have failed to hide – that of the unrestrained power of the judge, or other legal decision-maker, as a political actor. Various rationalisations have been offered but none has really solved the problem. Modern positivist analytical jurisprudence postulates a clear distinction between a 'core' and 'penumbra' of meaning of legal rules[10]. As long as the existence of a core of indisputable meaning of legal doctrine could be accepted, judicial decision-making could be seen to have at least *some* realm distinct from the expression of personal judicial values or preferences, or from policy-making judicial legislative activity. But it was noted in Chapter 4 that this claim could be maintained only through sociological inquiries into the nature of the judicial role which Hart's analytical jurisprudence was not prepared to undertake. Much other modern theory discussed in this book has tried to find the solution to the problem of explaining the judicial role within the confines of normative legal theory by postulating an overarching structure of legal values within which judicial decisions in hard cases are to be made. But, as has been argued in previous chapters, it may require a leap of faith to recognise these values and see them controlling actual judicial behaviour.

Legal realism has been marginalised in Britain partly because much of its literature does, indeed, reflect a distinctively American context and distinctively American problems while making little serious effort to address its arguments to wider issues and theoretical debates about Anglo-American law. But its most rigorous and least parochial writings have performed the invaluable service of demonstrating the problematic character of any attempt by normative legal theory to explain the character of law as doctrine without serious empirical examination of the social and political conditions within which that doctrine is developed and invoked.

Post-Realist Policy-Science

Llewellyn's work offers perhaps the most instructive form of constructive doctrinal realism. The critique of normative legal theory which it implies will be considered further in the last chapter of this book. It remains to consider briefly the way in which the other two types of realism – which I call its policy-science and radical sceptical forms – have evolved in recent legal scholarship.

Las-dougalism

As noted earlier, policy-science realism is compatible with a variety

---

[10] See Chapter 4, above, pp. 105–6.

of attitudes to legal doctrine. In the 1940s, the Yale law professor Myres McDougal and his political scientist colleague Harold Lasswell began a long term collaboration founded in the conviction that the discipline of law should become a policy science – a technology for achieving social goals and realising democratic values in practice through the use of legal doctrine and institutions. In this way legal realism's critique of traditional legal analysis for failing to see doctrinal logic's subservience to considerations of policy could be made constructive. It could become a prescription for realistic legal education, scholarship and advocacy in which the rational elaboration of techniques of policy-formulation and implementation would be central (Lasswell and McDougal 1943). 'Las-dougalism' (cf. Schlegel 1979: 461) has been appropriately described by William Twining as 'a combination of utilitarianism and Freudian psychology, supplemented by some of the insights of American social science, and encased in an elaborate terminology' (Twining 1973: 385). Perhaps partly because of the last of these elements, McDougal and Lasswell's policy-science of law has had little enduring or widespread influence, except among some scholars of international law. Probably a more important reason for its limited impact is that it did not really address the practical problems of doctrinal rationality and predictability which realism had emphasised, but rather tried to persuade lawyers to avoid them by adopting new and unfamiliar modes of analysis.

Law and Society

Much more important in its scale and influence is the 'law and society' movement which developed in the United States and other countries from the 1960s as a multidisciplinary movement committed to social scientific research on law. In its broadest sense this is a modern phase in the continuing international development of sociology of law – sociologically informed empirical and theoretical research on law – which has a long history and a rich and varied theoretical tradition (see generally Cotterrell 1984). But, in the context of this chapter's concerns, an important unifying element in the early development of law and society researches was their (relatively atheoretical) concern with legal 'impact' or effectiveness; that is, with studies of the effects on behaviour of particular legal rules or other doctrine, or the effects of legal institutions in practice. This kind of 'impact' study of law in action is a direct successor of the pioneer empirical researches of legal realists such as Underhill Moore, Charles Clark and William Douglas in the 1920s and 1930s. Law and society research in this form – not directly concerned with the nature of legal doctrine in general or with engaging with general theories of the nature of law – has little direct bearing on the concerns of normative legal theory. Thus, much law and society research has posed no challenge to this theory. It has restricted its concern to behaviour and left the theoretical analysis of the nature of legal doctrine to legal philosophers. Until relatively recently, the long tradition in the sociology of law of what I call empirical legal theory – concerned to explain theoretically the nature of law as doctrine and behaviour in historical and social context – has not been a central concern for law and society studies, at least in the homeland of American realism.

Economic Analysis of Law

Finally, among policy-science realism's successor movements it is important to mention the recent rapid development of economic analysis of law; a form of legal scholarship now widely established and recognised in American law schools and of increasing significance in the British academic legal world. That the application to law of the theories and methods of economics has achieved a significant penetration of the law school world is a tribute to the versatility of economic analysis. Thus, techniques of positive (that is, essentially explanatory rather than prescriptive) economic analysis can be used in legal impact studies by considering law's contribution to shaping the behaviour choices which rational, self-interested individuals are likely to make in particular situations. For example, to the extent that crime is an option rationally chosen by the criminal, economic analysis can ask in what circumstances law can provide disincentives which make the choice for criminal behaviour no longer a rational one (weighing up likely benefits and detriments) for the potential offender.

Beyond this kind of inquiry, normative (or welfare) economics assumes a goal of allocative efficiency – optimum allocation of resources for the maximum overall benefit of those amongst whom the allocation is to be made – and seeks to identify situations of inefficiency and prescribe means of correcting them. Thus, legal doctrine can be examined for its contribution to this kind of allocation. Much literature considers the allocative efficiency of liability rules in tort law and a variety of other doctrinal fields. In this kind of writing, policy analysis from a social scientific field is being used to supplement established types of justifications in legal logic for existing doctrine. Thus, economic analysis appears exceptionally useful in doctrinal analysis. It does not undermine legal discourse. It offers a parallel commentary of justification or critique which seems to provide a powerful answer to realist claims about the inadequacy of doctrinal rationality. Economics is invoked to provide the rationality which realism found wanting.

The high point of this is probably found in the descriptive theory that the implicit goal of judicially developed common law doctrine is to promote an efficient allocation of resources in society. This is a kind of 'invisible hand' theory insofar as it claims that, whether or not the judges knew what they were doing in terms of economic rationality in developing common law rules, the case-by-case evolution of common law has in fact led to outcomes with a high degree of allocative efficiency (Posner 1972). Thus, a kind of unstated and often unrecognised economic rationality is claimed to lie beneath the rationality of legal logic. The invisible hand of economic reality is portrayed as guiding judicial development of common law rules. This kind of analysis has some affinities with constructive doctrinal realism insofar as it seeks to supplement and enhance ordinary doctrinal analysis by reinterpreting it in a wider social scientific context. But economic analysis of law is probably, in general, better seen as a kind of modern policy-science approach insofar as much of it seems little concerned to illuminate through behavioural study the way doctrine is actually developed, interpreted and applied in legal contexts. The logic of economic analysis is considered to explain important aspects of the way law is or should be, irrespective of empirical study of the range of determinants of judicial behaviour in relation to doctrine.

Economic analysis of law has attracted strong criticism: for example, that its emphasis on cost-benefit efficiency is inappropriate or inadequate in explaining or evaluating legal policy; that its postulates of rational action are too unreal to provide the basis of explanatory models or theories; that its adherents tend to claim far more significance for economic analysis than is justified by its narrow inquiries; that while claiming to be empirical it does not actually examine people's preferences but deduces them from premises of rationality which sometimes lead to tautologies; that it is biased towards market solutions and unable to attach sufficient weight to non-market relationships. And the matter is complicated by the fact that several competing schools of economic analysis of law exist. But the merits of this burgeoning movement need not be considered here. What is important is to recognise that in the United States, and to an increasing extent in Britain, economic analysis of law has seemed to offer to many legal scholars a means of confronting a post-realist world in which legal logic no longer seems sufficient.

Post-Realist Radical Scepticism

Radical sceptical realism – wholly rejecting traditional forms of legal doctrinal analysis as pointless and mystificatory – can be seen as having two strongly contrasting post-realist successor movements, one in the law school environment and one almost entirely outside it in American political science.

Judicial Behaviouralism

The latter has come to be called judicial behaviouralism. In essence, it involves efforts to predict or explain the outcome of judicial decisions through systematic analysis of the behavioural characteristics of the judges involved. Computer analyses of the interrelations of such variables as judges' educational backgrounds, religious and political attitudes and a vast array of specific characteristics are used. Legal doctrine may provide variables for this kind of analysis insofar as published judgments in previous cases decided by the judges being studied, may be thought to provide important sources of information on their personal values. But otherwise judicial behaviouralism is best seen as an effort to bypass doctrinal analysis and treat what judges do as all-important and what they say as a triviality to be left for analysis to the lawyers. Since judicial behaviouralism does not at any point address any of the concerns of normative legal theory it is of little relevance here, except insofar as it seems to hold doggedly to the view that law (as a socially significant phenomenon) is behaviour *and not* doctrine.

Critical Legal Studies

A much more significant form of radical scepticism in this context is represented by some of the work of what has come to be known, since the 1970s, as the American Critical Legal Studies (CLS) movement. The first of the annual meetings of the Conference on Critical Legal Studies took place in 1977 as a result of a circular letter proposing 'a gathering of colleagues who are pursuing a critical approach toward the study of law in society' (Kelman 1987: 297). CLS writing reflects a diversity of influences from modern radical philosophy and social theory (Schlegel 1984) but is also 'in many ways. . . a direct descendant' of legal realism (Tushnet 1986: 505).

It has taken to heart the realist idea that general concepts in legal doctrine do not determine outcomes. As Holmes put it:

'General propositions do not decide concrete cases'[11]. Just as Felix Cohen saw much of the general conceptual apparatus of legal doctrine as transcendental nonsense, CLS writers tend to see it as mystification. Arguments purporting to follow the logic of concepts could lead in diametrically opposed directions. In CLS jargon, concepts are 'flippable' equally in one direction or another. Some CLS writers go further to argue that, because of the manipulability of concepts, legal texts are infinitely interpretable; there simply is no way of deciding that one reading is necessarily better than another (Tushnet 1983). Everything depends on how one wishes to string together doctrinal logic in arguments in which all the crucial concepts used are subject to a variety of possible interpretations. The interesting question is what determines 'possible' interpretations, and for most CLS writers this is not something determined by the logic of doctrine itself but by the *political context* in which the interpretations are being offered.

To this extent CLS is consistent in its outlook with radical sceptical realism and shares with it an active interest in pouring scorn on lawyers' faith in legal logic (Kelman 1984). But this scepticism has not caused CLS writers to lose interest in doctrine. The general CLS position is that while orthodox legal reasoning often seems to produce radically indeterminate, even arbitrary, outcomes, legal doctrine is not as a result insignificant. Quite the opposite. It is one of the important means by which social life is constituted; that is, it provides categories of thought (for example, property, liability, binding agreement, good faith, crime, corporation, fiduciary relationship) by means of which we make sense of the social world and impose a kind of moral and intellectual order on it. So legal doctrine has important ideological and legitimating effects, helping to 'teach' us how to think about society and convincing us of the 'naturalness' of the social relationships which law defines (e.g. Gabel 1980). The legal historian Morton Horwitz, reacting to some extent against the oversimple idea of the 'flippability' of legal concepts, has argued that particular conceptions of corporate personality – the highly abstract legal idea to which we have returned several times in discussions in this book – had special importance in legitimating the concentration of economic wealth and power in big business in the United States in the late nineteenth century. The 'natural entity' conception, which saw the corporation not as a legal creature of the state or as the agent of its members but as an autonomous abstract entity in law, made it possible, Horwitz argues, to justify freeing corporations

---

[11] *Lochner v New York* (1905) 198 US 45, 76.

from legal restraints, for example on their ability to own the stock of other corporations. In this manner doctrinal development cleared the way for corporate economic concentration, without ever admitting that this was what really lay behind the changes in legal ideas and the abstract arguments used to justify them (Horwitz 1985).

Horwitz' essay is a good example of the most productive kind of work which has arisen from the CLS movement. Doctrine and its development is taken very seriously, but the motor of doctrinal development is not considered to lie in legal logic, or overarching values or traditions of the legal system (Pound, Dworkin), or mere judicial discretion as proposed by positivist analytical jurisprudence. The impetus for change in doctrine comes from outside the professional legal domain, especially in political struggle and the economic conditions, changes or crises of capitalist society. But these real forces are not usually revealed in doctrine itself nor in legal reasoning. Part of CLS' objective is to reveal 'hidden motives that the judges themselves would treat as illegitimate if forced to confront them'; it 'requires the analysis of the coherence of judicial explanations of outcomes. . ... But the goal is neither an alternative rationale nor a criticism of the outcome' (Kennedy 1979: 219, 220). Instead it is to show how a judge's formal rationale of the decision (which presents itself as mere *legal* reasoning) obscures the real political significance of what is being decided.

Another example of this kind of analysis is found in Karl Klare's examination of American judges' interpretation of the 1935 National Labor Relations Act, 'perhaps the most radical piece of legislation ever enacted by the United States Congress' (Klare 1978: 265) and one which ostensibly gave major rights to employees as against employers and greatly strengthened the role of collective bargaining in American labour law. Klare shows how, in a series of decisions widely regarded as employee victories, courts applied the Act to shape an institutional structure of collective bargaining which gave unions power at the expense of individual workers and helped shape 'the modern administered, and regulated system of class relations' (Klare 1978: 336). Again the essence of the CLS method here is to show that what doctrine appears to say is not what it does; the narrow 'logic' of the cases is exploded by revealing in detail the economic and political context in which it is developed and how case outcomes relate to wider tendencies in American society and politics.

To the extent that this kind of inquiry is intended to increase understanding of the role and character of legal doctrine it can be seen as related to constructive doctrinal realism and certainly to the effort to develop empirical legal theory. But in much CLS work the analysis of doctrine is destructive rather than constructive. CLS is not concerned to make of doctrine a rational system or structure; or to make case outcomes more predictable; or even, in general, to develop any general theories about the nature of doctrine in its institutional contexts. Its broad aim is to expose the hollowness of claims for legal doctrinal rationality. This is seen as important because orthodox legal reasoning and the doctrine it produces hide the repressions, contradictions and alienating conditions of life of contemporary Western societies. At the heart of these problems is the 'fundamental contradiction' which Western 'liberalism' tries to obscure (Kennedy 1979: 211–3; cf. Gabel and Kennedy 1984) – the contradiction that individual freedom and autonomy is possible only under conditions of collective constraint and coercion. The project of CLS is to demystify the legal ideas which obscure the contradictions of liberal capitalist society. Often, in CLS writing, these contradictions (as well as the concept of liberalism which is the focus of most CLS attack) remain frustratingly vague; it is probably significant that critical legal scholarship in Britain (which has developed contemporaneously with and for the most part independently of the American movement) has generally avoided reliance on such concepts. But at least it can be said that CLS gives legal doctrine (and presumably the normative legal theory which helps to rationalise it) the backhanded compliment of asserting its great social importance – an importance which makes a concerted attack on its pretensions all the more necessary.

Legal Professionalism and the Legacy of Realism

It would be pointless to try to offer here a general evaluation of the vast range of 'sceptical' approaches to legal inquiry which have been discussed in this chapter. Their importance in the context of this book is, first, in their confrontations with normative legal theory and, secondly, in the insight they offer into relationships between normative legal theory and the political and professional environment of Anglo-American law. The former matter has been discussed throughout this chapter; but what of the professional ramifications of legal realism?

It has often been said in the American context that 'we are all realists now' (cf. Schlegel 1979: 460). The most plausible meaning to give to this is that, whatever normative legal theory might suggest, many practicing lawyers find no difficulty in accepting much of the substance of realism's scepticism about legal logic and general legal concepts, as well as its view that law as doctrine cannot be understood without seriously analysing the behavioural contexts in which doctrine is developed and applied. Lawyers (in Britain no less than in the United States) cope with the indeterminacy of rules; they are well aware of the 'human factors' in judging, the personality characteristics of judges, the importance of advocacy styles in affecting decisions, and the 'leeways of precedent'. For many lawyers, everyday experience of practice teaches that law in operation is much more a matter of behaviour (threat and compromise, negotiation and confrontation, bluff and counterbluff, timing and strategy) and economics (the relative cost to opposing parties of particular legal strategies) than of doctrinal logic.

But throughout this book it has been argued that law as a profession and as an intellectual discipline has often sought to present itself in quite different terms and normative legal theory has aided in the effort to portray law as an integrated structure of ideas, as a body of distinct, esoteric knowledge. The flourishing of American legal realism in the late 1920s and 1930s seems like a moment when 'the dam broke' and the uncertainties over law's rational systematic structures of knowledge became a crisis of confidence in law as an intellectual field and a profession. In the early 1930s there was already a relatively well developed structure of university legal education in the United States, staffed by a substantial number of scholars ready and competent to think through the theoretical implications of this crisis. By contrast, in Britain, university legal education at that time was in a fledgling state. It held nervously to a vaguely Austinian conception of legal science (cf. Dowdall 1926) and was presumably hardly ready to face the challenges of realism, even if they had presented themselves in the stark form in which they appeared in the United States. Only much later, from the 1960s, when a sizeable profession of full-time academic lawyers had been established in British universities, was a belated start made in addressing the challenges posed by American realism and its aftermath. Thus, now, in Britain as in the United States normative legal theory is confronted by a variety of scepticisms which fundamentally challenge the idea that law can be understood as a systematic structure of doctrine.

Normative legal theory was portrayed in the earlier chapters of this book as a unifying element in the intellectual world of law. Now, in the form of modern legal philosophy's theories of law, it tends to appear increasingly, in a post-realist context, as a marginalised outpost of speculation on law's ultimate rationality.

The consequences and the significance of this situation remain to be considered in the final chapter of this book.

8 The Uses of Theory

Previous chapters have traced the outlines of the most influential types of Anglo-American normative legal theory which have established themselves in the period of modern professionalisation of law. And this theory has been considered, to some extent, in the context of the political and professional conditions in which it arose. In addition, the book has discussed what might be called the pre-history of normative legal theory in classical common law thought (Chapter 2), and various modern challenges to normative legal theory which are represented by realist and post-realist currents of legal thought (Chapter 7). In this last chapter it remains to offer some general assessment of the intellectual path which has been traced.

Some Political and Professional Uses of Theory

This book has argued that normative legal theory has not been able to give a convincing explanation of judicial creativity and of legal development generally. This theory has tried to explain law as a structure or system of doctrine without being able to dismiss difficult empirical questions about the behavioural conditions under which it makes sense to think in terms of such a system or structure. Realist and post-realist legal thought is a recognition and expression of this continuing problem for any theory which attempts to treat law merely as doctrine or ideas. It can be argued that, in this respect, normative legal theory has not provided an adequate theoretical basis for understanding the nature of Anglo-American law.

To leave that as the sole conclusion here would, however, be unduly negative, misleading and unfair. A major claim made in Chapter 1 was that, despite normative legal theory's frequent pretensions to the contrary, it should *not be* understood as seriously attempting to provide general theories of the nature of law. Typically, normative legal theory *assumes* that law is centrally, and perhaps exclusively, legal doctrine. It does not address the possibility that law as an object of inquiry might better be considered to be a field of experience, a rather heterogeneous subject of study centred on a variety of types and problems of regulation potentially involving a wide diversity of practices, techniques, modes of thought and forms of knowledge (Cotterrell 1986b: 83). Hence it sets itself an agenda different from that which would need to be adopted if a genuinely open, provisional concept of law were taken as the starting point for inquiry; if the assumption that law is to be equated with legal doctrine were not treated as virtually sacrosanct. Normative legal theory rules out most systematic behavioural inquiries about law; it treats legal theory as largely distinct from social scientific inquiry; it commits itself to discussion of the integrity of legal ideas and legal reasoning because treating doctrine as almost the sole object of inquiry virtually dictates the necessity of trying to prove some rational structure or systematic unity of that doctrine. Most of the material in the previous chapters of this book has been concerned with normative legal theory's search for this structure or unity.

If the real importance and value of normative legal theory are to be appreciated, this theory must be understood in relation to the primary tasks which it has actually attempted, which are narrower than the ones often attributed to it. Anglo-American normative legal theory has focussed almost exclusively on legal doctrine because it has tended to see law from the standpoint of a lawyer concerned directly with the question of the rationality and integrity of legal doctrine. Thus, one of its most important roles has been to provide a rational framework within which legal doctrine can be ordered and presented as the systematic knowledge of a learned profession and as a distinctive intellectual field or an intellectual discipline. In addition, as previous chapters have sought to demonstrate, it has often provided the means of rationalising the place of legal knowledge and legal practice in a broader political context. One very important aspect of this has been the effort to show how law and politics can remain distinct fields; how judging is *not* like legislating; how legal advocacy is different from political activity; how legal principle differs from mere policy; how courts can remain impartial in protecting the political rights and freedoms of citizens *although* in the Anglo-American world they are indisputably agencies of state power. Insofar as law can be portrayed as distinct from politics, politics can in some degree be conducted in such a way as avoid interference with the stable structures of legality. Hence law as the embodiment of stability can co-exist with politics as the means of change. In this way, normative legal theory's efforts to demonstrate the independence of law from politics are also, as has been seen[1], attempts to provide justifications and explanations of the idea of the Rule of Law.

Of course, contributors to normative legal theory have not necessarily viewed their work in these terms. But the writings of most of the theorists discussed in this book show clearly the specific professional and political concerns which have animated them. Austin viewed his theory of law and sovereignty as the key to a science of law upon which modern legal practice could be securely based (Austin 1863: 379-85). Bentham saw expository jurisprudence as a prerequisite for systematic reform to enable the legal system to meet the need for rational and efficient government in the modern state. While he had generally little commitment to legal professional prerogatives and spent much of his career attacking them, he was acutely aware of the political uses of legal theory. The writings of Pound and Fuller continually reveal their concern with the status and condition of the legal profession. Pound's work, as has been seen, shows an anxiety about the risk of the legal profession being displaced from its central place among the governing elites of American society. The refurbishment of common law methods in new, enlightened forms appears in Pound's writings as a means to retrieve the situation and re-establish the role of legal 'experts'. For Fuller, a concern with professionalism is not so much celebratory and defensive of prerogatives as critical and exhortatory. Fuller's discussions of the morality of law can be seen as inspired by a passionate belief in the need for heightened professional awareness of the moral responsibilities of legal practice in the mid- and late twentieth century, when arbitrariness in government and abuse of official power have not disappeared with Nazi tyranny but surface also in various forms in the Anglo-American world. Accordingly, Fuller's theory seeks to demonstrate how law must be interpreted to realise within it the potential of reason as a moral and not merely intellectual virtue.

Hart and Dworkin, locked in combat over the model of rules and the place of principles in legal analysis, are also justifiably seen as defenders of a professional faith; above all, faith in the distinctiveness of the intellectual world of the lawyer and the separation of law from politics. Of all the theorists discussed in this book Hart seems the least 'contextual'; the one who writes least, or least concretely, about the political and social consequences, presuppositions and concerns of his major contributions to normative legal theory. Hart's commitment to a liberal legal and

[1]   See Chapter 4, pp 99-100, 112-7; and Chapter 5, pp 135, 148-9.

social order is made clear in his writings on punishment and responsibility in criminal law (Hart 1968). His defence of a form of utilitarianism is probably best expressed in debate with Lord Devlin on the role of law in enforcing morality (Hart 1963). But his elaboration of a concept of law within the traditions of positivist analytical jurisprudence is the part of Hart's work of primary concern in this book. It can be seen, with regard to its political and professional relevance, partly as a defence of the outlook of earlier English analytical jurisprudence and partly as an attempt to replace important elements in that outlook.

Thus, Hart's defence of legal positivism allies him with Bentham and Austin in insisting on precision in legal argument, which is seen to depend on an absolute defence of the distinctiveness of a realm of positive law and positive legal analysis separate from moral or political argument. To this extent, the central presupposition grounding Austin's science of law – that is, the science which represents the special systematic knowledge and methods of the lawyer – is carried down to the present day. But, if a *political* view of the transition from Austin's jurisprudence to Hart's is taken, the most important aspect of it is Hart's rejection of Austin's deliberate vagueness in distinguishing judicial from legislative or administrative functions. It seemed realistic to Austin to see judges as political decision-makers within the state. He was content merely to emphasise that they are *subordinate* decision-makers; delegates of the sovereign. The judge, for Austin, is a political actor but, as Fuller puts it, only the 'little sovereign' (Fuller 1940: 29). In Hart's concept of law, however, the emphasis switches from judges as subordinate law-makers to judges as rule-bound officials. The union of primary and secondary rules as a model of law removes a substantial political inconvenience of Austin's jurisprudential legacy – its lack of concern with the idea of the Rule of Law. For Hart, the most important point to make in normative legal theory about the role of the judge is that this role is defined and constrained by secondary rules. And the most important point (politically) to make about rules is that, properly drafted, they really *can* constrain the judge. They have, potentially, at least a core of settled meaning which cannot properly be ignored or misinterpreted[2].

Dworkin's work adopts a different, very sophisticated approach to the question of the relationship between law and politics. He discards the positivist separation of law and morals – a risky strategy, one might think, if, like most other theorists considered in this

---

[2] See Chapter 4, above, pp 104–6.

book, Dworkin is concerned to defend the intellectual autonomy of law. But the rejection of the separation of law and morals clears the way for a kind of legal imperialism. The lawyer is to be seen (and to see himself or herself) as far more than a technician who knows how to find and interpret vast numbers of rules and regulations. The lawyer is a moral entrepreneur entrusted with the wellbeing of the community's law, which is also the repository of its most important political values. Hence, the lawyer's responsibility for the law is also a moral and political responsibility to engage in the development and fulfilment of those values which morally define the community. Yet law does not dissolve into politics; legal practice is not, in this conception, merely political activity in the sense of struggles over the control and use of power[3]. The distinction between principle and policy marks, for Dworkin, the boundary between the lawyer's interpretation of existing law and the legislator's creation of new law.

Politically, the significance of Dworkin's work is to suggest how law can still be considered to control politics (that is, the Rule of Law can prevail) and yet, at the same time, the Rule of Law itself can be considered a creative, flexible notion of evolving values expressed in regulatory forms. Seen in this way the law which rules politics and society is not merely something for lawyers to identify (as through the use of such positivist tests as Hart's rule of recognition) but something for lawyers and judges to *build* out of the best legal traditions of their society. In this outlook, Dworkin seems to encompass something of what Fuller struggled to grasp – how it is that law can be described as a distinctive professional and intellectual field and, at the same time, one which requires, above all, that its practitioners remain permanently sensitive to certain moral and political demands. These are demands which citizens assume must be met through law and which, if not met, make it, 'a pure abstraction instead of. . . an effective discipline of wills' (Durkheim 1933: 427).

Who is Listening?

In suggesting these political and professional uses of normative legal theory no claim is made here that they exhaust its significance, but only that they have powerfully shaped its scope and its priorities. As will be argued later in this chapter, the theories considered in this book have a value not dependent on any influence they

[3]   Cf. Chapter 1, above) pp 12–3.

may have had on professional thought about law, or on wider currents of thought about the relations of law and politics and about the status of legal professions. But what professional and political influence *have* they had? It might be suggested that there is little evidence that normative legal theory has had any significant influence on practising lawyers in the Anglo-American world. Further, this esoteric literature has generally inhabited an intellectual milieu of its own in which few connections have been made between legal philosophy and broader intellectual currents. How could it have had any significance either professionally or politically?

To some extent this question needs to be answered differently for each of the types of theory which have been considered in this book. It seems clear, for example, that Maine's historical jurisprudence connected relatively easily with broader intellectual currents in Victorian British society. It could be treated as 'a species of the theories of social evolution which became popular in the 1850s and 1860s. They were attractive to Victorians who were conscious, and a little apprehensive, despite optimistic assertions of confidence, of the great social changes taking place around them, and who were ready to embrace theories that ascribed these changes to inevitable impersonal laws' (Stein 1980: 99). Historical jurisprudence, in the form Maine presented it, seems to have had considerable cultural influence. Yet, as shown in Chapter 2, it failed to provide a solution to the more specific problems of legal professionalisation of its time and quickly lost professional influence as a result.

Most of the other theory discussed in this book seems much more clearly to have reflected lawyers' professional interests in the rational organisation or systematic explanation of legal doctrine. It has avoided the kind of broad cultural reference which gave Maine's work its wide interest and resonance outside the legal professional world. Hence, if this narrower theory has, itself, had influence, it is likely to have been primarily an influence in the professional world of law, and through that, perhaps beyond into the wider political arena. But it is important to recognise that if influence has been exerted this is likely to have been in oblique, highly indirect ways. Austin, for example, undoubtedly influenced the English legal scholar A. V. Dicey's conception of legal science, its scope, components and methods (Cosgrove 1980: 23–8). Dicey and like-minded academic lawyers, in turn, produced textbooks and other writings reflecting these ideas and which offered models of legal analysis adopted by numerous other lawyers (cf. Sugarman 1986: 42–3). In more recent times, academic lawyers writing and teaching in many different fields have sometimes adopted the concepts and theoretical outlook of jurists such as Pound, Kelsen, Hart or Dworkin. These theories, even if appropriated in piecemeal form or merely plundered for plausible rhetoric, have presumably been of some help in defining a kind of intellectual universe within which serious scholarly discussion of law can take place. They have formed part of an available, presupposed storehouse of ideas for organising legal knowledge.

As Anglo-American academic lawyers have sought to establish their credentials as primary interpreters, organisers, critics and teachers of legal doctrine they have often felt, collectively as a professional community, the need for such general frameworks of legal thought. Academic commentators and expositors have frequently adopted ideas (for example, those such as sovereignty or *Grundnorm* conceptualising the ultimate authority of a legal system) which have received full elaboration in legal theory and which can be relied upon without further explanation simply because of this. The modern law school in both Britain and the United States provides analysis and explanation at many levels: precise technical examination of the legal-logical relationships of rules; formulation and exemplification of general legal principles; discussion of policy from a variety of standpoints; examination of legal issues or institutions in terms of a variety of 'external' disciplines, such as economics, sociology or philosophy; essentially political debate on constitutional issues (especially in the American context); and broad jurisprudential inquiries about the nature of law in general, or in particular kinds of society. The teaching and the study of law thus embrace a wide continuum of legal thought from the most narrow and precise issues of rule application to the most general speculation on legal affairs. Within this continuum, normative legal theory, at least in its most discussed and widely publicised forms considered in this book, has reflected and indirectly reinforced – and in some measure helped to crystallise and elaborate – assumptions about the character of law and legal thinking which have exerted, through the education and training of lawyers, influence on the intellectual outlook of lawyers as a professional group.

In one sense, the effort to develop normative legal theory remains central to the notion of law as an intellectual discipline. As the scope of law and the mass of its technical detail increase at what is often considered to be an alarming rate, normative legal theory continues the task of trying to impose rational order on legal doctrine as a whole. Much of it still seeks conceptualisations of law in general which will make it possible to continue to treat law as a unified, coherent intellectual discipline, and not just as a mass of unconnected regulations, practices or procedures. It still commits itself to the demonstration that lawyers possess a body of structured, principled and distinctive knowledge which entitles them to claim to be members of a scholarly profession. It attempts to provide some overall sense of direction within the bewildering complexities of legal thought.

Normative Legal Theory and Modern Legal Practice

In another sense, however, as suggested at the end of the previous chapter, normative theory seems in various respects marginalised in relation to professional legal knowledge and to the progress of law as professional practice and intellectual field (cf. Brunet 1988). It is surely significant that, in Britain and the United States since the 1960s, legal philosophy has become increasingly sophisticated and self-consciously professionalised as a branch of the discipline of philosophy rather than as a continuing integral part of academic legal studies.

What has really changed in this respect? No-one could suggest that legal theory has at any time been necessary to help the lawyer earn a living in everyday practice. But has it now ceased to be significant in helping to define an overall conception of law's character as intellectual discipline or professional field? I suggest that two somewhat related historical developments in the Anglo-American legal world have gradually contributed to an increased marginalisation of normative legal theory in this context. The result is not that theoretical ideas have been, in any way, banished from legal thinking but that the kind of theoretical ideas which normative legal theory has worked with seem, in some important respects, less helpful than at various times in the past.

One significant development is, simply, the remarkable proliferation of legal rules and regulations. The bulk of legal doctrine expands inexorably and rapidly, and seemingly irrespective of the political ideologies of governments. A consequence is that the task of explaining some overall, rational structure of legal doctrine has seemed increasingly difficult to many lawyers. It was seen in Chapter 7 that the strain put on the American case-law system by the vast increase in the number and range of potential precedents can be considered to be one of the significant contributing causes of the realist crisis of confidence in normative legal analysis. But the proliferation is not only, or even mainly, one of judicial precedents.

It affects numerous types of legislation and regulation at all levels of government.

Considered in isolation, however, this development might suggest that normative legal theory is more necessary than ever to provide some general framework of thought within which to encompass this mass of doctrinal minutiae. Here the second historical development comes into play. Law has not only increased in doctrinal bulk but it has appeared to change its general character and its fundamental relationship with the legal professions which serve and depend upon it. And these changes, as will appear, may have helped to make theoretical justifications of a unified or structured legal sphere seem unnecessary and even impossible.

Today, the lawyer's professional claim is primarily a claim to be able to find, interpret, advise about, creatively invoke, warn or defend against, or pre-emptively avoid governmental regulations of numerous kinds and affecting an immense range of social and especially economic arrangements and relationships. This claim may not depend on possession of an apparently integrated body of distinctive knowledge expressed in systematic form, or identifiable as a special professional field, or organised around fundamental principles of one kind or another. Perhaps, indeed, the very idea of law as a profession is giving way to the idea that the practice of law is a business of selling a very varied range of facilitative or defensive technical services, or performing them as employee of a business corporation or government agency (see e.g. Abel 1986). Law, as a cluster of techniques for achieving certain purposes, is eminently useful. Maybe legal practice seeks no grander justification to maintain its status and prerogatives than its obvious utility in an immense diversity of seemingly unrelated contexts.

At the same time, academic legal studies are now apparently secure in higher education in both Britain and the United States. Conditions have changed very markedly since Thorstein Veblen, the iconoclastic American social critic, was able to declare, early in this century, that a school of law no more belongs in the university than a school of dancing (cf. Stevens 1983: 51). In the United States, in many universities, the scale of legal studies in terms of numbers of students and resources dwarfs that of studies in many other disciplines. Again, law can apparently justify its status as a field of study purely in terms of its unquestionable practical utility. It may not need the luxury of demonstrated ultimate theoretical foundations of an intellectual discipline. It may not depend for its intellectual status on theoretical justification of its methods, of its scope and structure, or of its underlying principles and rationale. Its vocational relevance is self-evident.

However, the idea of the obvious utility of legal knowledge and practice is maintainable only because certain relatively stable conceptions of the nature of law are widely accepted and acted upon by lawyers and those whom they represent. It is unlikely that the specific theories discussed in this book have directly influenced legal practice. Nevertheless, the broad dichotomy in legal thought which has been drawn from these theories in these pages may well have practical significance. The dichotomy is between, on the one hand, views of law (reflected, for example, in classical common law thought and in the theories of Fuller, Pound and Dworkin) which understand it primarily or essentially as an expression of values derived from natural reason, community life, political history or some such source and, on the other hand, positivist approaches to law which treat it essentially as the regulatory expression of political power. Broadly speaking, for most legal practitioners in complex industrialised societies it is usually convenient and realistic to think of modern law, for practical purposes, in the latter sense, as the directives of numerous governmental agencies which include legislatures, courts, regulatory and administrative boards and agencies and individual officials.

The material discussed in this book essentially provides a theoretical commentary on the historical transformation of law, and the dilemmas arising from that transformation, which have encouraged this kind of legal outlook in the Anglo-American environment. The emergence of modern positivist analytical jurisprudence described in Chapters 3 and 4 is a recognition in theory of a historical fact around which modern lawyers organise their practice: the power of the modern state and its numerous governmental agencies acting by means of many kinds of regulation. The change in lawyers' outlook necessary to accept the idea of legal doctrine as a deliberate political creation, theoretically unlimited in scope, was a switch from the classical common law emphasis on the *content* or substance of legal doctrine as its defining essence, to an emphasis on the *form* of law. For classical common law thought the essence of law lay in the idea that the content of legal doctrine represented community values, experience or wisdom, as interpreted by lawyers. By contrast, positivist legal thought finds the essence of law in its form (as sovereign's command, rule or norm). In this way the essence of law is divorced from *substantive rationality* (the elaboration of values) and reduced to a *formal rationality* (each element of legal doctrine is identifiable as law because of its distinctive form and the distinctive formal source of its authority).

As has been seen, positivist theory could not explain (and

therefore legally control) how the content of legal doctrine is determined. Positivist analytical jurisprudence admits that the making of law is a political act; that what determine the content of legal doctrine are legislatures' choices and judges' discretions. And so legal analysis has to become, strictly speaking, technical analysis of the regulatory forms through which government acts. Hence the lawyer's domain of useful knowledge becomes essentially this technical knowledge. There is no reason why the legal professional must avoid any concern with policy or values. Nevertheless, the broad outcome to which the positivist recognition of law as an instrument of government tends to lead is a conception of legal practice as one of neutral technicality. Such a practice may – but, most importantly, *need not* – make any judgments about the fundamental rationality of the substance of legal doctrine (the consistency or appropriateness of its values, principles or underlying policy). Its obvious utility is a purely technical one.

Law was clearly an instrument of governmental power even in the heyday of classical common law thought. But the lawyer's understanding of law in this way has surely been made less ambiguous, first, by the establishment of modern positivist legal thought with the growth of modern state power and, secondly, by the proliferation of forms of legislation and regulation and the vast production of modern legal doctrine.

The result may be that this purely technical conception of law has progressively freed legal practice from an often unstated but important earlier dependence on theory. Classical common law thought depended on the idea that the content of legal doctrine embodied *reason*. It had to address the theoretical problem that this reason was supposed to be rooted in community life and, at the same time, accessible only to lawyers. The idea of the 'artificial reason' of the law[4], was an essential theoretical underpinning of common law practice, as was the broader idea of some necessary fundamental relationship between law and the values of the community. The combination of these ideas gave common lawyers (especially judges) the authority to control the rational content of legal doctrine. But with the positivisation of law – the recognition of law as a purely political creation having no necessary connection to a consistent framework of values – the primary concern with substantive reason found in the rhetoric of classical common law thought disappears. Thereafter it returns only in critical guise, as in the theories of Fuller, Finnis and Dworkin.

Ultimately, it seems that, in a practical, positivist, legal

[4] See Chapter 2, above, pp 33–5.

professional view, the essential systematic rationality of law can be reduced to a capacity to identify the formal origins of each rule or regulation in some specific, unambiguous and accepted governmental source. As regards the substance of legal doctrine, law's rationality appears merely 'piecemeal' or localised[5]. If the substantive rationality of law, in classical common law thought, was assumed to lie in stable, enduring principles grounded in the community's values, a positivist outlook treats that rationality only as the pragmatic explanations of particular legislative policies of the moment and the temporary reconciliations of the content of numerous unrelated legislative interventions. Hence, the effect of this positivisation of law is that the 'obvious utility' of legal practice tends to appear as one of *atheoretical technique*, rather than theoretically justified reason.

In relatively stable legal and political conditions, such as the Anglo-American legal professions have enjoyed for a considerable time, a particular professional conception of law may be increasingly self-sustaining. In unstable conditions the situation may be otherwise. In Chapter 5 it was suggested that crises of political and legal authority are often associated with the emergence of natural law theories which demand that a theoretically justified reason be included in legal technique. The historical conditions, discussed in Chapter 7, which gave American legal realism its greatest prominence in the 1930s were those of political and social instability which made it seem no longer realistic to many lawyers to treat legal and judicial practice as concerned merely with regulatory *techniques* for policy implementation. At a time when correct *policy* seemed all-important, and highly elusive, some lawyers and legal scholars saw legal technique as unimportant, at least if considered to be somehow separate from policy-formation.

Apart from such crises of confidence, the problem of explaining how change in legal doctrine occurs has certainly been relevant to the world of legal practice. The most pressing aspect of this problem for the legal practitioner is that of predicting how doctrine will be interpreted by judges and other legal authorities faced with the task of applying it in new situations. In the previous chapter it was suggested that many of the lessons of at least some versions of legal realist thought are likely to be very familiar to legal practitioners. But the problem of explaining doctrinal change is centrally significant in everyday practice only for certain kinds of lawyers: for example, those involved in appellate advocacy, or in long term legal planning where much is at stake; or for those

---

[5] Cf. Chapter 1, above, pp 5–6.

academic lawyers concerned to explain long-run trends of legal development. For many other lawyers it may be possible, in times of political and legal stability, to work pragmatically with legal doctrine as it stands at any given time. They may not need to be concerned with the difficulties which processes of doctrinal change and interpretation raise for the idea of law as a systematic rational structure of doctrine.

Thus, the idea of legal practice's obvious utility *does* presuppose certain theoretical views of law. But, today, historical conditions of legal development may have inspired practical legal notions which, by their nature, make explicit reference to normative theory less important than in the past. One such development, I have argued, is the positivisation of law which has removed from legal professions (including, for this purpose, professional judges) a great deal of control over the rational content of doctrine and encouraged a purely technical view of law. But another, related development, the vast and continuous proliferation of regulation in modern times, has intensified this technical outlook. The content of legal doctrine often changes so quickly and is so complex and extensive that lawyers tend to assume that no more than a piecemeal, localised rationality can be imposed on it. Further, the sources of law in governmental agencies are so numerous and varied that its *formal* rationality tends to appear merely as the requirement that a specific rule be traceable to some decision or procedure of an ostensibly authoritative governmental agency.

Normative Legal Theory as a Partial Perspective

If, as a result of these developments, normative legal theory seems professionally marginalised in some important respects, its search for reason in law is not thereby invalidated. It remains what it has always been: the preserve of the doubters, the seekers after something more, the intellectually curious who are restless at the suggestion that obvious utility provides, in itself, sufficient intellectual and moral foundation for the field they profess.

Indeed, this kind of stance which unites, despite all other differences, the theorists discussed in this book, may suggest to some readers that normative legal theory has been a rather noble enterprise even if its broader claims to general explanation or illumination of the nature of law have been much overstated. And this is the message I want this book to convey. The effort to explain the possibility of system and structure in legal ideas is not just an effort to give status to legal practice and legal analysis as something distinctive and autonomous. It is also an attempt to show how law can be envisaged as a great human achievement of reason, and how lawyers must work and think with it to strengthen the potential of rationality within it. Normative legal theory is, from this point of view, an effort to examine seriously how law can gain integrity as the means by which human beings impose reason, to the limits of their ability, on the otherwise chaotic conditions of their social existence.

The reason why this may sound pretentious is that normative legal theory has too often been presented as if it represented *truth* about the nature of law, when what it actually represents is a certain partial perspective or cluster of closely related perspectives on law. Primarily, but certainly not exclusively, the perspective of Anglo-American normative legal theory has been simply that of a lawyer trying to make sense of legal doctrine. Seen in that light, normative legal theory has been of considerable value insofar as it has tested, in a great variety of ways, the rationality of lawyers' ways of developing, interpreting and applying legal doctrine. It has made explicit many commonly implicit assumptions of legal thought; for example, with regard to the systematic character of legal doctrine, the nature of judicial creativity, the essence of common law method, the place of policy and principle in legal reasoning, the ultimate criteria of legal validity, the distinctions between legal and political argument, and the basis of the Rule of Law. Insofar as these assumptions actually are widely made they are important foundations of legal practice. It follows that the elaboration and analysis of them in normative legal theory is not mystification but rather clarification and explication of certain existing facets of the reality of legal practice in the Anglo-American world. Equally, normative legal theory's failures are often no less interesting than its successes in explaining the rational structures and systematic character of doctrine. Failures may indicate with special clarity the limits of reason in legal ideas, and the incoherences of doctrine.

Normative legal theory's examination of these matters becomes mystificatory only when it is assumed that what is being discussed is not primarily the particular mode of thought of lawyers about law in a certain context but, in some general and timeless sense, *the nature of law*. Then, normative legal theory, assuming itself to be not a specific, partial perspective or limited range of perspectives on law but a somehow complete perspective, turns into professional ideology. It purports to explain the way law *is*, rather than the way lawyers may think of it. It is ideological precisely because it does not even notice that its own perspective is inevitably limited and incomplete (cf. Cotterrell 1984: 121, 127, 238). It understands its limited view as a total one; the royal route to legal understanding.

To write of the lawyer's perspective is, of course, to gloss over the fact that lawyers' perspectives on law can themselves be very varied, that judges' perspectives may be significantly different from those of practising lawyers, that those of appellate judges may be significantly different from those of trial judges, and that the viewpoints of academic lawyers may also show much diversity and vary widely from those of practitioners. Since most normative legal theory has been produced by academic lawyers these points are important. Nevertheless, what unifies all of these legal professionals of different kinds is their generally substantial interest in and knowledge of law as doctrine; an interest which suggests a broadly different general perspective from that of many social scientists, for example, whose focus might be primarily on behaviour, and patterns of social relations, associated with law as a field of experience and practice.

Many contributors to normative legal theory have been aware, in one way or another, of a need to transcend a perspective which treats law as structured and systematised doctrine in order to extend understanding of law as a social phenomenon. Normative legal theory represents often only a part of these writers' work in the field of legal theory. Fuller, for example, seeking to understand better the range of regulatory mechanisms available in Western societies and to discover some of their inherent limitations and potentialities, was drawn increasingly to the study of sociology and anthropology, as noted in Chapter 5. Kelsen recognised in a clearer, more rigorous manner than have most other writers discussed in this book, the partial nature of normative legal theory's perspective. He came to accept sociology of law as a parallel but quite distinct enterprise of inquiry about the legal field, alongside what he viewed as legal science – the normative analysis of legal doctrine guided by the concepts of the pure theory of law. Kelsen's writings recognise that normative legal theory cannot merely collect the data of law and put it in systematic order. It must deliberately construct a perspective on reality appropriate to its object. Hence his conceptualism, discussed in Chapter 4, presupposes that each science constructs its own methods and its own way of seeing reality. Indeed its special perspective determines what that reality is, since, for Kelsen, there is no way of understanding reality except through a structure of concepts devised for that purpose. While Kelsen's position suggests no way of linking different sciences or disciplines, his intellectual curiosity led him to researches in several of them, including especially anthropology and political theory, alongside normative legal theory.

The Destiny of Legal Theory

The claim made here that normative legal theory represents a *partial* perspective on law does entail the further claim that different perspectives can be related in some way. For something to be partial, after all, it must relate to a larger whole of which there are other parts. Thus we reach the extremely difficult question of how the insights of normative legal theory can somehow be integrated with ideas developed by viewing law from other perspectives. Indeed, what other perspectives might these be? In Chapter 1 a broad distinction was drawn between normative legal theory and empirical legal theory. By empirical legal theory I mean theory which seeks to explain the character of law in terms of historical and social conditions and treats the doctrinal and institutional characteristics of law emphasized in normative legal theory as explicable in terms of their social origins and effects (Cotterrell 1983: 241–2). Empirical legal theory is concerned with the systematic explanation of law as a field of experience; as behaviour as well as doctrine, with both of these being treated as components and determinants of each other. Adopting this definition it is clear that several of the writers whose work has been considered in this book for its relevance to normative legal theory have also directly contributed to the development of empirical legal theory in various ways.

Perhaps the most interesting link figure is Karl Llewellyn whose constructive realist critique of orthodox legal doctrinal analysis was considered in Chapter 7. Llewellyn's commitment to the orthodox lawyer's quest for integrity and rationality of doctrine is clear. At the same time, a realist perspective which refuses to accept that legal analysis can *only* be analysis of doctrine frees Llewellyn to suggest ways in which the processes of development, interpretation and application of legal doctrine can be viewed behaviourally. The insights of normative analysis are not to be overthrown. But it is made clear that they represent, at best, a partial perspective on the 'reality' of law. And, perhaps what is most important about this constructive realist claim is that it makes clear that it is not enough for the lawyer to be satisfied with the partial perspective which a focus on doctrinal rationality represents, and to leave other perspectives to other observers of law (for example, social scientists or politicians). Once the partial character of the doctrinal rationality focus is revealed, the incompleteness of the knowledge which it offers is thereby also revealed. Unless it can be shown in what respects that knowledge is reliable and in what respects it is not, its utility is wholly undermined. And the only way to determine the extent of its reliability is to examine and understand (from various behavioural perspectives) the conditions under which doctrine is developed and applied.

If the normative legal theory discussed in this book can be considered, despite its variety, to represent one kind of perspective or perhaps a cluster of closely related perspectives on law it is still very much an open question how far any productive dialogue or integration of normative legal theory with empirical legal theory is possible. It seems significant, however, that the ideas of many of the theorists discussed in this book have led them beyond normative legal theory itself into inquiries about the social or political context in which legal doctrine exists. Again, Fuller's serious involvement with social science is an excellent example. In earlier times, as discussed in Chapter 3, Austin, with his single-minded commitment to the development of a science of law which would show the distinctive structure of legal doctrine, saw the need for a theoretical understanding of the character of the modern state. Equally, he made some effort to analyse the actual conditions which determine the obedience of a population to political authorities. So did Maine, who located the unity of legal doctrine in a conception of culture and set out to study it from historical and anthropological standpoints. Bentham, too, recognised the need for some kind of speculation on psychology and behaviour to complement and fulfil the conceptual analysis of his jurisprudence. By contrast, Hart largely ignores inquiries about actual social or political conditions and tries to avoid making his conceptual analysis dependent on specific empirical claims about existing societies. Yet, in Chapter 4, it was seen that the method of his normative legal theory demands a concern with these matters and the lack of it undermines the clarity of some of his most important concepts. Thus, there might be good grounds for suggesting that the kind of perspective which normative legal theory usually reflects is not self-sufficient and, when developed in a rigorous and open-minded fashion, tends to provoke questions which encourage a broadening of view and a concern with empirical questions about the social and political environment of legal doctrine.

In this respect, Kelsen's and Dworkin's approaches to normative legal theory represent the sole exceptions to this tendency among the theories discussed in this book. Dworkin's method presupposes a participants' discourse of law. It sees the legal world entirely through the eyes of practical interpreters of legal doctrine and refuses explicitly to admit any other perspective on law into its field of concerns. In this way it firmly excludes all external (sociological) perspectives. As has been seen, the price paid for this is a theory of judicial interpretation which necessarily cannot rely at all on sociological information about the nature of judiciaries as interpretive communities. Thus, it cannot really recognise social constraints on judges arising from the institutional settings of judging.

Kelsen's legal philosophy, unlike Dworkin's interpretive theory, retains a concern to develop an objective 'scientific' explanation of the nature of law as doctrine. Like Dworkin, however, Kelsen claims the total irrelevance of sociological inquiries to his legal theory, and sets it up in such a way as to justify this. As noted earlier, Kelsen's conceptualism makes possible a distinct and self-contained normative legal theory because it can *postulate* the concepts upon which such a theory can be founded. It does not seek to find them in experience and it claims that, being deliberately *constructed* for theoretical purposes, they are in no way dependent upon specific empirical conditions. Because Kelsen is clear that the pure theory of law is not concerned with behaviour, such as the judicial activity of deciding cases, but solely with the logic of norms, the separation of normative legal theory from empirical theory in this form seems largely unassailable. What Kelsen offers is a pure science of normative logic. By explicitly and firmly separating this science from all others which might aid the understanding of law, he marks out a distinct field for normative theory. While its scope is narrow and its integrity is defended by excluding most of the practical life of the law which enters into other theories discussed in this book, this is, for Kelsen, the price which must be paid for analytical rigour.

Various kinds of theory discussed in this book, therefore, suggest a resistance to or denial of the possibility of integrating normative and empirical legal theory, while other kinds seem to push towards a broadening perspective on law. But unless one is prepared to accept the limitation of view inherent in Dworkin's or Kelsen's approaches (and Kelsen's work in anthropology and political theory shows that he was not willing to accept such a limitation), there seem good reasons to seek to broaden or transcend the perspectives of normative legal theory. Quite apart from any general intellectual justification for attempting this, the current situation of legal practice may demand it if the virtues of normative legal theory are not to be undervalued in the professional world of Anglo-American law.

Normative legal theory's most important failing, according to this book's argument, has been its inability to explain the processes of legal change. Yet it has been suggested in this chapter that it is precisely legal change (change in the character of doctrine and forms of regulation, and corresponding changes in the conditions of legal practice and legal education) which seems to suggest the danger of normative legal theory being marginalised insofar as it continues to claim that law does or should exhibit something more than what I call a piecemeal rationality. Empirical legal theory, which has a rich and varied literature and which now flourishes in a wide variety of forms, treats law as a social phenomenon to be examined through systematic empirical analysis of the political, economic and social conditions in which it exists. I have described much of its central literature elsewhere (Cotterrell 1984). Examination of it here would be out of place. It is enough to say that empirical legal theory potentially offers the means of examining legal change in systematic fashion. It recognises that the impetus for change is not usually to be found in legal doctrine but in the social, economic and political conditions in which that doctrine exists. Empirical legal theory is, thus, necessary to explain the changing situation of law (and perhaps of normative legal theory itself) in a way that normative legal theory is unable to do.

But this is not to supersede normative legal theory. The heritage of this theoretical literature provides a storehouse of ideas about the nature of law viewed from a certain standpoint. That standpoint is not rendered inappropriate by the fact that there are others which must be taken into account in order to achieve a more adequate understanding. Debate rages in modern philosophy and elsewhere as to what 'adequate' can mean in this kind of context. No answer has been given in these pages to the general question of how, in general terms, it is possible to confront partial perspectives on experience with others so as to extend knowledge. Some writers doubt that this is possible because no partial perspective can necessarily provide the means of declaring any other 'wrong'. Can empirical legal theory show that normative theory is wrong? I make no claim here that it can or that there is any reason why it should try to do so. For the purposes of this book it is enough to say that taken on its own terms, judged in terms of what it has apparently attempted to do in clarifying and making explicit the rational structure or system of legal doctrine, normative legal theory has certain strengths and weaknesses. Its weaknesses seem to open the way to types of theory, drawing on social scientific traditions and methods, which offer the prospect of explaining what, according to the arguments of this book, it apparently cannot explain.

Its greatest strengths, however, have been its commitment to make legal knowledge a system of reason; a great structure of thought which does justice as an intellectual creation to the efforts of multitudes of legal minds which have been occupied with providing solutions to practical problems of social regulation through the ages. The primary purpose of this book has been to describe some of the most valuable products of that commitment.

Notes and Further Reading

In the following notes sources included in the list of text references are cited by author and date only.

Chapter 1: Legal Philosophy in Context

JURISPRUDENCE, LEGAL PHILOSOPHY AND LEGAL THEORY: The definitions of jurisprudence, legal philosophy and legal theory given in the text are controversial but convenient for the purposes of demarcating this book's concerns. There is, indeed, no clear uniformity in general usage of these terms. For different usages from those adopted here see e.g. Twining 1984; and the useful discussion in E.W. Patterson, *Jurisprudence* 1953, pp. 7-10. Tur 1978 adopts a definition of jurisprudence which treats it as broadly similar to what is described in the text as normative legal theory. The idea that jurisprudence is concerned with generalisation in contrast with particularistic legal studies is emphasised in e.g. J. Hall, *Foundations of Jurisprudence* 1973, pp. 11-4. The designations 'normative legal theory' and 'empirical legal theory' roughly parallel Kelsen's designations of normative and sociological jurisprudence (Kelsen 1941b) but, unlike Kelsen, I see these not as different sciences with different subject-matter but as elaborations of different perspectives on law as a field of experience. Both are concerned, in one way or another, with the nature of law as a normative and empirical phenomenon. Typically, however, they conceptualise this phenomenon differently, seek knowledge of it in different ways and use this knowledge for different purposes.

LEGAL PHILOSOPHY AND LEGAL PRACTICE: On legal philosophy and legal practice see also R. H. S. Tur, 'Jurisprudence and Practice' (1976) 14 Journal of the Society of Public Teachers of Law (n.s.) 38; W. Friedmann, 'Legal Theory and the Practical Lawyer' (1941) 5 Modern Law Review 103. On the utility of legal philosophy in clarifying essential concepts used in legal practice see e.g. A.L. Goodhart, 'An Apology for Jurisprudence' in P. Sayre (ed), *Interpretations of Modern Legal Philosophies* 1947.

JUSTIFYING NORMATIVE LEGAL THEORY: On the functions of legal philosophy see also W. Twining, 'Some Jobs for Jurisprudence' (1974) 1 British Journal of Law and Society 149; Stone 1964, pp. 53-5. P. Soper, 'Making Sense of Modern Jurisprudence' (1988) 22 Creighton Law Review

67 is a helpful recent discussion. On lawyers as legal philosophers see W. Friedmann, *Legal Theory* 5th ed. 1967, pp. 3-4, noting that the dominance of lawyers in this enterprise has occurred since the nineteenth century: 'The decisive shift from the philosopher's or politician's to the lawyer's legal philosophy is of fairly recent date. It follows a period of great developments in juristic research, technique and professional training. The new era of legal philosophy arises mainly from the confrontation of the professional lawyer, in his legal work, with problems of social justice.' I should want to modify this only by suggesting also (i) that legal philosophy may have aided as well as reflected some of the developments Friedmann refers to and (ii) that problems of explaining the integrity of law as an intellectual field and as the basis of a learned professional practice may have been as important as those of social justice in determining the shape and influence of modern Anglo-American legal philosophy. On philosophy in relation to jurisprudence see Stone 1964, pp. 7-10.

LEGAL PHILOSOPHY IN SOCIAL AND POLITICAL CONTEXT: A contextual view provides its own special criteria of relevance. Since the context with which this book is concerned is an Anglo-American one it follows that discussion in these pages is confined to theory which has had most prominence in this legal professional and political context. The fact that intellectual quality certainly does not guarantee wide political and professional influence is amply demonstrated by the fate of the jurisprudential teachings of Adam Smith, as of much other advanced, legally-relevant literature of the Scottish Enlightenment (for example, writings by Adam Ferguson and John Millar). Smith's Glasgow lectures in the 1760s on jurisprudence have, until relatively recently, suffered unjustified neglect in jurisprudential discussion in Britain. First published from student notes in 1896, they are now available in A. Smith, *Lectures on Jurisprudence* 1978.

HOW SHOULD LEGAL PHILOSOPHY BE INTERPRETED CONTEXTUALLY? : On related 'contextual' approaches in other intellectual fields, see e.g. James Tully ed., *Meaning and Context* 1988. Karl Mannheim's writings on the sociology of knowledge also contain many invaluable guides to productive interpretation of currents of ideas in social context: see e.g. *Ideology and Utopia* 1936; *Essays on the Sociology of Knowledge* 1952; Mannheim 1956; *Structures of Thinking* 1982. Properly used, the sociology of knowledge should not require that ideas be reduced to – or explained away in terms of – social conditions. It should force us to keep in mind at all times the dialectic between intellectual imagination and determining conditions. The possible relevance of approaches such as Quentin Skinner's for the study of legal philosophy is noted in W. Twining, 'Talk About Realism' (1985) 60 New York University Law Review 329, at p. 336.

Chapter 2 : The Theory of Common Law

THE CHARACTER OF COMMON LAW THOUGHT: By far the best recent discussion of classical common law thought is in Postema 1986. While Postema's emphasis on the importance in common law thinking of the idea of community as the foundation of law parallels an important theme in the text, his interpretation differs from mine in two ways. First, it suggests a relatively explicit appeal to community as characteristic of common law reasoning. But it seems to me that this appeal is usually implicit and many terms (for example, realm, commonwealth, subjects, people, nation) are used to indicate the social entity from which law draws authority and relevance. Secondly, Postema's discussion tends to imply a more developed conception of the nature of community and of the relationship between law and community than the limited theoretical vision of common law thought in general might warrant. Common law thought does not present a theory of law. It merely provides the elements from which a rudimentary theory can be constructed.

THE COMMON LAW JUDGE: See generally Levy-Ullmann 1935, Part 1 ch 3. For Blackstone's views on precedent and the judge's role see especially Blackstone 1809 I, pp. 69-71.

CAN COMMON LAW THOUGHT EXPLAIN LEGAL DEVELOPMENT?: On common law as custom see Simpson 1973; Postema 1986, pp. 4-13. On records and reporting of common law see F. Pollock, *Essays in the Law* 1922, chs 9 and 10; Levy-Ullmann 1935, Part 1 ch 4.

COMMON LAW AND LEGISLATION: See Levy-Ullmann 1935, Part 2; Postema 1986, pp. 15-9; C. K. Allen, *Law in the Making* 7th ed. 1964, pp. 444-69; Sommerville 1986, pp. 95-100; McIlwain 1910, ch 4; T. F. T. Plucknett, *Statutes and Their Interpretation in the First Half of the Fourteenth Century* 1922.

THE POLITICAL AND SOCIAL ENVIRONMENT: Sommerville 1986 summarises the typical outlook of common lawyers during the crucial years of the early seventeenth century in which modern conceptions of the sovereignty of Parliament began to establish themselves firmly in legal theory. Also of considerable value on the political significance of common law ideas of immemorial custom is Pocock 1957. See also J. U. Lewis, 'Coke's Theory of Artificial Reason' (1968) 84 Law Quarterly Review 330. Gough 1955 is the standard modern account of the use of natural law conceptions in English legal history. See also T. F. T. Plucknett, 'Bonham's Case and Judicial Review' (1926) 40 Harvard Law Review 30; S. E. Thorne, 'Dr. Bonham's Case' (1938) 54 Law Quarterly Review 543; C. M. Gray, 'Bonham's Case Reviewed' (1972) 116 Proceedings of the American Philosophical Society 35; Grey 1878. An important discussion of political authority from within the tradition of classical common law thought is

Matthew Hale's neglected mid-seventeenth century critical analysis of Hobbes' ideas on sovereignty and legal authority. See on this, Yale 1972.

SAVIGNY: A THEORY FOR COMMON LAW?: On historical jurisprudence generally see Stein 1980. Savigny's general influence was enormous 'due not only to the power of his intellect, his aristocratic birth and bearing, the key positions that he held (professor in the University of Berlin, later Prussian minister of legislation), but above all to the timeliness of the ideas he advanced': J. P.Dawson, *The Oracles of the Law* 1968, p. 451. See also E.W. Patterson, 'Historical and Evolutionary Theories of Law' (1951) 51 Columbia Law Review 681. For the background and consequences of the codification controversy in Germany see Dawson, above, ch 6, and J. W. Jones, *Historical Introduction to the Theory of Law* 1940, ch 2.

In England, Bentham advocated codification as a means of banishing what he saw as the archaism and irrationality of common law methods: see text Chapter 3, pp. 54, 76–7. The German codification controversy was substantially replayed in the United States, ultimately with results very different from those in Germany (codification did not finally gain much of a foothold, whereas the major German codification of civil law occurred – despite Savigny's powerful delaying influence – with effect from 1900). Harold Reuschlein notes: 'No more significant warfare has ever been waged in the history of American juristic thought than the bitter warfare between codification and custom which ranged over the second half of the nineteenth century': Reuschlein 1951, p. 69. For general discussions see Reuschlein 1951, pp. 63-71; Patterson, above, pp. 295-8; P. J. King, *Utilitarian Jurisprudence in America* 1986, ch 5.

On Savigny's influence in England see Stein 1980, pp. 72ff. For an illustration of the reflection of his ideas in some American legal scholarship see Carter 1907, which bears the imprint of Savigny's thinking throughout. See also, on the influential American Savignian legal scholar T.M. Cooley, Reuschlein 1951, pp. 58-63.

MAINE'S HISTORICAL JURISPRUDENCE: See e.g. Stone 1966, ch 3 part 1; P. Vinogradoff, 'The Teaching of Sir Henry Maine' (1904) 20 Law Quarterly Review 119; W. A. Robson, 'Sir Henry Maine Today' in W. I. Jennings (ed), *Modern Theories of Law* 1933; R. Cocks, 'Sir Henry Maine: 1822-1888' (1988) 8 Legal Studies 247. Feaver 1969 is an excellent biography. R. Cocks, *Sir Henry Maine: A Study in Victorian Jurisprudence* 1988, was not available to me in time for account to be taken of it in the text. It provides a concise but detailed account of Maine's jurisprudence and is of special interest in attempting to assess both the relevance of Maine's work for later legal theory and its connections with issues of legal practice and professionalisation in his times.

MAINE ON POLITICS AND SOCIETY: See e.g. Collini, Winch and Burrow 1983, ch 7; Burrow 1966, ch 5; G.A. Feaver, 'The Political Attitudes of Sir Henry Maine' (1965) 27 Journal of Politics 290; B. Smith, 'Maine's

Concept of Progress' (1963) 24 Journal of the History of Ideas 407; Barker 1928, ch 6. Maine's 'administrative' view of legal problems was no doubt influenced by his experience in colonial government in India from 1862-9 as legal member of the Governor-General's Council. One consequence of it was his clear appreciation of the value of codification of law as an instrument of modernisation in the Indian context (See Feaver 1969, pp. 76-7). Understandably, James Carter, adhering closely to orthodox common law thought, criticises Maine for being too prepared to see law as a political creation. See Carter 1907, pp. 187-90.

HISTORICAL JURISPRUDENCE AND THE LEGAL PROFESSION: On the relative conservatism of common law thought see e.g. Dicey 1905, p. 367. Professionalisation of law can mean various things and some writers confidently assert that by the seventeenth century 'the English bench and bar had become professionalised': White 1976a, p. 19. What seems to be meant is that specialised legal tasks allocated to barristers, attorneys and solicitors had become established. My concern with professionalisation, however, centres on the self-conscious development of modern professional organisation entailing the claim to esoteric but scientific knowledge, associated training and well defined qualifications for entry into the professional group.

THE FATE OF MAINE'S NEW SCIENCE: With regard to Maine's influence in sociology, Ferdinand Toennies was apparently first led to the idea of his classic work on *Gemeinschaft* and *Gesellschaft*, one of the foundations of modern sociology, by his reading of *Ancient Law*, and spoke of Maine as his teacher: see Feaver 1969, pp. 58, 282. For a modern anthropological assessment see R. Redfield, 'Maine's *Ancient Law* in the Light of Primitive Societies' (1950) 3 Western Political Quarterly 574. See generally G. Stocking, *Victorian Anthropology* 1988.

Chapter 3: Sovereign and Subject: Bentham and Austin

Bentham's most important work of normative legal theory is Bentham 1970. The manuscript, substantially completed by 1782 but put aside by its author, lay buried among the mass of Bentham's papers for one and a half centuries until rediscovered by Charles Everett in 1939. Everett edited the work and published it as *The Limits of Jurisprudence Defined* in 1945. The story of the origins of Bentham's manuscript and the scholarly detective work which led to its identification and publication is told in Everett's preface to the 1945 edition and H. L. A. Hart's introduction to the revised and expanded 1970 version, published as *Of Laws in General*.

Austin was a member of Bentham's circle and a profound admirer of his ideas, although the personal relationship between the two seems to have cooled by the time Austin gave his London University lectures between 1829 and 1833 (cf. Rumble 1985, pp. 15-8, 34-5). On the general relationship between Bentham's and Austin's work see Morison 1982, pp. 38-48, 130.

The first few lectures of Austin's course were published in expanded form as *The Province of Jurisprudence Determined* in 1832. The rest remained unpublished until after his death in 1859. In 1861 a second edition of *The Province* was published by Sarah Austin and in 1863 she published the remaining lectures insofar as they could be reconstructed from Austin's notes. There are three contrasting recent full-length studies of Austin's work. Rumble 1985 deals with Austin's career as a whole including his later political writings and his work as a Royal Commissioner in Malta. It contains profound discussions of many aspects of Austin's thought. Hamburger and Hamburger 1985 is a more conventional biography, providing a valuable portrait of both John and Sarah Austin. Morison 1982 is perhaps most closely geared to the interests of students of normative legal theory, but tends to adopt a rather narrow interpretation of Austin's aims and methods.

THE EMPIRE OF DARKNESS AND THE REGION OF LIGHT: For Bentham's views on codification see Postema 1986, ch 12. For Austin's views on the subject see Austin 1885, pp. 660-81, 1098-1100. On German influences on Austin, see especially A. B. Schwarz 'John Austin and the German Jurisprudence of his Time' (1934) 1 Politica 178; Morison 1982, pp. 60-3; Rumble 1985, pp. 31-4. It should be noted that despite Austin's dismissal of most of Savigny's criticisms of codification as absurd and irrational (Austin 1885, pp. 675-80), he had the highest regard for some of Savigny's other writings, especially his influential book on the concept of possession. For Austin, this exemplified the kind of rational, systematic German Romanist juristic scholarship which he admired for the manner in which it distilled succinct logical principles from historically developed doctrine. Austin viewed Savigny's *Of the Vocation* as an unfortunate, emotionally inspired aberration. Bentham's principle of utility is expounded in his *An Introduction to the Principles of Morals and Legislation*, originally published in 1789 (Athlone Press edn. 1970). See also e.g. R. Harrison, *Bentham* 1983, ch 7; A. J. M. Milne, 'Bentham's Principle of Utility and Legal Philosophy' in M.H. James (ed), *Bentham and Legal Theory* 1973.

POSITIVE LAW AND POSITIVE MORALITY: The insistence on treating positive law as the sole or distinct object of study for legal scholarship is characteristic of the approach to legal thought known as legal positivism. See below, Chapter 4.

THE COERCIVE STRUCTURE OF A LAW: The now classic critique of Austin's command theory of law is in Hart 1961, chs 2-4. On Austin's discussion of sanctions see C. Tapper, 'Austin on Sanctions' [1965] Cambridge Law Journal 271.

SANCTIONS AND POWER CONFERRING RULES: Hart 1961 provides by far the most influential modern critique of Austin's treatment of power conferring rules. See also the thoughtful discussion of the nature of power conferring rules in MacCormick 1981a, ch 6. For a recent attempt to provide elements of a defence of Austin see Moles 1987, pp. 65-70. While Moles' approach seems to me to be, in this respect, broadly along the right lines it does not address major criticisms which Hart and others raise and fails to make clear the particular crucial difference of aims (reflecting different political philosophies) as between Austin and Hart which I try to bring out in the text of this chapter and the next. See also R. Ladenson, 'In Defense of a Hobbesian Conception of Law' (1980) 9 Philosophy and Public Affairs 134.

SOVEREIGNTY: Hinsley 1986 offers a useful general account of the development of the concept of sovereignty. See also M. Francis, 'The Nineteenth Century Theory of Sovereignty and Thomas Hobbes' (1980) 1 History of Political Thought 517; W. J. Rees, 'The Theory of Sovereignty Restated' (1950) 59 Mind 495; S. I. Benn, 'The Uses of "Sovereignty"' (1955) 3 Political Studies 109. On the abstract character of Austin's sovereign see also Manning 1933, p. 207; Moles 1987, p. 71; and cf. Fuller 1940, p. 46 insisting on Austin's ambiguity. On Bentham's ideas see also J. H. Burns, 'Bentham on Sovereignty: An Exploration' in M. H. James (ed), *Bentham and Legal Theory* 1973.

SOME CHARACTERISTICS OF AUSTIN'S SOVEREIGN: For a sample of commentary and criticism see e.g. Buckland 1949, ch 9; Maine 1875a, chs 12 and 13. Despite the apparent problems stressed by many critics in applying Austin's theory of sovereignty to the case of the United States, American Austinians of the nineteenth century seemed to find no great difficulty in doing so. See P. J. King, *Utilitarian Jurisprudence in America* 1986, ch 7. For critiques see *ibid.* ch 8 and J. Dewey, 'Austin's Theory of Sovereignty' (1894) 9 Political Science Quarterly 31.

MUST THE SOVEREIGN BE LEGALLY ILLIMITABLE?: On Bentham's views see Postema 1986, pp. 237-56; Hart 1982, ch 9.

THE JUDGE AS DELEGATE OF THE SOVEREIGN: For Austin's views on 'judiciary law' see especially Austin 1885, pp. 641-60. See also the detailed, sympathetic examination in Rumble 1985, ch 4. For Bentham's views on the matter see the excellent in-depth analysis in Postema 1986, chs 10-13.

AUSTIN'S THEORY OF THE CENTRALISED STATE: Austin's views on centralised state organisation and delegation (which he saw as its correlate) are expressed in his review essay 'Centralization' (1847) 85 Edinburgh Review 221. For a thoughtful discussion of his later political ideas see Rumble 1985, ch 6. A general discussion of the relevance of changes in Austin's outlook for the ideas expressed in his lectures is contained in Hamburger and Hamburger 1985, ch 9.

AUSTIN AND THE LEGAL PROFESSION: For general background see the excellent discussion of relationships between trends in jurisprudence and legal professionalism in England in Sugarman 1986. Also of interest is W. Twining, '1836 And All That: Laws in the University of London 1836-1986' (1987) 40 Current Legal Problems 261. For illustration of Austin's influence on legal scholarship see Cosgrove 1980, pp. 23-8.

Chapter 4: Analytical Jurisprudence and Liberal Democracy: Hart and Kelsen

EMPIRICISM AND CONCEPTUALISM: For Kelsen's own comparison of his work with Anglo-American analytical jurisprudence see Kelsen 1941b. For the methods-debate around Austin's work see Morison 1958 and Morison 1982; Hart 1958, especially at p. 65 (broadly empiricist interpretations); Manning 1933; Stone 1964, ch 2; Moles 1987, ch 1; Campbell 1988 (broadly conceptualist interpretations). Rumble 1985 wisely equivocates: while Austin would have tended to adopt the empirically oriented view typical of the utilitarians, 'his actual approach to the problems of jurisprudence is not nearly as empirical as Morison suggests' (p. 96). It should be noted that often the antagonists in this debate seem to be talking of a variety of ambiguities in Austin's methods and not necessarily of the specific methodological distinction around which this chapter is organised. Hart's own rejection of conceptualism is made clear in Hart 1970.

HART'S LINGUISTIC EMPIRICISM: Hohfeld's major work is *Fundamental Legal Conceptions as Applied in Judicial Reasoning* 1923. For a detailed discussion of his contribution to analytical jurisprudence see Stone 1964, ch 4, in which some of Kocourek's ideas are also discussed. On Kocourek see also Reuschlein 1951, pp. 173-9. The best study of Hart's work as a whole is MacCormick 1981a, which also contains biographical details, and generally adopts a sympathetic and constructively critical view. See also W. Twining, 'Academic Law and Legal Philosophy' (1979) 95 Law Quarterly Review 557. Leith and Ingram (eds) 1988 is a valuable collection of essays offering a generally much less sympathetic critique. Moles 1987 is also strongly critical of the methods and orientation of Hart's work. See also e.g. M. Kramer, 'The Rule of Misrecognition in the Hart of Jurisprudence' (1988) 8 Oxford Journal of Legal Studies 401.

THE CHARACTER OF RULES: See Hart 1961, pp. 54-60 on the nature of rules, and pp. 79-88 on obligation. On the internal aspect of rules see also especially D. N. MacCormick, *Legal Reasoning and Legal Theory* 1978, pp. 275-92.

SOCIOLOGICAL DRIFT: There is now a considerable literature which attacks, in one way or another, the lack of sensitivity of Hart's legal philosophy to the sociological questions it suggests. See e.g. Hughes 1962; J. P. Gibbs, 'Definitions of Law and Empirical Questions' (1968) 2 Law and Society Review 429; S. Roberts, *Order and Dispute* 1979, pp. 24-5;

M. Krygier, '*The Concept of Law* and Social Theory' (1982) 2 Oxford Journal of Legal Studies 155; B. Edgeworth, 'Legal Positivism and the Philosophy of Language' (1986) 6 Legal Studies 115. A serious attempt to meet these criticisms would, however, force Hart's normative legal theory to become integrated with empirical legal theory of the kind associated with sociology of law. See, however, E. Colvin, 'The Sociology of Secondary Rules' (1978) 28 University of Toronto Law Journal 195. That such criticisms have been made continuously with little effect on the reputation of Hart's theory despite the lack of satisfactory answers to many of them may be testimony to the appeal, among legal scholars, of a normative legal theory which apparently provides unity and system in legal ideas while doing so in the explicitly 'legal common sense' terms of conformity with ordinary legal linguistic usage.

THE STRUCTURE OF A LEGAL SYSTEM: See Hart 1961, pp. 89-107. Doubts about the viability or utility of the distinction between primary and secondary rules as Hart describes them have long been expressed. See e.g. L. J. Cohen, Book Review (1962) 71 Mind 395; C. Tapper, 'Powers and Secondary Rules of Change' in A. W. B. Simpson (ed) *Oxford Essays in Jurisprudence*, second series, 1973; Fuller 1969a, pp. 134-7. For an argument that law should be understood in terms of duty-imposing and duty-excepting rules see J. W. Harris, *Law and Legal Science* 1979, pp. 92-106.

THE EXISTENCE OF A LEGAL SYSTEM: See Hart 1961, pp. 107-20.

HART'S HERMENEUTICS: See also the excellent discussion in J. Jackson, 'The Concept of Fact' in Leith and Ingram (eds) 1988.

JUDICIAL DECISIONS AND THE 'OPEN TEXTURE' OF RULES: See Hart 1961, ch 7; Hart 1977; MacCormick 1981a, ch. 10. See also S. Livingston, 'Of the Core and The Penumbra' in Leith and Ingram (eds) 1988; E. Hunter Taylor, 'H. L. A. Hart's Concept of Law in the Perspective of American Legal Realism' (1972) 35 Modern Law Review 606.

KELSEN'S CONCEPTUALISM: The current lack of an adequate biography of Kelsen in English is a serious and regrettable gap in the literature of legal scholarship. For a biography in German see R. A. Metall, *Hans Kelsen: Leben und Werk* 1969. Among studies of Kelsen's work see e.g. W. Ebenstein, *The Pure Theory of Law* 1945; R. Moore, *Legal Norms and Legal Science* 1978; R. Tur and W. Twining (eds), *Essays on Kelsen* 1986. The periodical literature on Kelsen's work is immense and ever-growing.

'THE MACHINE NOW RUNS BY ITSELF': On the concept of the basic norm (*Grundnorm*) see Kelsen 1945, pp. 115-22; Kelsen 1967, ch 34; and the revised formulation in Kelsen, 'The Function of a Constitution' in

Tur and Twining, above. On Kelsen's views on contradiction between norms see e.g. J. W. Harris, 'Kelsen and Normative Consistency' in Tur and Twining, above.

DEMOCRACY AND THE RULE OF LAW: For Kelsen's ideas on democracy see Kelsen 1945, pp. 284-300 and, especially, the brilliant discussion of democracy as an ideal in Kelsen 1955, a remarkable and unjustly neglected essay. The link between philosophical and political relativism is elaborated also in 'Absolutism and Relativism in Philosophy and Politics' in Kelsen 1957. For Kelsen's conception of the identity of the state and the legal order see Kelsen 1967, pp. 284-319; and Kelsen 1945, pp. 181-92: 'The result of our analysis is that there is no sociological concept of the state different from the concept of the legal order' (Kelsen 1945, p. 192). Kelsen's rejection of God as well as the state as transcendent entities may suggest a straightforward atheism. In fact, however, issues raised in theological literature are frequent concerns of his writings. Kelsen's insistence, here as elsewhere, seems to be that the responsibility for actions and the consequences of beliefs, including issues of conscience and faith, should be borne directly and personally by individuals, not assigned elsewhere.

On concerns about the legal frameworks of modern state intervention in Western societies see e.g. W. G. Friedmann, 'The Planned State and the Rule of Law' (1948) 22 Australian Law Journal 162 and 207; H. W. Jones, 'The Rule of Law and the Welfare State' (1958) 58 Columbia Law Review 153; Friedmann, *The State and the Rule of Law in a Mixed Economy* 1971; Cotterrell 1984, pp. 168-87; T. Lowi, 'The Welfare State, the New Regulation and the Rule of Law' in A. C. Hutchinson and P. Monahan (eds), *The Rule of Law* 1987; Cotterrell, 'The Rule of Law in Corporate Society' (1988) 51 Modern Law Review 126.

Chapter 5: The Appeal of Natural Law

LEGAL POSITIVISM AND NATURAL LAW: The best-known concise summation of the legal positivist tradition is Hart 1958. See also generally on the issues discussed in this chapter, S. I. Shuman, *Legal Positivism* 1963. Austin's views on natural law are in Austin 1885, lecture 32. For the history of natural law theory see e.g. A. P. D'Entreves, *Natural Law* 2nd edn, 1970; M. B. Crowe, *The Changing Profile of the Natural Law* 1977; H. A. Rommen, *The Natural Law* 1948, Part 1; H. McCoubrey, *The Development of Naturalist Legal Theory* 1987; Weinreb 1987. For a highly distinctive treatment see E. Bloch, *Natural Law and Human Dignity* 1986. D. Beyleveld and R. Brownsword, *Law as a Moral Judgment* 1986 is an ambitious if sometimes tortuous work containing discussions of the implications for many issues of modern legal theory of rejection of the analytical separation of law and morality. On natural law and common law see Gough 1955; J. C. H. Wu, *Fountain of Justice* 1955, Part 1, Section

1. On natural law in American constitutional development see Haines 1930 (which contains a valuable bibliography of the older literature); E. S. Corwin, 'The "Higher Law" Background of American Constitutional Law' (1928–9) 42 Harvard Law Review 149 and 365; Wu, above, Part 1, Section 2; Grey 1978.

IS NATURAL LAW DEAD?: See e. g. Rommen, above, ch 6. On the 'piecemeal rationality' of modern law see Cotterrell, 'English Conceptions of the Role of Theory in Legal Analysis' (1983) 46 Modern Law Review 681 at pp. 691-2, 698-9; and on conditions which make possible, nevertheless, a frequent denial of this state of affairs and the claim that legal science is a unified and autonomous field, see Cotterrell 1986a, pp. 15-20. See further Chapter 8, below.

NATURAL LAW AND LEGAL AUTHORITY: Among convenient recent British and American discussions of Aquinas' legal theory see e.g. Crowe, above, chs 6 and 7; W. E. May, 'The Meaning and Nature of the Natural Law in Thomas Aquinas' (1977) 22 American Journal of Jurisprudence 168 (and literature cited therein); A. Battaglia, *Toward a Reformulation of Natural Law* 1981; N. Kretzmann, 'Lex Iniusta Non Est Lex' (1988) 33 American Journal of Jurisprudence 99; and the very valuable commentary in Finnis 1980.

THE 'REBIRTH' OF NATURAL LAW: See generally J. Stone, *Human Law and Human Justice* 1965, ch 7; Haines 1930, especially Parts 2 to 5; and on the rebirth of natural law in continental Europe especially around the beginning of the twentieth century see also J. Charmont, *La renaissance du droit naturel* 2nd edn, 1927; and Rommen, above, ch 7.

ANGLO-AMERICAN LESSONS FROM THE NAZI ERA: On the Hart-Fuller debate see e.g. P.Soper, 'Choosing a Legal Theory on Moral Grounds' in J. Coleman and E. F. Paul (eds), *Philosophy and Law* 1987. On post-war legal problems arising from the legacy of the Nazi regime see H. O. Pappe, 'On the Validity of Judicial Decisions in the Nazi Era' (1960) 23 Modern Law Review 260; McCoubrey, above, ch 7; *Oppenheimer* v *Cattermole* [1975] 1 All. E. R. 538 (HL). On the Nazi legal system, among convenient sources in English, K. Loewenstein, 'Law in the Third Reich' (1936) 45 Yale Law Journal 779; E. Fraenkel, *The Dual State* 1941 (which argues that a regime of legality existed as a cloak for the parallel regime of arbitrariness); Kirchheimer 1941; Neumann 1986, ch 16 (originally written in the 1930s); Neumann 1944, pp. 440-58; N. S. Marsh, 'Some Aspects of the German Legal System Under National Socialism' (1946) 62 Law Quarterly Review 366; Krausnik *et al* 1968, especially ch 2. There is also much valuable translated material in S. P. Simpson and J. Stone, *Cases and Readings on Law and Society* 1949, vol 3. On legal positivism in Nazi Germany see also A. Kaufmann, 'National Socialism and German Jurisprudence from 1933 to 1945' (1988) 9 Cardozo Law Review 1629 which argues persuasively (pp. 1644-5) that legal thought pragmatically combined a positivist attitude to Nazi law with an anti-positivist view of the surviving remnants of pre-Nazi law. Kaufmann also shows the widespread prostitution of legal philosophy to support the aims of the regime. I am grateful to Judith Koffler for bringing this essay to my attention.

THE IDEAL OF LEGALITY AND THE EXISTENCE OF LAW: Franz Neumann's major work on the Rule of Law (Neumann 1986) was written as a London University Ph.D. thesis after he left Germany in 1933. It was published in German translation in 1980, but the original English version appeared in book form only in 1986. The major themes of the thesis are, however, reiterated in Neumann's other published works, especially 'The Change in the Function of Law in Modern Society' (originally published in German in 1937) in F. Neumann, *The Democratic and the Authoritarian State* 1957, and *Behemoth*, his classic wartime study of the Nazi political order (Neumann 1944). On Neumann's ideas see Cotterrell, 'The Rule of Law in Corporate Society' (1988) 51 Modern Law Review 126. For an interesting discussion of the consequences for the German civil service of the kind of legal conditions which Neumann and Kirchheimer highlight see J. Caplan, 'Bureaucracy, Politics and the National Socialist State' in P. Stachura (ed), *The Shaping of the Nazi State* 1978.

A PURPOSIVE VIEW OF LAW: Summers 1984 is a clear and thoughtful study of Fuller's work as a whole, and includes much helpful biographical information and a bibliography of his writings. See also the posthumously published *The Principles of Social Order* (K. Winston, ed) 1981 which collates many of Fuller's important later papers. There is an extensive periodical literature by and about Fuller. Some discussions of Fuller's *The Morality of Law* are listed in the revised edition: see Fuller 1969a, pp. 188-9, 243-4. For recent discussion see e.g. K. I. Winston, 'Is/Ought Redux' (1988) 8 Oxford Journal of Legal Studies 329; P. R. Teachout, 'The Soul of the Fugue' (1986) 70 Minnesota Law Review 1073 which argues that Fuller should be understood not as a system-building theorist but as an ethical critic; and the symposium in (1978) 92 Harvard Law Review, no. 2.

FULLER AND THE COMMON LAW TRADITION: For Fuller's conception of the varieties of social ordering see also e.g. his 'Some Unexplored Social Dimensions of the Law' in A. E. Sutherland (ed), *The Path of the Law from 1967* 1968; 'Two Principles of Human Association' in J. R. Pennock and J. W. Chapman (eds), *Voluntary Associations* 1969; 'The Law's Precarious Hold on Life' (1969) 3 Georgia Law Review 530; 'Law as an Instrument of Social Control and Law as a Facilitation of Human Interaction' [1975] Brigham Young University Law Review 89; 'Mediation: Its Forms and Functions' (1971) 44 Southern California Law Review 305; 'Some Presuppositions Shaping the Concept of "Socialization"' in J. L. Tapp and F. J. Levine (eds), *Law, Justice and the Individual in Society* 1977.

POLITICS AND PROFESSIONAL RESPONSIBILITY: On legal positivism's moral myopia in other contexts see M. Tushnet, *The American Law of Slavery 1810-1860* 1981, pp. 54-65; R. M. Cover, *Justice Accused* 1975. Among Fuller's other writings on law and political values are 'Freedom: A Suggested Analysis' (1955) 68 Harvard Law Review 1305; 'Irrigation and Tyranny' (1965) 17 Stanford Law Review 1021; 'Freedom as a Problem of Allocating Choice' (1968) 112 Proceedings of the American Philosophical Society 101; 'Some Reflections on Legal and Economic Freedoms' (1954) 54 Columbia Law Review 70.

NATURAL LAW TAMED?: On Hart's 'minimum content of natural law' see also Hart 1958, pp. 78-81 and his further remarks in *Law, Liberty and Morality* 1963, p. 70: 'It is indeed arguable that a human society in which. . . [such universal values as individual freedom, safety of life, and protection from deliberately inflicted harm] are not recognised at all in its morality is neither an empirical nor a logical possibility. . .'. For commentary and criticism see e.g. Fuller 1969a, pp. 184-6; D'Entreves, above, pp. 185-203. On Finnis see e.g. J. W. Harris, 'Can You Believe in Natural Law?' (1981) 44 Modern Law Review 729; D. N. MacCormick, 'Natural Law Reconsidered' (1981) 1 Oxford Journal of Legal Studies 99; McCoubrey, above, pp. 179-86; Weinreb 1987, pp 108-15. R. Hittinger, *A Critique of the New Natural Law Theory* 1987 is a study of the work of Finnis and of that of the theologian Germain Grisez upon which he relies substantially.

Chapter 6: The Problem of the Creative Judge: Pound and Dworkin

POUND'S REJECTION OF THE MODEL OF RULES: Wigdor 1974 is a superb biography of Pound, providing not only a richly detailed account of his career but also an incisive study of the evolution of his ideas. Paul Sayre's *The Life of Roscoe Pound* 1948, is idiosyncratic, sometimes eloquent, richly anecdotal, written in an attractively warm and personal style, and unashamedly biased towards its subject. There are bibliographies by F. C. Setaro (1942) and G. A. Strait (1960) of Pound's writings through six decades of prolific scholarship. For his own account of the antecedents and development of sociological jurisprudence see Pound 1911 and the other parts of this essay in 24 Harvard Law Review 591 and 25 Harvard Law Review 489. In 'The Need of a Sociological Jurisprudence' (1907) 19 Green Bag 607, sociological jurisprudence is advocated as a response to popular disrespect for law and the need to keep legal processes in tune with popular aspirations of the time; if this is not achieved lawyers may lose 'their legitimate hegemony in legislation and politics to engineers and naturalists and economists' (p. 612). For Pound's views on positivist analytical jurisprudence see e.g. *Law and Morals* 1924, ch 2. For a late statement of his views on natural law see 'The Revival of Natural Law' (1942) 17 Notre Dame Lawyer 287. Pound was careful to distinguish sociological jurisprudence from sociology of law, which he recognised as a branch of social science concerned with explanation of law as a natural phenomenon in terms of behaviour. See his introduction to G. Gurvitch, *Sociology of Law* 1947; and Pound, 'Sociology of Law' in G. Gurvitch and W. E. Moore (eds), *Twentieth Century Sociology* 1945.

THE OUTLOOK OF SOCIOLOGICAL JURISPRUDENCE: On Pound's St. Paul address and its consequences see Wigdor 1974, pp. 123-30; J. H. Wigmore's celebrated account of the event is reprinted in Sayre, *Life of Roscoe Pound*, pp. 146-51; and in A. Kocourek, 'Roscoe Pound as a Former Colleague Knew Him' in P. Sayre (ed), *Interpretations of Modern Legal Philosophies* 1947, pp. 424-7. For Pound's early firm defence of legislation as entitled to full recognition as a source of principle in common law reasoning see also 'Common Law and Legislation' (1908) 21 Harvard Law Review 383; and 'Liberty of Contract' (1909) 18 Yale Law Journal 454.

A THEORY OF INTERESTS: See also Pound 1959 III, ch 14 and e.g. Patterson, 'Pound's Theory of Social Interests' in Sayre (ed), *Interpretations of Modern Legal Philosophies*. Pound acknowledged the influence of the German jurist Rudolf von Jhering in developing a theory of interests as a foundation for legal theory. See on the relationship between Pound's and Jhering's ideas, Reuschlein 1951, pp. 107-12. For the broader European development and context of Jhering's ideas see e.g. Stone 1964, pp. 227-9. M. Schoch (ed), *The Jurisprudence of Interests* 1948 provides translations of some of the major works of this movement.

THE SEARCH FOR A MEASURE OF VALUES: The view that legal philosophy must not desert the task of establishing and systematising values is developed in Pound 1940, ch 2. On relationships between Kohler's theories and Pound's sociological jurisprudence see e.g. Reuschlein 1951, pp. 117-20. For statements of the content of the jural postulates of Anglo-American law at various times in Pound's career see Pound 1942, ch 4; Pound 1959 III, pp. 8-10 and references there to earlier writings.

THE WIDER CONTEXT OF POUND'S JURISPRUDENCE: On Pound's essentially conservative political views see Sayre, *Life of Roscoe Pound*, ch 6. On the reform philosophies of the Progressives see e.g. R. M. Crunden, *Ministers of Reform* 1984. M. White, *Social Thought in America* 1949 is widely cited as authority for the existence of a general 'revolt against formalism' in American intellectual life from the beginning of the twentieth century and including – as its legal aspect – a rejection in legal thought of the apparently exclusively legal-logical concerns of positivist analytical jurisprudence. I remain unconvinced that the anti-positivist writings considered in this chapter are best understood as part of this general intellectual trend. Rather they may be merely specific responses to the inadequacies of positivist analytical jurisprudence's explanations of legal change in the context of the American legal system, especially in periods of rapid social change. Conflation of diverse intellectual developments is often misleading even though it may well be instructive and important to identify cross-influences. A comparably misleading result certainly arises, in my view, from attempts (especially in Summers 1982) to link Pound with many other influential mid-twentieth century American jurists as part of a relatively unified school of 'pragmatic instrumentalists'.

DWORKIN AND POUND: Burnet 1985 is a rare attempt to compare the two writers systematically, although it does not link them specifically to a common defence of the common law outlook as does the text of this chapter. Dworkin seems more ready to acknowledge a debt to Fuller than to Pound if only in the most general terms: 'But for the example of his dissatisfaction, others would have been content with the positivist's truism that the validity of law is one thing and its morality another': Dworkin 1965, p. 668.

PRINCIPLES AND POLICIES: For criticism of and commentary on Dworkin's work see e.g. M. Cohen (ed), *Ronald Dworkin and Contemporary Jurisprudence* 1984. There is an already large and rapidly growing periodical literature discussing his legal philosophy. The key passage in Earl J.'s judgment in *Riggs* v *Palmer* notes that 'all laws as well as all contracts may be controlled in their operation and effect by general, fundamental maxims of the common law. No one shall be permitted to profit by his own fraud, or take advantage of his own wrong, or to found any claim upon his own iniquity, or to acquire property by his own crime. These maxims are dictated by public policy, have their foundation in universal law administered in all civilised countries, and have nowhere been superseded by statutes.' (1889) 115 NY 506 at pp. 511-2. This suggests that applicable principles are the maxims of common law as discussed in Chapter 2, above. Further, these principles are seen as founded in policy, a view not obviously compatible with Dworkin's attempted separation of policy and principle (but cf. Dworkin 1977, pp. 22-3). Finally, their roots are in universal (natural?) law beyond that of the legal system which the court serves, whereas Dworkin sees legal principles as grounded in the historical values of the legal system to which they belong.

For an interesting attempt to defend a version of positivist analytical jurisprudence founded on Hart's ideas, while recognising much of the substance of Dworkin's claims about the significance of principles, see D. N. MacCormick, *Legal Reasoning and Legal Theory* 1978. MacCormick argues that in hard cases judges are constrained by what he calls persuasive legal sources (pp. 163-4). When deductive legal logic runs out, judicial arguments are consequentialist in nature, but within the constraints of overriding institutional demands for coherence and consistency of values. Further, like Dworkin, MacCormick claims that no clear analytical line can be drawn between hard and clear cases (p. 197). Against Dworkin, however, MacCormick claims (i) that a descriptive legal theory of principles – no less than of rules – is possible, since legal principles have a positive source in legislation and reported judgments of courts; (ii) because of this, the legal validity of principles can be tested in the same way as that of any legislative provision or judicial rule; hence (iii) Hart's idea of an ultimate rule of recognition within a legal system is not rendered incoherent by an acceptance of the analytical importance of legal principles. Finally, (iv), principle and policy are part of, implicated in, and the basis of legal rules; they are not separate components of a legal system: 'to explicate the principles is to rationalize the rules' (p. 157).

Although MacCormick's thesis is a valuable attempt to remedy the absence in Hart's legal philosophy of an analysis of judicial reasoning in hard cases, it seems open to the objection that principles governing coherence and consistency are not given by rules of law, as MacCormick seems to suggest, but must be *imposed* on them. Thus, for Dworkin, the process of applying and developing principles is creative and constructive; it is not already bounded by a criterion of legal validity but is part of the ongoing process of determining legal validity. MacCormick seeks to retain the positivist idea of discretion, but to bound it with principle: 'It is the interaction of arguments from principle and consequentialist arguments which fully justifies decisions in hard cases' (p. 194). This seems to be to have one's cake and eat it if, for MacCormick, discretion *beyond rules* is to be *controlled* by principles *governed by rules*. If it is not so controlled, the positivist problem of the inability legally to explain discretion remains. On the other hand, if principles are admitted not to be governed conclusively by a rule of recognition, MacCormick's positivist defence of the centrality of this ultimate validating rule seems hard to sustain.

THE CLOSED WORLD OF LEGAL INTERPRETATION: Dworkin has long recognised the frequent vagueness of the rule-principle distinction. See Dworkin 1977, pp. 27-8. As regards the idea of community, there is no doubt about the kind of community Dworkin favours, even though his legal theory does not give him a direct means of analysing it. It is one strongly committed to both individual autonomy and social justice for all its members. Thus, he is explicit that the social order of Britain since the fundamental change of government philosophy in 1979 is 'better off as measured by national economic indicators and worse off, in my view, in most other ways'. See Dworkin, 'The New England' New York Review of Books, October 27 1988, at p. 59; and cf. Dworkin 1986, ch 11.

POLITICS, PROFESSIONALISM AND INTERPRETIVE COMMUNITIES: See also the similar conception of the citizen's right of civil disobedience in J. Rawls, *A Theory of Justice* 1972, especially pp. 382-91 (citizen's right in a 'nearly just' society to judge the legal rendering of basic principles on which the political order as a whole is founded). Unlike Dworkin, Rawls sees civil disobedience as a breach of law to assert higher political principle, not as an alternative interpretation of the proper legal situation (p. 365). His statement that the 'final court of appeal is not the court, nor the executive, nor the legislature, but the electorate as a whole' (p. 390) seems to be meant in a looser, more rhetorical sense than Dworkin might argue for. But the closeness of the two writers' positions is striking. On the Dworkin-Fish debate see also S. Fish, *Is There a Text in This Class?* 1980; Dworkin 1985, chs 6 and 7; Fish, 'Dennis Martinez and the Uses of Theory' (1987) 96 Yale Law Journal 1773; J. M. Schelly, 'Interpretation in Law: The Dworkin-Fish Debate (or Soccer Among the Gahuka-Gama)' (1985) 73 California Law Review 158.

Chapter 7: Varieties of Scepticism

Scepticism about normative analysis of law: for the parallel Scandinavian literature see especially, A. Hagerstrom, *Inquiries Into the Nature of Law and Morals* 1953; K. Olivecrona, *Law as Fact* 1939, and the completely rewritten second edition 1971; A. V. Lundstedt, *Superstition or Rationality in Action For Peace?* 1925, *Law and Justice* 1952 and *Legal Thinking Revised* 1956; A. Ross, *On Law and Justice* 1958 and *Directives and Norms* 1968.

American legal realism has often been criticised for an indifference to values (e.g. Pound 1931, p. 703), but this hardly applies to some of its most eminent theorists, such as Felix Cohen and Karl Llewellyn. Most realists denied the existence of any moral absolutes. Cohen, however, claimed insistently that the relativity of moral values in no way undermined their importance as guides to law in a particular time and place. See generally, his *Ethical Systems and Legal Ideals* 1933, and L. K. Cohen (ed) *The Legal Conscience* 1960. Llewellyn expressed sympathy for natural law theory's search for legal ideals but rejected its attempts to demonstrate moral absolutes and its claims that law and morality could not be analytically separated. See 'One "Realist's" View of Natural Law for Judges' in Llewellyn 1962; and Twining 1973, pp. 185-8. These positions suggest no greater indifference to legal values than is exhibited in the writings of many positivist analytical jurists.

On views of American legal realism in Britain see Twining 1968, pp. 5-7 discussing dismissive attitudes at Oxford University and in legal literature in the 1950s. That this approach is still current in some circles is suggested by a recent, and otherwise excellent, brief primer on legal studies in which the only guidance offered, about the massive and diverse literature of American legal realism, is: 'The flavour of American realism is best caught from Jerome Frank's *Law and the Modern Mind* (London, 1949), and if you read it you need to know that Frank, in spite of his odd views, was a very good judge' (A. W. B. Simpson, *An Invitation to Law* 1988, p. 216). But the example of American legal realism seems to have provided significant inspiration among the small group of progressive academic lawyers who founded the Modern Law Review in 1937 to invigorate legal scholarship in Britain; see C. Glasser, 'Radicals and Refugees: The Foundation of the Modern Law Review and English Legal Scholarship' (1987) 50 Modern Law Review 688. For Hart's views on American legal realism see Hart 1961, ch 7; Hart 1977; and for criticism of these views see references under the heading 'Judicial Decisions and the "Open Texture" of Rules' in notes to Chapter 4, above.

For valuable general assessments of realism see especially L. Kalman, *Legal Realism at Yale 1927-1960* 1986; Twining 1973; Rumble 1968; Stevens 1983.

PRAGMATISM AND REALISM: C. S. Peirce introduced pragmatism as a philosophical term and doctrine in the late nineteenth century. For James' doctrines see his *Pragmatism* 1907. Dewey's synthesis of Peirce's and James's ideas is reflected in his *Reconstruction in Philosophy* 1920, *Experience and Nature* 1925 and *The Quest for Certainty* 1929. See generally e.g. E. C. Moore, *American Pragmatism* 1961; J. Passmore, *A Hundred Years of Philosophy* 2nd ed 1966, ch 5. On Felix Cohen's essay see also G. Peller, 'The Metaphysics of American Law' (1985) 73 California Law Review 1151, at pp. 1227-32; and on Cohen generally, M. P. Golding, 'Realism and Functionalism in the Legal Thought of Felix S. Cohen' (1981) 66 Cornell Law Quarterly 1032. Close parallels with Cohen's discussion of 'transcendental nonsense' and 'magic solving words' in law can be found in the Swedish philosopher Axel Hagerstrom's discussions of 'word magic' in his *Inquiries*, above, and in the works by Lundstedt and Olivecrona. On the Marxist notion of 'reification', appropriated in much recent critical legal studies literature, see especially the classic analysis in G. Lukacs, 'Reification and the Consciousness of the Proletariat' in his *History and Class Consciousness* 1971.

REALISM AND NORMATIVE LEGAL THEORY: On the background to Pound's 'spring offensive of 1931 against the realists' (cf. Llewellyn 1931a, p. 54), and Llewellyn's reply which supplies the nine generalisations discussed in the text, see also N. E. H. Hull, 'Some Realism About the Llewellyn-Pound Exchange Over Realism' [1987] Wisconsin Law Review 921. On Moore's approach to empirical research on law see also e. g. W. U. Moore and C. C. Callahan, 'My Philosophy of Law' in Julius Rosenthal Foundation 1941. Schlegel's essays on realism (Schlegel 1979; 1980) are superbly rich and detailed accounts of the fate of some of the most significant legal realist efforts at serious social scientific research. On Holmes' 'bad man' see W.Twining, 'The Bad Man Revisited' (1973) 58 Cornell Law Quarterly 275. On caricatures of Llewellyn's view of the significance of rules see Twining 1968, ch 2, and for a clear statement of his actual position, in mid-career, on their importance within the broader concept of law as an institution see Llewellyn 1941.

Jerome Frank's enigmatic character has inspired several studies: see J. Paul, *The Legal Realism of Jerome N. Frank* 1959; W. Volkomer, *The Passionate Liberal* 1970; R. J. Glennon, *The Iconoclast as Reformer* 1985. Probably the best known source of radical realist claims about the impenetrability of subjective psychological factors ultimately determining how a judge reaches his decision is J. C. Hutcheson, 'The Judgment Intuitive' (1929) 14 Cornell Law Quarterly 274. Written by an experienced American judge, it stressed in the most direct terms the central role of 'hunches' or 'intuitions' in deciding cases. This kind of radical realism naturally had the effect of emphasising the special importance of psychology, among the human sciences, in helping to explain judicial and administrative behaviour. Cf. E. S. Robinson *Law and the Lawyers* 1935, p. v: 'This book attempts to show that jurisprudence is certain to become one of the family of social sciences – that all its fundamental concepts will have to be brought into line with psychological knowledge'. See also Frank 1949, chs 10 and 11; also the appeal to psychoanalytic theory in Frank 1930, and to psychiatry in Arnold 1935, pp. 269-70.

Peller, in 'The Metaphysics of American Law', above, characterises Llewellyn's approach as 'constructive realism' in contrast to the 'deconstructive realism' exemplified by Felix Cohen's attack on 'transcendental nonsense'. The constructive-deconstructive opposition might, however, be somewhat too stark, taken alone. Cohen's essay, for example, seeks to deconstruct existing legal doctrine in order to construct more realistic functional doctrinal forms. I prefer to treat as the basic variable the degree of seriousness with which orthodox doctrinal reasoning is taken by the writers in question. Those realists who attach substantial significance to it can be called 'constructive' merely insofar as their efforts are directed towards a better understanding of its working, or to improvements in the manner of using legal doctrine.

LLEWELLYN'S CONSTRUCTIVE DOCTRINAL REALISM: On Llewellyn's work the best general source is Twining 1973, an excellent, deeply sympathetic intellectual biography. There is also an interesting personal account of Llewellyn in Twining 1968, pp. 5-23. Many of his most important papers are collected in the posthumously published *Jurisprudence* (Llewellyn 1962). Llewellyn's important contributions to the sociology of law, while not directly the concern of this book, are discussed in Cotterrell 1984, ch 3 and in more detail in Twining 1973, ch 9.

THE POLITICAL CONTEXT OF AMERICAN LEGAL REALISM: Purcell 1973 locates the development of legal realism as part of a broader range of political and cultural developments in the United States. See also, generally, Kalman, above, and for legal realism's place in the development of American legal education Stevens 1983 and Twining 1973, Part 1. On the involvement of lawyers in the New Deal see P. Irons, *New Deal Lawyers* 1982 and G. E. White's review essay 'Recapturing New Deal Lawyers' (1988) 102 Harvard Law Review 489. The movement for 'free judicial decision' associated with the German *Freirechtslehre* advocates was not confined to Germany. See generally, *The Science of Legal Method: Select Essays by Various Authors* 1917, especially essays by Eugen Ehrlich and Francois Geny.

POST-REALIST POLICY-SCIENCE: On the collaboration of McDougal and Lasswell see Kalman, above, pp. 176-87; J. N. Moore, 'Prolegomenon to the Jurisprudence of Myres McDougal and Harold Lasswell' (1968) 54 Virginia Law Review 662. Among general statements and applications of the McDougal-Lasswell approach see Lasswell and McDougal, 'Legal Education and Public Policy' (1943) 52 Yale Law Journal 203; McDougal, 'The Law School of the Future' (1947) 56 Yale Law Journal 1345, and 'Law as a Process of Decision' (1956) 1 Natural Law Forum 53; Lasswell, *Power and Personality* 1948; R. Arens and H. D. Lasswell, *In Defense of Public Order* 1961. Cf. J. H. Schlegel's description of legal realists as 'forging a more contemporary notion of the law professor's role, that of the policy maker – the omni-competent member of the academic-governmental "Commissions to Study the Causes of Almost Anything"' (Schlegel 1980, pp. 315-6). For examples and criticisms of legal impact studies in the law and society literature see Cotterrell 1984, pp. 37-8, 337. On the law and society movement in the United States see L. M. Friedman, 'The Law and Society Movement' (1986) 38 Stanford Law Review 763; R. L. Abel, 'Redirecting Social Studies of Law' (1980) 14 Law and Society Review 805. The standard American text on economic analysis of law is R. A. Posner, *Economic Analysis of Law* (3rd edn) 1986. P. Burrows and C. G. Veljanovski (eds), *The Economic Approach to Law* 1981 offers a good introduction to alternative approaches developed by British writers. M. Kuperberg and C. Beitz (eds), *Law, Economics, and Philosophy* 1983 collects together some seminal papers expounding and applying economic approaches to law.

POST-REALIST RADICAL SCEPTICISM: On judicial behaviouralism see further Cotterrell 1984, pp. 230-4, 359-60. On the American Critical Legal Studies movement see generally the very useful collection of papers in (1984) 36 Stanford Law Review, no. 1 (special issue on CLS); Kelman 1987; R. Unger, 'The Critical Legal Studies Movement' (1983) 96 Harvard Law Review 563; and other symposia in (1984) 52 George Washington Law Review, (1985) 6 Cardozo Law Review and (1985) 34 American University Law Review. There is a bibliography, by D. Kennedy and K. Klare, of American CLS work in (1984) 94 Yale Law Journal 461, and a shorter one by A. Hunt in (1984) 47 Modern Law Review 369. D. Kairys (ed) *The Politics of Law* 1990 is a useful introduction to and, in a sense, manifesto of CLS ideas. Important philosophical underpinnings of the movement are expressed in R. Unger, *Knowledge and Politics* 1975. For the controversy provoked by Karl Klare's essay on the Wagner Act (Klare 1978) see (1984) 43 Maryland Law Review 23, (1985) 44 Maryland Law Review 731, 1100, 1111.

For representative samples of writing from Britain which adopt broadly critical approaches to legal scholarship see R. Fryer et al (eds), *Law, State and Society* 1981; D. Sugarman (ed), *Legality, Ideology and the State* 1983; W. Twining (ed), *Legal Theory and Common Law* 1986 (especially papers by Sugarman, Cotterrell, Lewis, Collins, Stokes and O'Donovan); P. Fitzpatrick and A. Hunt (eds), *Critical Legal Studies* 1987 (also published as 14 Journal of Law and Society, no. 1, special issue); R. Cotterrell and B. Bercusson (eds), *Law, Democracy and Social Justice* 1988 (also published as 15 Journal of Law and Society, no, 1, special issue). Much of this British writing has a different orientation from American CLS and reflects different influences and priorities. It generally shares, however, a scepticism about any idea of a pure legal logic divorced from the specific social contexts of its use; and, like the American movement, it tends to focus on the ideological importance of legal doctrine and to emphasise the inseparability of law and politics.

As in the case of legal realism, it is dangerous to generalise about American CLS. Some recent American writing has seemed concerned to examine professional constraints on judicial behaviour in a manner clearly compatible with constructive doctrinal realism. See e.g. D. Kennedy, 'Freedom and Constraint in Adjudication' (1986) 36 Journal of Legal Education 518.

LEGAL PROFESSIONALISM AND THE LEGACY OF REALISM: A good idea of the bewilderment which realism caused among some sections of the legal profession in America can be gathered from P. Mechem, 'The Jurisprudence of Despair' (1936) 21 Iowa Law Review 669. A comparable anguish about the 'nihilism' of critical legal studies is expressed in P. Carrington, 'Of Law and the River' (1984) 34 Journal of Legal Education 222. On the situation of legal education in Britain at the time of the realist 'ferment' in America see e.g. Glasser, 'Radicals and Refugees', above.

Chapter 8: The Uses of Theory

The idea that normative legal theory's professional role is made problematic by the changing forms of Western law is discussed also in Cotterrell, 'English Conceptions of the Role of Theory in Legal Analysis' (1983) 46 Modern Law Review 681. The idea that one discourse, or one perspective on reality, cannot necessarily provide a grounding for, invalidate or even evaluate another originating in a different practice (in other words, that all 'truth' claims are specific to the discourse in which they are made) is a theme of much modern writing in philosophy and social theory. Within recent Anglo-American philosophy one of the clearest and most influential statements is R. Rorty, *Philosophy and the Mirror of Nature* 1979. See also e. g. J.-F. Lyotard, *The Postmodern Condition* 1984. For a broad view of important parts of the relevant European continental tradition see A. Megill, *Prophets of Extremity* 1985.

I have tried to suggest, with reference to the disciplines of law and sociology, some conditions under which fields of knowledge *can* sometimes confront each other directly in the specific historical circumstances of particular intellectual and professional practices: see Cotterrell 1986a. Elsewhere I have tried to defend the view that knowledge can and does progress by the overcoming of partial perspectives, through their confrontation with other perspectives which come to be widely accepted as having more explanatory power. Broader perspectives can subsume (interpret and incorporate) narrower ones and so give rise to explanations which seem to have greater overall plausibility, richness, range and rigour in the light of historical experience and competing theories. See e.g.

Cotterrell 1984, p. 4; 1986b, p 84-5. But this confrontation of perspectives will always be a social and, in some sense, political confrontation; never a purely intellectual one: see generally Cotterrell 1986a.

References

(Dates in brackets are those of the original publication of the work or edition cited.)

ABEL, R. L. (1986) 'The Decline of Professionalism?' 49 Modern Law Review 1–41.

ARNOLD, T. W. (1935) *The Symbols of Government* (New York: Harcourt Brace and World edn, 1962).

ARTHURS, H. W. (1985) *Without the Law: Administrative Justice and Legal Pluralism in Nineteenth-Century England* (Toronto: University of Toronto Press).

AUSTIN, J. (1832) 'The Province of Jurisprudence Determined' reprinted in *The Province of Jurisprudence Determined and The Uses of the Study of Jurisprudence* pp. 1–361 (London: Wiedenfeld and Nicolson edn, 1955).

AUSTIN, J. (1863) 'The Uses of the Study of Jurisprudence' reprinted in *The Province of Jurisprudence Determined and The Uses of the Study of Jurisprudence* pp. 363–93 (London: Wiedenfeld and Nicolson edn, 1955).

AUSTIN, J. (1885) *Lectures on Jurisprudence or the Philosophy of Positive Law* 5th edn, edited by R. Campbell (London: John Murray).

BARKER, E. (1928) *Political Thought in England 1848–1914* 2nd edn. (Westport, Conn.: Greenwood Press reprint 1980).

BENTHAM, J. (1970) *Of Laws in General*, edited by H. L. A. Hart (London: University of London Athlone Press).

BENTHAM, J. (1977) *A Comment on the Commentaries and A Fragment on Government*, edited by J. H. Burns and H. L. A. Hart (London: University of London Athlone Press).

BLACKSTONE, W. (1809) *Commentaries on the Law of England* 15th edn, edited by E. Christian (London: Cadell and Davies). For convenience page references in the text are to the pagination of the 1765–9 edition as indicated in Christian's edition.

BRACHER, K. D. (1971) *The German Dictatorship: The Origins, Structure, and Effects of National Socialism*, translated by J. Steinberg (London: Weidenfeld and Nicolson).

BRUNET, E. (1988) 'The Need for Legal Theory at All Stages of

Legal Education' in J. P. Grant, R. Jagtenberg and K. J. Nijkerk (eds) *Legal Education: 2000* pp. 187–99 (Aldershot: Avebury).

BRUNNER, H. E. (1945) *Justice and the Social Order*, transl. by M. Hottinger (London: Lutterworth Press).

BRYCE, J. (1901) *Studies in History and Jurisprudence* Vol. 2 (Oxford: Clarendon).

BUCKLAND, W. W. (1949) *Some Reflections on Jurisprudence* (Hamden, Conn.: Archon reprint 1974).

BURNET, D. A. (1985) 'Dworkin and Pound' 71 Archiv fur Rechts- und Sozialphilosophie 234–45.

BURROW, J. W. (1966) *Evolution and Society: A Study in Victorian Social Theory* (Cambridge: Cambridge University Press).

CAMPBELL, C. M. (1988) 'The Career of the Concept' in Leith and Ingram (eds) (1988) pp. 1–25.

CARTER, J. C. (1907) *Law: Its Origin Growth and Function* (New York: Da Capo reprint 1974).

CASTBERG, F. (1955) 'Philosophy of Law in the Scandinavian Countries' 5 American Journal of Comparative Law 388–400.

CLARK, E. C. (1885) 'Jurisprudence: Its Uses and Its Place in Legal Education' 1 Law Quarterly Review 201–6.

COCKS, R. (1983) *Foundations of the Modern Bar* (London: Sweet and Maxwell).

COHEN, F. S. (1935) 'Transcendental Nonsense and the Functional Approach' reprinted in L. K. Cohen (ed) *The Legal Conscience: Selected Papers of Felix S. Cohen* pp. 33–76 (New Haven: Yale University Press, 1960).

COHEN, M. R. (1933) *Law and the Social Order: Essays in Legal Philosophy* (New York: Archon reprint 1967).

COLLINI, S., WINCH, D. and BURROW, J. (1983) *That Noble Science of Politics: A Study in Nineteenth-Century Intellectual History* (Cambridge: Cambridge University Press).

COSGROVE, R. A. (1980) *The Rule of Law: Albert Venn Dicey, Victorian Jurist* (London: Macmillan).

COTTERRELL, R. B. M. (1983) 'The Sociological Concept of Law' 10 Journal of Law and Society 241–55.

COTTERRELL, R. B. M. (1984) *The Sociology of Law: An Introduction* (London: Butterworth).

COTTERRELL, R. B. M. (1986a) 'Law and Sociology: Notes on the Constitution and Confrontations of Disciplines' 13 Journal of Law and Society 9–34.

COTTERRELL, R. B. M. (1986b) 'The Law of Property and Legal Theory' in Twining (ed) (1986) pp. 81–98.

CRAIG, P. (1983) *Administrative Law* (London: Sweet and Maxwell).

DAINTITH, T.C. (1982) 'Legal Analysis of Economic Policy' 9 Journal of Law and Society 191–224.

D'ENTREVES, A. P. (1967) *The Notion of the State: An Introduction to Political Theory* (Oxford: Oxford University Press).

DEWEY, J. (1924) 'Logical Method and Law' 10 Cornell Law Quarterly 17–27.

DICEY, A. V. (1905) *Lectures on the Relation Between Law and Public Opinion in England During the Nineteenth Century* (London: Macmillan).

DICEY, A. V. (1959) *An Introduction to the Study of the Law of the Constitution* 10th edn. (London: Macmillan).

DINWIDDY, J. R. (1975) 'Bentham's Transition to Political Radicalism, 1809–10' 36 Journal of the History of Ideas 683–700.

DOWDALL, H. C. (1926) 'The Present State of Analytical Jurisprudence' 42 Law Quarterly Review 451–70.

DUMAN, D. (1983) *The English and Colonial Bars in the Nineteenth Century* (London: Croom Helm).

DURKHEIM, E, (1933) *The Division of Labour in Society*, transl. by G. Simpson (New York: Free Press 1964 edn).

DWORKIN, R. M. (1965) 'Philosophy, Morality and Law: Observations Prompted by Professor Fuller's Novel Claim' 113 University of Pennsylvania Law Review 668–90.

DWORKIN, R. M. (1967) 'The Case For Law: A Critique' 1 Valparaiso University Law Review 215–7.

DWORKIN, R. M. (1971) 'Philosophy and the Critique of Law' in R. P. Wolff (ed) *The Rule of Law* pp. 147-70 (New York: Simon and Schuster).

DWORKIN, R. M. (1977) *Taking Rights Seriously* (London: Duckworth 1978 reprint with new appendix).

DWORKIN, R. M. (1982) '"Natural Law' Revisited' 34 University of Florida Law Review 165–88.

DWORKIN, R. M. (1985) *A Matter of Principle* (Cambridge, Mass.: Harvard University Press).

DWORKIN, R. M. (1982) ' "Natural Law" Revisited' 34 University of Florida Law Review 165–88.

ELLIOTT, G. (1987) *Althusser: The Detour of Theory* (London: Verso).

EVANS, M. O. (1896) *Theories and Criticisms of Sir Henry Maine* (London: Stevens and Haynes).

FEAVER, G. (1969) *From Status to Contract: A Biography of Sir Henry Maine 1822–1888* (London: Longmans, Green).

FINNIS, J. (1980) *Natural Law and Natural Rights* (Oxford: Oxford University Press).

FISH, S. (1982) 'Working on the Chain Gang: Interpretation in Law and Literature' 60 Texas Law Review 551–67.

FISH, S. (1983) 'Wrong Again' 62 Texas Law Review 299-316.

FRANK, J. (1930) *Law and the Modern Mind* (Garden City, NY: Anchor reprint 1963, including 1948 preface to sixth printing).

FRANK, J. (1949) *Courts on Trial: Myth and Reality in American Justice* (Princeton: Princeton University Press).

FULLER, L. L. (1940) *The Law in Quest of Itself* (Chicago: Foundation Press).

FULLER, L. L. (1946) 'Reason and Fiat in Case Law' 59 Harvard Law Review 376-95.

FULLER, L. L. (1958) 'Positivism and Fidelity to Law – A Reply to Professor Hart' 71 Harvard Law Review 630–72.

FULLER, L. L. (1969a) *The Morality of Law* 2nd edn (New Haven: Yale University Press).

FULLER, L. L. (1969b) 'Human Interaction and the Law' 14 American Journal of Jurisprudence 1–36.

FULLER, L. L. (1978) 'The Forms and Limits of Adjudication' 92 Harvard Law Review 353–409.

GABEL, P. (1980) 'Reification in Legal Reasoning' 3 Research in Law and Sociology 25–51.

GABEL, P. and KENNEDY, D. (1984) 'Roll Over Beethoven' 36 Stanford Law Review 1–55.

GILMORE, G. (1961) 'Legal Realism: Its Cause and Cure' 70 Yale Law Journal 1037-48.

GOODRICH, P. (1983) 'The Rise of Legal Formalism; Or the Defences of Legal Faith' 3 Legal Studies 248–266.

GOODY, J. (1977) *The Domestication of the Savage Mind* (Cambridge: Cambridge University Press).

GORDON, R. (1981) 'Historicism in Legal Scholarship' 90 Yale Law Journal 1017-56.

GOUGH, J. W. (1955) *Fundamental Law in English Constitutional History* (Oxford: Oxford University Press).

GREY, T.C. (1978) 'Origins of the Unwritten Constitution: Fundamental Law in American Revolutionary Thought' 30 Stanford Law review 843-93.

HABERMAS, J. (1974) *Theory and Practice*, transl. by J. Viertel (London: Heinemann).

HACKER, P. M. S. (1977) 'Hart's Philosophy of Law' in Hacker and Raz (eds) (1977) pp. 1–25.

HACKER, P. M. S. and RAZ, J. (eds) (1977) *Law, Morality and Society: Essays in Honour of H. L. A. Hart* (Oxford: Oxford University Press).

HAINES, C. G. (1930) *The Revival of Natural Law Concepts: A*

Study of the Establishment and of the Interpretation of Limits on Legislatures with Special Reference to the Development of Certain Phases of American Constitutional Law (New York: Russell and Russell edn, 1965).

HAMBURGER, L. and HAMBURGER, J. (1985) *Troubled Lives: John and Sarah Austin* (Toronto: University of Toronto Press).

HARNO, A. J. (1932) 'Social Planning and Perspective Through Law' Handbook and Proceedings of the Association of American Law Schools 1932 Annual Conference pp. 8–22.

HARRIS, D. R. (1961) 'The Concept of Possession in English Law' in A. G. Guest (ed) *Oxford Essays in Jurisprudence* 1st series pp. 69–106 (Oxford: Oxford University Press).

HART, H. L. A. (1953) 'Definition and Theory in Jurisprudence' reprinted in Hart (1983) pp. 21–47.

HART, H. L. A. (1955) 'Introduction' to J. Austin, *The Province of Jurisprudence Determined and the Uses of the Study of Jurisprudence* (London: Wiedenfeld and Nicolson).

HART, H. L. A. (1958) 'Positivism and the Separation of Law and Morals' reprinted in Hart (1983) pp. 49–87.

HART, H. L. A. (1961) *The Concept of Law* (Oxford: Oxford University Press).

HART, H. L. A. (1963) *Law, Liberty and Morality* (Oxford: Oxford University Press).

HART, H. L. A. (1965) 'Lon L. Fuller: The Morality of Law' reprinted in Hart (1983) pp. 343–63.

HART, H. L. A. (1968) *Punishment and Responsibility: Essays in the Philosophy of Law* (Oxford: Oxford University Press).

HART, H. L. A. (1970) 'Jhering's Heaven of Concepts and Modern Analytical Jurisprudence' reprinted in Hart (1983) pp. 265–77.

HART, H. L. A. (1972) 'Legal Powers' reprinted in Hart (1982) pp. 194–219.

HART, H. L. A. (1977) 'American Jurisprudence Through English Eyes: The Nightmare and the Noble Dream' reprinted in Hart (1983) pp. 123–44.

HART, H. L. A. (1982) *Essays on Bentham: Studies in Jurisprudence and Political Theory* (Oxford: Oxford University Press).

HART, H. L. A. (1983) *Essays in Jurisprudence and Philosophy* (Oxford: Oxford University Press).

HART, H. L. A. (1987) 'Comment' in R. Gavison (ed) *Issues in Contemporary Legal Philosophy: The Influence of H. L. A. Hart* (Oxford: Oxford University Press).

HINSLEY, F. H. (1986) *Sovereignty* 2nd edn (Cambridge: Cambridge University Press).

HOBBES, T. (1962) *Leviathan*, edited by J. Plamenatz (Glasgow: Collins).

HOLDSWORTH, W. S. (1928) *The Historians of Anglo-American Law* (Hamden, Conn.: Archon reprint 1966).

HOLMES, Jr., O. W. (1897) 'The Path of the Law' 10 Harvard Law Review 457-78.

HOLMES, Jr., O. W. (1899) 'Law in Science and Science in Law' 12 Harvard Law Review 443-63.

HONORÉ, A. M. (1973) 'Groups, Laws and Obedience' in A. W. B. Simpson (ed) *Oxford Essays in Jurisprudence* 2nd series pp. 1-21 (Oxford: Oxford University Press).

HONORÉ, A. M. (1987) *Making Law Bind: Essays Legal and Philosophical* (Oxford: Oxford University Press).

HORWITZ, M. J. (1977) *The Transformation of American Law 1780-1860* (Cambridge, Mass.: Harvard University Press).

HORWITZ, M. J. (1985) 'Santa Clara Revisited: The Development of Corporate Theory' 88 West Virginia Law Review 173-224.

HOWE, M. deW. (ed) (1953) *Holmes-Laski Letters: The Correspondence of Mr. Justice Holmes and Harold J. Laski 1916-1935* (London: Geoffrey Cumberlege, Oxford University Press).

HUGHES, G. (1962) 'Professor Hart's Concept of Law' 25 Modern Law Review 319-33.

HUNT, A. (1978) *The Sociological Movement in Law* (London: Macmillan).

JAMES, M. H. (1973) 'Bentham on the Individuation of Laws' 24 Northern Ireland Legal Quarterly 357-82.

JULIUS ROSENTHAL FOUNDATION (1941) *My Philosophy of Law: Credos of Sixteen American Scholars* (Boston: Boston Law Book Co.).

KELMAN, M. G. (1984) 'Trashing' 36 Stanford Law Review 293-348.

KELMAN, M. G. (1987) *A Guide to Critical Legal Studies* (Cambridge, Mass.: Harvard University Press).

KELSEN, H. (1941a) 'The Law as a Specific Social Technique' reprinted in Kelsen (1957) pp. 231-56.

KELSEN, H. (1941b) 'The Pure Theory of Law and Analytical Jurisprudence' reprinted in Kelsen (1957) pp. 266-87.

KELSEN, H. (1945) *General Theory of Law and State*, transl. by A. Wedberg (New York: Russell and Russell edn, 1961).

KELSEN, H. (1955) 'Foundations of Democracy' 66 Ethics 1-101.

KELSEN, H. (1957) *What is Justice?; Justice, Law and Politics in the Mirror of Science* (Berkeley: University of California Press).

KELSEN, H. (1967) *Pure Theory of Law*, transl. by M. Knight (Berkeley: University of California Press).

KELSEN, H. (1973) 'God and the State', transl. by P. Heath, in O. Weinberger (ed) *Hans Kelsen – Essays in Legal and Moral Philosophy* (Dordrecht: D. Reidel).

KENNEDY, D. (1979) 'The Structure of Blackstone's Commentaries' 28 Buffalo Law Review 205–382.

KIRCHHEIMER, O. (1941) 'The Legal Order of National Socialism' reprinted in F. S. Burin and K. L. Shell (eds) *Politics, Law and Social Change: Selected Essays of Otto Kirchheimer* (New York: Columbia University Press, 1969).

KIRCHHEIMER, O. (1961) *Political Justice: The Use of Legal Procedure for Political Ends* (Princeton: Princeton University Press).

KLARE, K. E. (1978) 'Judicial Deradicalization of the Wagner Act and the Origins of Modern Legal Consciousness, 1937–1941' 62 Minnesota Law Review 265–339.

KOCOUREK, A. (1928) *Jural Relations* 2nd edn (Indianapolis: Bobbs-Merrill).

KRAUSNIK, H., BUCHHEIM, H, BROSZAT, M., and JACOBSEN, H-A. (1968) *Anatomy of the SS State*, transl. by R. Barry, M. Jackson and D. Long (London: Collins).

LARSON, M. S. (1977) *The Rise of Professionalism: A Sociological Analysis* (Berkeley: University of California Press).

LASKI, H. J. (1967) *A Grammar of Politics* 5th edn (London: George Allen and Unwin).

LASSWELL, H. D. and McDOUGAL, M. S. (1943) 'Legal Education and Public Policy: Professional Training in the Public Interest' 52 Yale Law Journal 203–95.

LEITH, P. and INGRAM, P. (eds) (1988) *The Jurisprudence of Orthodoxy: Queen's University Essays on H. L. A. Hart* (London: Routledge).

LEVY, L. W. (ed.) (1987) *Essays on the Making of the Constitution* 2nd edn (New York: Oxford University Press).

LEVY-ULLMANN, H. (1935) *The English Legal Tradition: Its Sources and History*, transl. by M. Mitchell (London: Macmillan).

LLEWELLYN, K. N. (1930a) 'A Realistic Jurisprudence: The Next Step' reprinted in Llewellyn (1962) pp. 3–41.

LLEWELLYN, K. N. (1930b) *Cases and Materials on the Law of Sales* (Chicago: Callaghan).

LLEWELLYN, K. N. (1931a) 'Some Realism About Realism' reprinted in Llewellyn (1962) pp. 42–76.

LLEWELLYN, K. N. (1931b) 'Frank's Law and the Modern Mind' reprinted in Llewellyn (1962) pp. 101–10.

LLEWELLYN, K. N. (1940) 'On Reading and Using the Newer Jurisprudence' reprinted in Llewellyn (1962) pp. 128– 65.

LLEWELLYN, K. N. (1941) 'My Philosophy of Law' in Julius Rosenthal Foundation (1941) pp. 183–97.

LLEWELLYN, K. N. (1942) 'On the Good, the True, the Beautiful, in Law' reprinted in Llewellyn (1962) pp. 167–213.

LLEWELLYN, K. N. (1951) *The Bramble Bush: On Our Law and Its Study* 2nd edn (Dobbs Ferry, NY: Oceana).

LLEWELLYN, K. N. (1960) *The Common Law Tradition: Deciding Appeals* (Boston: Little, Brown).

LLEWELLYN, K. N. (1962) *Jurisprudence: Realism in Theory and Practice* (Chicago: University of Chicago Press).

LLEWELLYN, K. N. and HOEBEL, E. A. (1941) *The Cheyenne Way: Conflict and Case Law in Primitive Jurisprudence* (Norman: University of Oklahoma Press).

LUHMANN, N. (1982) *The Differentiation of Society*, transl. by S. Holmes and C. Larmore (New York: Columbia University Press).

MacCORMICK, D. N. (1981a) *H. L. A. Hart* (London: Edward Arnold).

MacCORMICK, D. N. (1981b) 'Law, Morality and Positivism' 1 Legal Studies 131–45.

MacCORMICK, D. N (1985) 'A Moralistic Case for A-Moralistic Law' 20 Valparaiso Law Review 1–41.

McILWAIN, C. H. (1910) *The High Court of Parliament and Its Supremacy: An Historical Essay on the Boundaries Between Legislation and Adjudication in England* (New Haven: Yale University Press).

MAINE, H. S. (1861) *Ancient Law* (London: Dent edn 1917).

MAINE, H. S. (1875a) *Lectures on the Early History of Institutions* (London: John Murray).

MAINE, H. S. (1875b) 'The Effects of Observation of India on Modern European Thought', reprinted in Maine (1876) pp. 203–39.

MAINE, H. S. (1876) *Village Communities in the East and West* 3rd edn (London: John Murray).

MAINE, H. S. (1883) *Dissertations on Early Law and Custom* (London: John Murray).

MAINE, H. S. (1885) *Popular Government* (London: John Murray).

MAITLAND, F. W. (1888) 'Why the History of English Law is Not Written' reprinted in Maitland (1911) vol 1, pp. 480–97.

MAITLAND, F. W. (1893) 'Outlines of English Legal History, 560-1600' reprinted in Maitland (1911) vol 2, pp. 417–96.

MAITLAND, F. W. (1901) 'The Crown as Corporation' reprinted in Maitland (1911) vol 3, pp. 244–70.

MAITLAND, F. W. (1911) *The Collected Papers of Frederic William*

Maitland, edited by H. A. L. Fisher (Cambridge: Cambridge University Press).

MANCHESTER, A. H. (1980) *A Modern Legal History of England and Wales 1750–1950* (London: Butterworth).

MANNHEIM, K. (1956) *Essays on the Sociology of Culture,* transl. by E. Manheim and P. Kekcskemeti (London: Routledge and Kegan Paul).

MANNING, C. A. W. (1933) 'Austin Today: or "The Province of Jurisprudence" Re-examined' in W. I. Jennings (ed) *Modern Theories of Law* (London: Wildy reprint 1963).

MILL, J. S. (1859) *On Liberty* (New York: Liberal Arts Press edn 1956).

MOLES, R. N. (1987) *Definition and Rule in Legal Theory: A Reassessment of H. L. A. Hart and the Positivist Tradition* (Oxford: Basil Blackwell).

MORISON, W. L. (1958) 'Some Myth About Positivism' 68 Yale Law Journal 212–33.

MORISON, W. L. (1982) *John Austin* (London: Edward Arnold).

MURPHY, P. L. (1972) *The Constitution in Crisis Times 1918–1969* (New York: Harper and Row).

NEUMANN, F. L. (1944) *Behemoth: The Structure and Practice of National Socialism 1933–1944* (New York: Octagon reprint 1983).

NEUMANN, F. L. (1986) *The Rule of Law: Political Theory and the Legal System in Modern Society* (Leamington Spa: Berg).

NUSSBAUM, A. (1940) 'Fact Research in Law' reprinted in *Essays on Jurisprudence from the Columbia Law Review* pp. 185–215 (New York: Columbia University Press, 1963).

PAULSON, S. L. (1975) 'Classical Legal Positivism at Nuremburg' 4 Philosophy and Public Affairs 132–58.

POCOCK, J. G. A. (1957) *The Ancient Constitution and the Feudal Law: A Study of English Historical Thought in the Seventeenth Century* (New York: W. W. Norton reprint 1967).

POSNER, R. A. (1972) 'A Theory of Negligence' 1 Journal of Legal Studies 28–96.

POSTEMA, G. J. (1986) *Bentham and the Common Law Tradition* (Oxford: Oxford University Press).

POUND, R. (1906) 'The Causes of Popular Dissatisfaction with the Administration of Justice' reprinted in R. D. Henson (ed) *Landmarks of Law: Highlights of Legal Opinion* pp. 180–95 (New York: Harper, 1960).

POUND, R. (1908) 'Mechanical Jurisprudence' 8 Columbia Law Review 605–23.

POUND, R. (1911) 'The Scope and Purpose of Sociological Jurisprudence' (Part 2) 25 Harvard Law Review 140–68.

POUND, R. (1921) *The Spirit of the Common Law* (Francestown, N.H.: Marshall Jones).

POUND, R. (1923) *Interpretations of Legal History* (Cambridge: Cambridge University Press).

POUND, R. (1931) 'The Call For a Realist Jurisprudence' 44 Harvard Law Review 697–711.

POUND, R. (1940) *Contemporary Juristic Theory* (Littleton, Col.: Rothman reprint 1981).

POUND, R. (1941) 'My Philosophy of Law' in Julius Rosenthal Foundation (1941) pp. 249–62.

POUND, R. (1942) *Social Control Through Law* (New Haven: Yale University Press).

POUND, R. (1943) 'A Survey of Social Interests' 57 Harvard Law Review 1–39.

POUND, R. (1950) *New Paths of the Law* (Lincoln, Neb.: University of Nebraska Press).

POUND, R. (1959) *Jurisprudence* (St. Paul, Minn.: West Publishing Co.).

POUND, R. (1963) 'Runaway Courts in the Runaway World' 10 University of California at Los Angeles Law Review 729–38.

POUND, R. (1967) 'The Case For Law' 1 Valparaiso University Law Review 201–14.

PURCELL Jr., E. A. (1973) *The Crisis of Democratic Theory: Scientific Naturalism and the Problem of Value* (Lexington: University Press of Kentucky).

RAZ, J. (1980) *The Concept of a Legal System: An Introduction to the Theory of Legal System* 2nd edn (Oxford: Oxford University Press).

REUSCHLEIN, H. G. (1951) *Jurisprudence – Its American Prophets: A Survey of Taught Jurisprudence* (Westport, Conn.: Greenwood Press reprint 1971).

ROSEN, P. L. (1972) *The Supreme Court and Social Science* (Urbana: University of Illinois Press).

RUMBLE Jr., W. E. (1968) *American Legal Realism: Skepticism, Reform and the Judicial Process* (Ithaca, N. Y.: Cornell University Press).

RUMBLE Jr., W. E. (1985) *The Thought of John Austin: Jurisprudence, Colonial Reform, and the British Constitution* (London: Athlone Press).

SARTORIUS, R. (1966) 'The Concept of Law' 52 Archiv fur Rechts-und-Sozialphilosophie 161–90.

SAVIGNY, F. C. von (1831) *Of the Vocation of Our Age for*

Legislation and Jurisprudence, transl. by A. Hayward (New York: Arno Press reprint 1975).

SAVIGNY, F. C. von (1867) *System of the Modern Roman Law*, transl. by W. Holloway, vol 1 (Westport: Hyperion Press reprint 1979).

SCHLEGEL, J. H. (1979) 'American Legal Realism and Empirical Social Science: From the Yale Experience' 28 Buffalo Law Review 459–586.

SCHLEGEL, J. H. (1980) 'American Legal Realism and Empirical Social Science: The Singular Case of Underhill Moore' 29 Buffalo Law Review 195–323.

SCHLEGEL, J. H. (1984) 'Notes Toward an Intimate, Opinionated, and Affectionate History of the Conference on Critical Legal Studies' 36 Stanford Law Review 391–411.

SCHMITT, C. (1985) *Political Theology: Four Chapters On the Concept of Sovereignty*, transl. by G. Schwab. (Cambridge, Mass: MIT Press).

SELZNICK, P. (1969) *Law, Society, and Industrial Justice* (New Brunswick: Transaction reprint 1980).

SHKLAR, J. N. (1964) *Legalism* (Cambridge, Mass.: Harvard University Press).

SIMPSON, B. (1973) 'The Common Law and Legal Theory' reprinted in Twining (ed) (1986) pp. 8–25.

SKINNER, Q. (1978) *The Foundations of Modern Political Thought. Vol. 1: The Renaissance* (Cambridge: Cambridge University Press).

SKOLNICK, J. (1975) *Justice Without Trial: Law Enforcement in Democratic Society* 2nd edn (New York: Wiley).

SOMMERVILLE, J. P. (1986) *Politics and Ideology in England 1603–1640* (London: Longman).

STEIN, P. (1980) *Legal Evolution: The Story of an Idea* (Cambridge: Cambridge University Press).

STEPHEN, L. (1900) *The English Utilitarians. Volume 3: John Stuart Mill* (London: Duckworth).

STEVENS, R. (1983) *Law School: Legal Education in America from the 1850s to the 1980s* (Chapel Hill: University of North Carolina Press).

STOLJAR, S. J. (1958) 'The Corporate Theories of Frederic William Maitland' in L. C. Webb (ed) *Legal Personality and Political Pluralism* (Melbourne: Melbourne University Press).

STONE, J. (1964) *Legal System and Lawyers' Reasonings* (London: Stevens).

STONE, J. (1966) *Social Dimensions of Law and Justice* (Sydney: Maitland).

STRAUSS, L. (1953) *Natural Right and History* (Chicago: University of Chicago Press).

SUGARMAN, D. (1983) 'The Legal Boundaries of Liberty: Dicey, Liberalism and Legal Science' 46 Modern Law Review 102–111.

SUGARMAN, D. (1986) 'Legal Theory, the Common Law Mind and the Making of the Textbook Tradition' in Twining (ed) (1986) pp. 26–61.

SUMMERS, R. S. (1971) 'The Technique Element in Law' 59 California Law Review 733–51.

SUMMERS, R. S. (1982) *Instrumentalism and American Legal Theory* (Ithaca, N. Y.: Cornell University Press).

SUMMERS, R. S. (1984) *Lon L. Fuller* (London: Edward Arnold).

TUR, R. H. S. (1978) 'What is Jurisprudence?' 28 Philosophical Quarterly 149–61.

TUSHNET, M. (1983) 'Following the Rules Laid Down: A Critique of Interpretivism and Neutral Principles' 96 Harvard Law Review 781-827.

TUSHNET, M. (1986) 'Critical Legal Studies: An Introduction to its Origins and Underpinnings' 36 Journal of Legal Education 505-17.

TWINING, W. (1968) *The Karl Llewellyn Papers* (Chicago: University of Chicago Law School).

TWINING, W. (1973) *Karl Llewellyn and the Realist Movement* (London: Weidenfeld and Nicolson).

TWINING, W. (1984) 'Evidence and Legal Theory', reprinted in Twining (ed) (1986) pp. 62–80.

TWINING, W. (ed) (1986) *Legal Theory and Common Law* (Oxford: Basil Blackwell).

WEBER, M. (1948) 'Politics as a Vocation' in H. H. Gerth and C. Wright Mills (eds and transl.) *From Max Weber: Essays in Sociology* (London: Routledge and Kegan Paul).

WEBER, M. (1978) *Economy and Society*, edited by G. Roth and C. Wittich (Berkeley: University of California Press).

WEINREB, L. L. (1987) *Natural Law and Justice* (Cambridge, Mass.: Harvard University Press).

WHITE, G. E. (1972) 'From Sociological Jurisprudence to Realism: Jurisprudence and Social Change in Early Twentieth-Century America' reprinted in White 1978, pp. 99–135.

WHITE, G. E. (1976a) 'The Path of American Jurisprudence' reprinted in White 1978, pp. 18–73.

WHITE, G. E. (1976b) *The American Judicial Tradition: Profiles of Leading American Judges* (New York: Oxford University Press).

WHITE, G. E. (1978) *Patterns of American Legal Thought* (Indianapolis: Bobbs-Merrill).

WIGDOR, D. (1974) *Roscoe Pound: Philosopher of Law* (Westport, Conn.: Greenwood Press).

WISEMAN, Z. B. (1987) 'The Limits of Vision: Karl Llewellyn and the Merchant Rules' 100 Harvard Law Review 465–545.

YALE, D. E. C. (1972) 'Hobbes and Hale on Law, Legislation, and the Sovereign' 31 Cambridge Law Journal (supplementary volume) 121-56.

Index

American Law Institute, 159, 204
Aquinas, St. Thomas 126, 146
Aristotle, 146
Arnold, Thurman, 195
Austin, J.L., 89, 91
Austin, John
  advances of theory 116, 117
  centralised state, theory of, 77–9,
    232
  change in attitude to, 15
  codification, favouring, 54
  common law, hostility to, 54
  delegation, on, 75–6
  doctrine, view of, 232
  empiricist, as, 85–7
  government, law as, 61, 62
  influence of, 53, 79–82, 221
  influences on, 55
  judges, on, 76–7, 151, 184
  law—
    defining, 59, 104
    distinguishing, 57
    generality, requirement of, 60
    merit or demerit of, 119, 130
  legal theory, 7, 52, 183, 218
  legal profession, and, 79–82, 154
  liberty, on, 61
  positive law, on, 57–9, 120
  positive morality, on, 59
  power-conferring rules, view
    of, 63–7
  rules, concept of, 92
  sanctions, view of, 62–7
  sovereignty, theory of, 67–77
  utility, principle of, 55, 56
Austin, Sarah, 52, 77, 79

Bentham, Jeremy
  codification, on, 54, 76
  common law, hostility to, 23, 54
  empiricism, 86
  law and morals, opinion on, 57, 119
  legal theory, 7, 53, 218

Bentham, Jeremy – *continued*
  natural law, view of, 122
  sovereignty, theory of, 68, 72, 76
Blackstone, Sir William, 24, 25, 29,
  40, 57, 72, 119, 122
Brunner, Emil, 143
Buckland, William, 15

Carter, James, 33
Centralised state
  Austin's theory of, 77–9
Clark, Charles, 189, 207
Codification
  Austin, view of, 54, 76–7
  Bentham, view of, 54, 76
  Roman law, of, 38
  Savigny, opposition of, 38, 54
Cohen, Felix, 186, 187, 188, 195, 211
Coke, Sir Edward, 24, 27, 29, 32, 121
Common law
  ancient wisdom in, 27
  Austin and Bentham, hostility
    of, 54
  authority of, 27–30
  concepts in, 106
  custom, as, 28–30
  Dworkin, theories of, 30, 174, 175
  Fuller, views of, 138–42
  history of, 22
  judges, 25, 26
  judicial decisions, in, 23, 25, 26
  knowledge, as, 33, 34
  law of community, as, 27, 33–5
  legal development, role in, 26–30
  legal doctrine, content of, 225, 226
  legislation, and, 30–3
  linguistic history of, 34
  maxims, importance of, 24
  meaning, 22
  natural law, and, 36, 121, 122
  neo-classical thought, 183
  Parliamentary supremacy over, 31,
    32

Common law – *continued*
  political and social environment,
    in,   33–7
  political authority, and,   35–7
  reason, as,   34
  rules, in,   22–3
  Savigny, theory of,   37–41
  state, and,   35–6
  thought, character of,   22–5
  tradition of,   21
  unity of,   23, 24
  unwritten, being,   28, 29
  written law, transition to,   43
Conceptualism
  empiricism, and,   85
Critical Legal Studies,   188, 210–3
Custom
  common law as,   28–30

Daintith, Terence,   62
Darwin, Charles,   45
Democracy
  political relativism, recognition
    of,   114
  rule of law, and,   112–6
  suspicion of,   77, 167
Dewey, John,   185
Dicey, A.V.,   24, 117, 123, 221
Douglas, William,   189, 207
Dworkin, Ronald
  civil disobedience, justification
    of,   177
  common law thought, and,   30,
    167–8, 174–5
  community as basis of law,   175–7,
    225
  early writings,   166
  inadequacy of model of rules,
    showing,   166, 167
  interpretive communities,
    and,   177–81,
  law and politics, relationship
    of,   219, 220
  legal interpretation,   172–7, 232–3
  legal questions, view of,   11
  legal theory,   7, 102, 103, 232, 233
  organicist conception,   172, 173
  Pound, and,   151–2, 166–8,
  positivism, attack on,   152, 167
  principles and policies,   168–72
  professionalism, and,   177–8, 218
  rights, view of,   168

Economic analysis
  law, of,   208, 209
Empiricism
  Austin, theory of,   85–7
  conceptualism, and,   85–7
  linguistic, 87–92

Finnis, John,   126, 146–9, 176, 177,
    226
Fish, Stanley,   179, 180, 199
Frank, Jerome,   192, 195, 204
Fuchs, Ernst,   204
Fuller, Lon
  common law tradition, and,   138–42
  Hart debate,   129–32
  law—
    customary,   141–2
    definition of,   138, 225
    internal morality of,   137, 138
    non-law, demarcation from,   142
    purposive view of,   136–9, 226
    types of,   141, 142
  legal positivist theory, and,   135,
    138, 139, 142, 143
  legality of rules,   134, 148–9
  professionalism, concern with,   142–
    3, 218
  social life, views of,   140, 141
  social science, and,   230, 232

Gilmore, Grant,   202, 204, 205
Goody, Jack,   29
Government
  law as,   61, 62

Haines, Charles Grove,   128
Hale, Matthew,   25, 29, 30
Hart, H.L.A.
  Austin, and,   64, 86–7, 116, 117
  Concept of Law,   92, 93, 102
  empiricist approach,   96, 104
  Fuller debate,   129–32
  hermeneutics,   101–3
  inaugural lecture,   89
  insiders and outsiders of legal
    system, distinguishing,   94, 95,
    101
  judge's decisions, and,   151, 219
  Kelsen contrasted,   84, 85
  linguistic philosophy,   102, 103
  legal positivism, defence of,   219
  legal realism, and,   194

Hart, H.L.A. – *continued*
legal system, rule of, recognition
of, 100, 101
legal theory, justification of, 7
linguistic empiricism, 87–92, 185
linguistic philosophy, 89–91
natural law, acceptance of, 145
normative and predictive
language,use of, 93, 94
political theory, 115, 116
professionalism, and, 218
Rule of Law, and, 99, 100
rules—
internal and external views,
distinguishing, 10, 93–4
obligation imposing, 95
open texture of, 103–6
power-conferring, 64, 66
primary, 96–8
recognition, of, 97, 100–1, 110,
111
secondary, 97–100
theory of, 92–4
sociological drift, 94–6
utilitarianism, 219
work of, 83
Hobbes, Thomas, 57, 59, 67, 68, 75,
148
Hoebel, E.A., 197
Hohfeld, Wesley, 88, 89
Holmes, Oliver Wendell, 7, 191, 203,
210
Honoré, Tony, 14
Horwitz, Morton, 211–2

James, William, 185
Judges
common law, 25, 26
delegates of sovereign, as, 75–7
discretion, exercising, 104, 171
formal style judging, 199
grand style judging, 198, 200–2
intrumentalist approach, 156
interpretation by, 173–5
jurisdiction, exceeding, 65
organicist approach, 156
predictability of decisions, 191
principle, application of, 171, 172
Judicial behaviouralism, 210
Jural postulates
law, in, 163, 164, 179
Jurisprudence
analytical, 87–9

Jurisprudence – *continued*
definition, 2
fields of, 2
historical, 38–51
materials of, 8
Maine's, 41–4, 221
philosophy, differing from, 5
realistic, 188
sociological, *See* POUND, ROSCOE
Jurists
work of, 4

Kantorowicz, Hermann, 204
Kelsen, Hans
Anglo-American environment,
in, 84, 106
Austin, and, 84
basic norm, postulating, 110, 111
conceptualism, 106–9, 230, 233
concretisation, 109
democracy, on, 114
doctrine of sovereignty, view
of, 115
Hart contrasted, 84, 85
intellectual scope of work, 84
judge's decisions, and, 151
legal theory, 7, 84, 143, 232, 233
politicisation, protection of law
from, 127
professional relevance, 108
sociology of law, on, 108–9, 230
state, view of, 113
syncretism, rejection of, 107
theories, development of, 84
Kirchheimer, Otto, 133, 134
Klare, Karl, 212
Kocourek, Albert, 89
Kohler, Josef, 163

Lasswell, Harold, 207
Law
character of, 1
codification, time for, 38
coercive structure of, 59–63
changes in, 28
common, *See* COMMON LAW
community, relationship with, 175–
7
contractual ordering, 141, 142
customary, 141, 142
economic analysis, 208, 209
enacted, 141

Law – *continued*
  fiat, as, 139
  generality, requirement of, 60
  government, as, 61, 62
  hermeneutic understanding
    of, 101–3
  intellectual discipline, as, 222
  internal and external matters, 10–
    11
  internal morality, 132, 137
  interpretation, as, 173–5
  knowledge, as, 33, 34
  "law and society" movement, 207,
    208
  legality, ideal of, 132–6
  morality, separation, of, 119
  Nazi, 131–4
  other phenomena, and, 57–9
  own creation, regulating, 109–12
  politics, and, 12, 13, 217, 219–20
  positive, 58
  precepts of, 153, 154
  reason, as, 34
  sanction attached to, 62–7
  scientific, 59
  social practices, complex of, 92
  species of command, as, 59
  systematic rationality, 227
  unity of, 9
Legal authority
  natural law, and, 125–7
Legal doctrine
  organisation of, 6
  technicality of, 5–6, 124
Legal institutions
  meaning, 3
Legal philosophy
  conceptual clarification, importance
    of, 2
  contextual interpretation, 17–20
  legal practice, and, 4–6
  legal theory, contribution to, 3, 9
  materials of, 8
  matters encompassed by, 2
  modern state, law in, 3
  political significance, 12, 13
  sceptical tendencies, 8
  social and political context, in, 14–
    17
Legal positivism
  Fuller, views of, 135, 138, 139, 142,
    143
  Hart, defence of, 219

Legal positivism – *continued*
  inadequacies, 145
  legal decisions, no analysis of
    making, 149
  legal doctrine, content of, and, 225,
    226
  natural law, and, 118–22, 129, 149
  natural law writers, view of, 127,
    128
  other legal environments, in, 151
  use of term, 120
  values, approach to, 143
Legal practice
  legal philosophy, and, 4–6
Legal profession
  Austin, influence of, 79–82
Legal realism
  American, 184, 202–6
  causes of, 202–6
  certainty, abandonment of, 192
  common points of departure, 8,
    188
  constructive doctrinal, 193–202
  corporate personality, issues
    of, 186
  Germany, in, 204, 205
  Las-dougalism, 206, 207
  legal professionalism, and, 213–5
  New Deal, effect of, 203–5
  normative legal theory, and, 188–
    94
  policy-science, and, 192, 193, 206–9
  pragmatism, and, 185–188
  radical scepticism, 193, 210–213
  Scandinavian, 184, 205

Legal system
  moral content of, 130
  recognition, rule of, 100, 101
Legal theory
  empirical, 3, 15, 16, 208, 231, 234
  legal philosophy, contribution
    of, 3, 9
  normative, *See* NORMATIVE LEGAL
    THEORY
  sociology of law, contribution of, 3
  use of term, 3
Legislation
  common law, and, 30–3
  development in English law, 31
  role of, 40
Levy-Ullmann, Henri, 22

Llewellyn, Karl
behavioural perspective on
law, 196, 198
Cases and Materials on Sales, 195
Common Law Tradition, 197, 198,
199, 200
constructive doctrinal realism, 194–
202, 231–2
doctrine, view of, 231
formal style, 199–201
grand-style, 198, 200–2
native tribes, study of, 197
New Deal, not supporting, 205
paper rules, concept of, 191, 195
period-style, 198–200
realism, defence of, 188–90
realistic jurisprudence, 188
title, concept of, 195
Luhmann, Niklas, 124

Maine, Sir Henry
historical jurisprudence, 41–4, 232
legal profession, and, 47–9, 79, 221
new science, 49–51
politics and society, on, 44–7, 77,
78
MacCormick, Neil, 101, 102, 145, 250–1
McDougal, Myres, 207
McIlwain, Charles, 31
Maitland, Frederic, 35, 36
Mannheim, Karl, 18
Manning, C.A.W. 70
Mill, John Stuart, 77
Moore, Underhill, 189, 207
Morality
aspiration, of, 136
duty, of, 136
law, separation from, 119
positive, 59
Morison, W.L., 85

Natural law
appeal of, 127
classical common law thought,
and, 121, 122
decline of, 122–4
Finnis, philosophy of, 146–9
Fuller, strategy of, 131
legal authority, and, 125–7
legal positivism, and, 118–22, 127–
9, 149
minimum content of, 145
politics, in, 125

Natural law – *continued*
rebirth of, 127–9
taming of, 145–9
theory, 120
United States, in, 122
weaknesses, 149
Nazi Era
Anglo-American lessons,
from 129–32
law, use of, 131, 132
legal system, non-existence of, 133
passive view of legality, effect
of, 143
rule of law, and, 128
Neumann, Franz, 133, 134, 138, 143
Normative legal theory
Austin, contribution of, 53
clarification of concept of laws,
making, 16
destiny of, 231–5
failing of, 233, 234
interpretation, difficulties in, 14
judges, role of, 150, 151
justifying, 6–9
lawyers, perspectives of, 16
meaning, 3
modern legal practice, and, 223–8
partial perspective, as, 16–7, 19–20,
228–31
political and professional uses
of, 9–13, 216–20
presumptions, 216
professional context, in, 12, 13,
217–9, 220–8
realism, and, 188–94
social context of law,
excluding, 15, 16, 217
value of, 220–3

Parliament
supremacy of, 31, 32
Philosophy
legal, *See* LEGAL PHILOSOPHY
linguistic, 89–91, 102, 103
pragmatist, 185
Politics
common law thought, and, 35–7
professionalism, and, 12, 13, 142–4
Postema, Gerald, 33, 76
Pound, Roscoe
administration of justice, attack
on, 157

Pound, Roscoe
common law, and,   23, 155, 157,
    161, 162, 165–6
democracy, suspicion of,   167
Dworkin, and,   151–2, 166–8
early writings,   154, 155
intellectual reputation,   152
jural postulates, view of,   163, 164
law, definition of,   153–4
legal development, view of,   153,
    154, 225
legal profession, status of,   154–5,
    218
legal theory,   7
legal realism, attack on,   165, 188
legislation, defence of,   157–8
natural law, view of,   128, 154
pragmatism, appeal of,   165
Progressive movement,
    supporting,   164, 165
social engineering,   156
sociological jurisprudence—
    development of,   151, 152
    label, use of,   152, 153, 165
    measure of values, identification
        of,   162–64
    outlook of,   7, 156–9
    programme for,   159, 161
    wider context, in,   164–6
theory of interests,   159–62
Pragmatism
legal realism, and,   185–8
philosophy,   185
Pound, view of,   165
Progressive movement
legal theory,   165

Raz, Joseph,   99, 102
Realism
legal. *See* LEGAL REALISM
policy-science,   192, 193, 206–9
Roman law
Austin, influencing,   55
codification of,   38
Roosevelt, Franklin
New Deal,   203–5
Ross, Edward,   153
Rule of Law
alternative meanings,   128, 129, 135,
    148–9, 220
Austin and,   60, 74, 83
defence, as,   128
democracy, and,   112–6

Rule of Law – *continued*
doctrine of,   60, 83, 133
Hart's theory, and,   99, 100
Rules
centrality,   105
certainty, governing,   105
character of,   92–4
core and penumbra,   105
determinate,   105
insiders and outsiders,   94
legality of,   134
normative language about,   93
obligation-imposing,   95
open texture of,   103–6
paper and real,   190
power conferring,   63–7
predictive terms,   93
principles controlling applicability
    of,   170
primary,   96–8
procedural,   66
secondary,   97–100

Sanctions
Austin, view of,   62–7
power conferring rules, and,   63–67
punitive,   62
requirement of,   63
Savigny, Friedrich Carl, von,   38–41,
    44, 54
Scepticism,
fact and rule,   192
normative analysis of law, of,   183
post-realist radical,   210–3
radical,   193
rule,   194
Schlegel, J.H.   189
Schmitt, Carl,   112
Simpson, Brian,   23, 28
Skinner, Quentin,   17
Sociology of law,   2, 3
Sovereign
characteristics of,   69–72
commands of,   67
constitutional law, in,   70
illimitable, to be,   69, 72–4
independent political society, of,   68
institution, acceptance as,   74
Sovereignty
Austin's theory of,   67–77
delegation of,   75–7
Kelsen, view of,   115
location of,   71

Sovereignty – *continued*
   pre-legal notion, as, 70
   social contract, 68
   United States, location in, 71
Stone, Julius, 86
Strauss, Leo, 124

Theory
   legal, *See* LEGAL THEORY: NORMATIVE
     LEGAL THEORY
Twining, William, 207

United States
   natural law ideas, 122
   realist movement, 184
   sovereignty, location of, 71

Uniform Commercial Code, 196, 201–2
Unity
   common law, of, 23, 24
   culture, of, 50
   law, in, 9
Utility
   principle of, 55, 56

Veblen, Thorstein, 224

Waismann, Friedrich, 104
Weber, Max, 106, 123, 130, 145, 148
Wigdor, David, 156, 164
Wittgenstein, Ludwig, 89, 91